Experiments for Teaching Psychology

Student Guide

Version 2.0

James D. St. James
Millikin University

Walter Schneider
University of Pittsburgh

Amy Eschman
Psychology Software Tools, Inc.

PsychMate®
PST-100626
Rev 3

Copyright © 2003-2016, Psychology Software Tools, Inc.

Publisher: Psychology Software Tools, Inc.
             311 23rd Street Extension
             Suite 200
             Sharpsburg, PA 15215-2821 USA

Printed in the United States of America.

ISBN 1-880374-52-8

Table of Contents

Acknowledgements

PsychMate® represents the efforts of many individuals. We, the authors, greatly appreciate their efforts. The product concept and design team included Walter Schneider, Ph.D.; James St. James, Ph.D.; Anthony Zuccolotto; Caroline Pierce; Brandon S. Cernicky; and Amy Eschman. The major system programmers on the project were Brandon S. Cernicky (student experiment-launcher and data-submission software), Kimberly Rodgers (instructor analysis software), Chris Neff (PEAK), and Susan Campbell and Caroline Pierce (PsychMate package file). Most of the specific experiments were written by Susan Campbell and Amy Eschman. PEAK templates were created by Michael Hout. Graphics were provided for the software and documentation by Kristal Kamholz and Gregg Stangl. Debbie Gilkey, Leslie Kuntz, Rose Mann, Anthony Zuccolotto, and the staff of Psychology Software Tools, Inc. helped with the testing of the software and the editing of tasks and documentation. Document design and copyediting were provided by Barbara Riehle.

Additionally, we thank the beta sites, including The University of Pittsburgh, Millikin University, Austin College, St. Cloud State University, Albion College, and Carnegie Mellon University, for dealing with early versions of the system and for providing us with suggestions for improvement. We are also appreciative of the original researchers whose procedures have provided the basis for all of the enclosed experiments and, in some cases, for the specific material they provided to us. We thank Marilyn Welsh for providing us with the problem set for the TOL-R in Chapter 2.5, Executive Control, Planning, and the Tower of London. Thanks to Julia Huffman and Ericka Hamilton for developing the word lists used in the experiment in Chapter 3.4, Levels of Processing and the Self-Reference Effect. Thanks to Rainer Goebel, Geoffrey Boynton, Carolyn Meltzer, BIRC, and Electrical Geodesics, Inc. for contributions and illustrations used in Chapter 6.1, Introduction to Brain Imaging and Brain Tutor.

Getting Started Guide

Introduction

What distinguishes the sciences from other approaches to understanding the world is a reliance on empirical research. Scientific ideas must be tested against the world to determine their value. The science of psychology seeks to understand many aspects of human and animal behavior, including the mechanisms of perception, cognition, and social interaction that underlie those behaviors. The application of that knowledge to improve the conduct of human affairs is also a goal of psychology. PsychMate® was developed to acquaint you firsthand with many of the empirical methods used to test scientific ideas in psychology.

In support of that goal, PsychMate offers a set of experiments in many areas of psychology. Many are rightly regarded as "classics." These are experiments that have, in many ways, defined the field of experimental psychology, providing general methods of research as well as interpretation of data. In this guide we detail the many considerations that go into the designs of these experiments, including discussions of experimental control. The logic of how to interpret the results of experiments is also stressed.

We hope that you will gain from PsychMate a wide base of knowledge about empirical procedures in psychology and that you will be able to use that base to develop and extend psychological knowledge. The experiments included in PsychMate were chosen not only for their contributions to our knowledge of psychology, but also because they have provided the field with new approaches to gaining knowledge. We hope that you will consider, as you do the experiments and read about them, how you might extend the techniques you are learning to the study of other aspects of psychology.

Additionally, we feel that you cannot truly understand an experiment unless you know what the subjects in that experiment actually experienced. PsychMate gives you the opportunity to participate as a subject in many of the most important experiments from the last several decades in psychology. PsychMate deliberately contains more experiments than your instructor is likely to have you complete. This was done to permit some choice and flexibility, since each instructor will take a somewhat different approach to teaching experimental methodology. Please feel free to explore the other experiments, which may provide the basis for your own research project.

NOTE: PsychMate may be purchased as a site license by an institution, or as an individual license by a single user. If this manual was purchased as an individual license, it contains one CD for installing PsychMate, plus a Student Activation Code. We recommend that you do not use the CD or activation code until your laboratory section has met and you have discussed how to create your online PsychMate account.

You will not be able to join a class until the instructor has provided you with a Class Key. Individual licenses will also need the Student Activation Code, which is located with the PsychMate Student software CD. Each individual user must have a unique activation code. A single activation code may not be used by more than one student. Site licenses do not require individual Student Activation Codes.

Getting Started

PsychMate offers online creation and management of student accounts, as well as automatic submission of data when working online (i.e., connected to the Internet). To use PsychMate, you must first register to set up an online PsychMate account.

Create a PsychMate Account

Install the PsychMate Student software to your local machine. (NOTE: This requires administrator privileges.) If you are in a department or public lab, you may need to obtain permission to install PsychMate, or your instructor may have already taken care of this for you. In order to be able to program novel experiments, the Psychology Experiment Authoring Kit (PEAK) must be installed. View the PsychMate website (**www.psychmate.com**) for detailed installation instructions. Once PsychMate is installed, launch PsychMate from the Start menu.

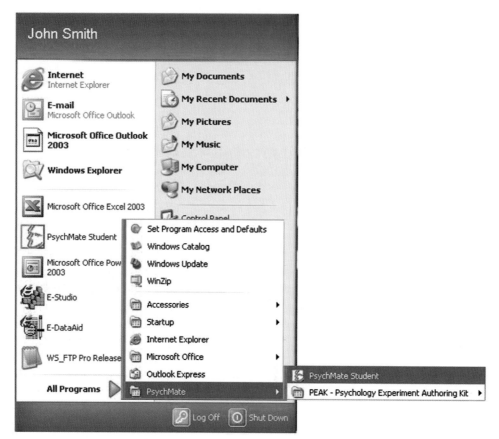

In order to complete the account creation and registration process, you must have the following information available:

- E-mail Address —> Necessary for receiving your PsychMate password

- Student Identifier —> Optional alternative for instructor to identify student in participation summary. Check with your instructor to determine if this value is necessary.

- Student Activation Code (not necessary for site licenses) —> Located with your PsychMate Student software CD, required to join a class (in combination with the Class Key).

- Class Key —> Provided by your instructor, required to join a class.

If you have previously created a PsychMate account, you can use your e-mail address and assigned password to log in. If you are a new user, you must first create a PsychMate account. Click the "New User?" link to create an account.

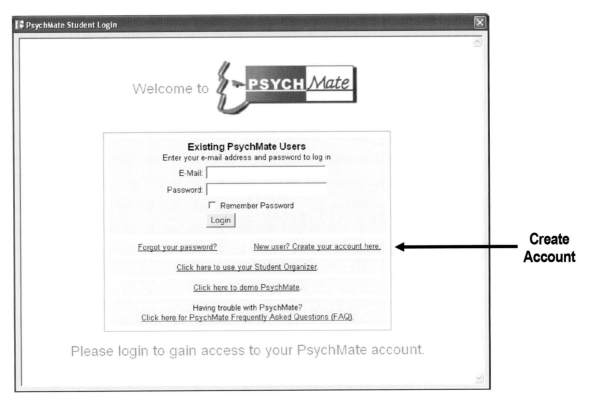

During the account creation process, you will be prompted to supply personal information (e.g., name, e-mail address, etc.). This information is necessary for creating an account and generating a password that is unique to you. In addition, information such as age or gender is useful for analyzing data according to population variables. Information you provide will not be distributed to anyone except your instructor, and can be used only for providing a summary of participation. No identifying information (including your name) will be stored with your data file, nor can it be used to identify a data file as belonging to you.

At the completion of the PsychMate registration, you will be assigned a subject number. You will have access to this subject number by viewing your online PsychMate Student Account information (see above). However, the subject number is used only for identification of a specific data set and is supplied to you for informational purposes only. A summary of experiment participation is provided to your instructor so that the instructor can determine who has completed each experiment, but the subject number is never provided to your instructor, nor can your subject number be linked to your name in the participant summary. Thus, your instructor is able to determine who has run each experiment, but is NOT able to link a specific data file to a specific student.

Your PsychMate account gives you access to useful information and resources. When you log in to PsychMate, click the Account button to access your account. Here you will find information relevant to your account, such as your user info (password, subject number, etc.), classes in which you are active, a Knowledge Base offering answers to frequently asked questions (FAQs), and downloads of updates available for the PsychMate software. User info may be changed for 30 days following the creation of your account.

Using PsychMate

Participate as a Subject in Experiments

Once you have created your PsychMate account and joined a class, you are ready to begin running experiments using the PsychMate Student experiment launcher. The launcher may be used while connected to the Internet (for automatic data submission), or it may be used with the Student Organizer to run offline and allow data submission at a later time. Refer to the **Create A Student Organizer** section (this chapter) for information concerning using the PsychMate Student Organizer.

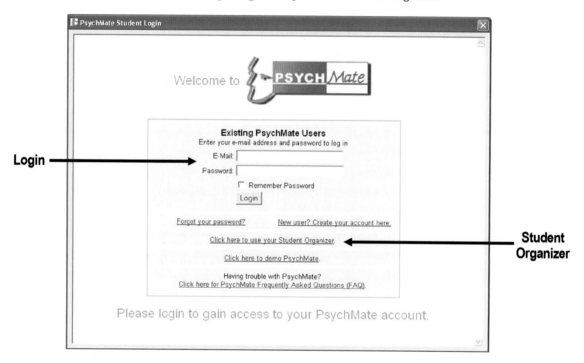

To run an experiment, launch PsychMate from the Start menu. If you are currently connected to the Internet, log into PsychMate using your e-mail address and password. If you wish to work offline, you may select the option of using the Student Organizer to log in.

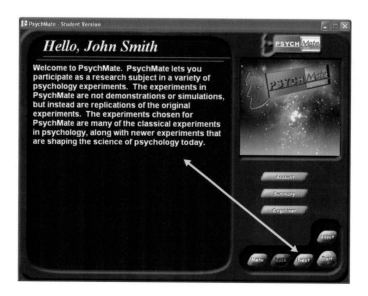

On the Welcome page, click Next to proceed to the Experiment Categories page. Experiments are grouped into categories. To run an experiment assigned by your instructor, you must use the launcher to select the category in which the experiment exists, and then select the specific experiment assigned.

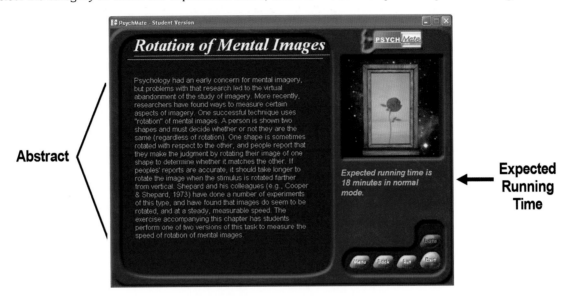

For each experiment, you are given an abstract and an estimated running time. The estimated running time is intentionally overestimated so that you will not run out of time during the experiment. Determine whether you have enough time to complete the experiment, read the experiment abstract, and click the Run button to launch the experiment.

Select the mode in which you wish to run. You may run PsychMate experiments in either of two modes: Normal or Demo. Use Normal mode for all class assignments, unless you are instructed otherwise. In this mode, you will serve as a subject in the entire experiment, and the data will be submitted to your class. The estimated running times refer to the time to complete the experiments in Normal mode only. Demo mode should be used only to review an experiment (for example, to refresh your memory for the details when writing it up for class) or to preview experiments. In Demo mode, the experiment lasts only about 5 minutes, and no data are submitted.

After you select the mode for the experiment, the experiment will begin. You will first see instructions for the particular experiment you are running. Carefully read those instructions, then follow the instructions on the screen to begin the experiment itself. After completion of the experiment, you will be returned to the experiment launcher.

Submit Your Data

If you are using PsychMate online, your data will be submitted to your instructor automatically. If you have been working from your Student Organizer, you will need to connect to the Internet and manually submit your data from your Student Organizer (see the **Using the Student Organizer** section in this chapter).

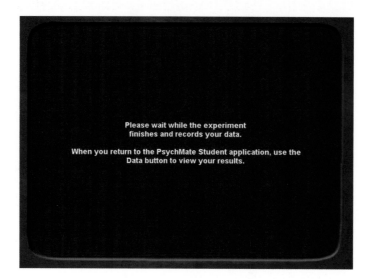

View Your Data

After running an experiment, you are given the opportunity to view your data, tables, and plots through the experiment launcher. This information summarizes your individual data. Your instructor may be compiling a group data file using all participants' data to be presented in class. To view your own data, click the Data button.

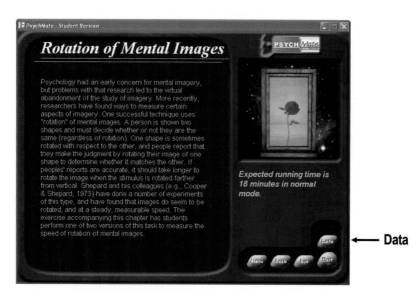

For most experiments, you may view raw data, plots, and tables. In the dialog presented, select the item you wish to view and click OK. The appropriate plot, table, or raw data spreadsheet will be displayed.

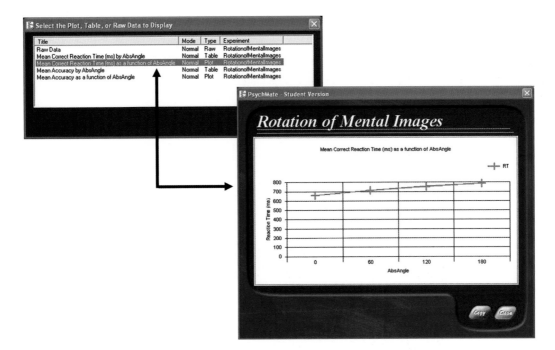

To print the display, click the Copy button, which copies the current display to the clipboard. After copying the plot, table, or raw data to the clipboard, you can paste the contents of the clipboard into another application (e.g., Word) for printing.

Ending an Experiment Early

Expected running times are provided for each PsychMate experiment so that you may determine if you have enough time available to complete a specific assignment. However, if the need arises, you can end any experiment early. To end an experiment, press CTRL+ALT+SHIFT simultaneously. You will be prompted as to whether or not you want to quit. Answering "Yes" will end the experiment at that point. No data will be recorded, and you will have to rerun the experiment from the beginning. You will also receive an error message indicating that the experiment was terminated by the user. Simply click OK to dismiss this dialog, and you will be returned to the experiment launcher.

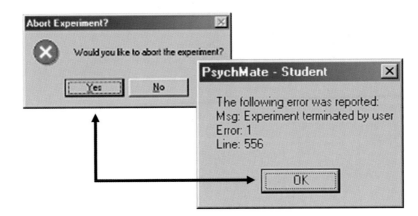

Your Student Account

The Account button in the PsychMate experiment launcher provides access to your online PsychMate account. Through your online account, you have access to announcements concerning the PsychMate software, a summary of your user information and the PsychMate classes for which you are enrolled, and answers to frequently asked questions. In addition, you always have access to the most recent version of the PsychMate software and any updates via the Download page.

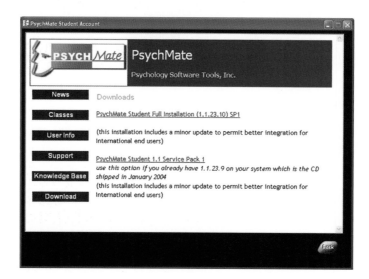

Editing User Info and Password

Your User Info and password may be edited within 30 days of creating your account. Log in to Psych-Mate, click the Account button to access your online PsychMate account, and click the User Info button to display your personal information. Follow the links provided to edit your user information or password. Your instructor does not have access to your user information, including your password. Refer to the **Create a PsychMate Account** section for more information concerning maintaining your anonymity while using PsychMate.

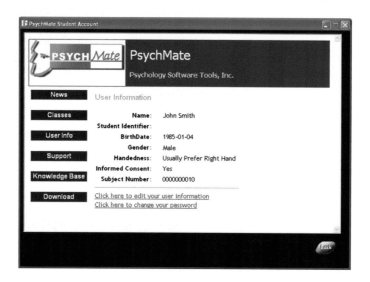

Activating Classes

The Classes button in your online PsychMate account displays all classes in which you are currently active, and a link to activate new classes. Each class you wish to join requires a unique Class Key.

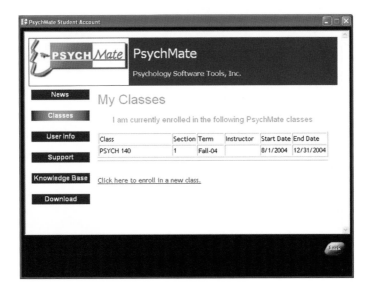

Getting Help

The Knowledge Base button in your online PsychMate account provides you with a link to answers to frequently asked questions. If you encounter errors or have questions concerning the use of PsychMate, first refer to the FAQs. If you are unable to resolve your problem, contact your instructor.

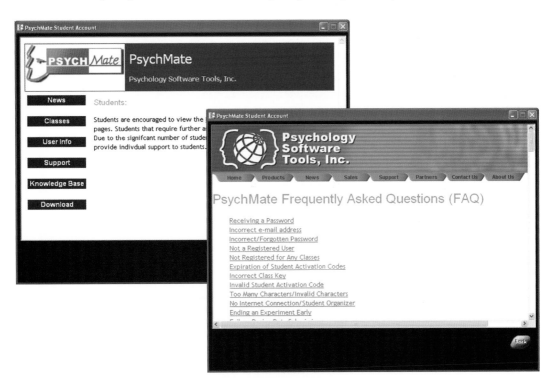

Participation Summary

PsychMate provides a summary of your participation in PsychMate experiments. To view the summary, log in to PsychMate and click the Summary button on the Welcome page.

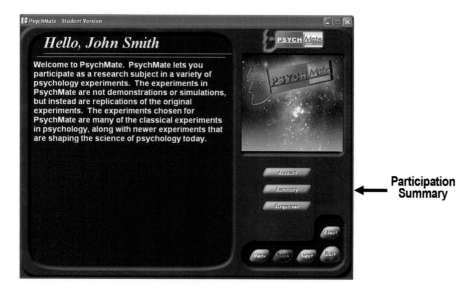

The Student Summary displays a listing of the PsychMate experiments sorted by category. The information in the Student Summary may be sorted otherwise by clicking on an individual column header. The Submitted column indicates whether or not a data file has been submitted for each experiment, and the Status column indicates the status of the data file submission (e.g., On Time, Not Due Yet, Late, etc.). For experiments offering multiple versions (e.g., Attentional Interference and the Stroop Effect), the Submitted and Status columns provide a comma-delimited listing of values for each version. Thus, if your instructor assigns multiple versions for an experiment, you can determine the status of each version independently.

Student Summary

Category	Experiment	Submitted	Status
Cognition	Mental Comparisons	No	Not Due Yet
Cognition	Additive Factors Methodology	No	Not Due Yet
Cognition	Automatic versus Controlled Processing	No	Not Due Yet
Cognition	Lexical Decisions	No	Not Due Yet
Cognition	Organization in Memory as an Aid to Recall	No	Not Due Yet
Cognition	Executive Control, Planning, and the Tower of London	No	Not Due Yet
Cognition	Recall, Recognition, and Encoding Specificity	No	Not Due Yet
Cognition	Scanning Short-Term Memory	No	Not Due Yet
Cognition	Sentence-Picture Comparison	No	Not Due Yet
Cognition	The Generation Effect	No	Not Due Yet
Cognition	Typicality in Categorization	No	Not Due Yet
Cognitive Neuroscience	Working Memory	Yes	On Time
Human Factors	Human Factors in Telephone Systems	No	Not Due Yet
Perception	Attentional Interference and the Stroop Effect	No, Yes, No	Not Due Yet, On Time,...
Perception	The Filling-In of Blind Spots: Induced Scotomas	No	Not Due Yet
Perception	Change Blindness	Yes	On Time
Perception	Iconic Memory	No	Not Due Yet
Perception	Perceptual Matching	No	Not Due Yet
Perception	Rotation of Mental Images	No, No	Not Due Yet, Not Due ...
Perception	Selective Attention and Response Competition	Yes	On Time
Perception	Signal Detection	No, No, No, ...	Not Due Yet, Not Due ...
Reaction Time Procedures	Number of Choices	No	Not Due Yet
Reaction Time Procedures	Stimulus Probabilities	No	Not Due Yet
Social Psychology	Automaticity and Stereotyping	No	Not Due Yet
Social Psychology	Impression Formation	No	Not Due Yet
Social Psychology	Levels of Processing and the Self-Reference Effect	No	Not Due Yet

Summary generated on 9/2/2004 9:01:56 AM

Using the Student Organizer

To run an experiment using a machine that does not have an Internet connection, use the Student Organizer. When using the Student Organizer, the experiment is run offline and the data files are saved to a removable medium (e.g., floppy, memory stick). Using a Student Organizer requires you to submit the data files as a separate step once you have accessed a computer with an Internet connection.

Create a Student Organizer

To run experiments offline, you must first create a Student Organizer while using PsychMate online. After launching PsychMate, click the Organizer button. In the Student Organizer Management dialog, click the Create a Student Organizer button.

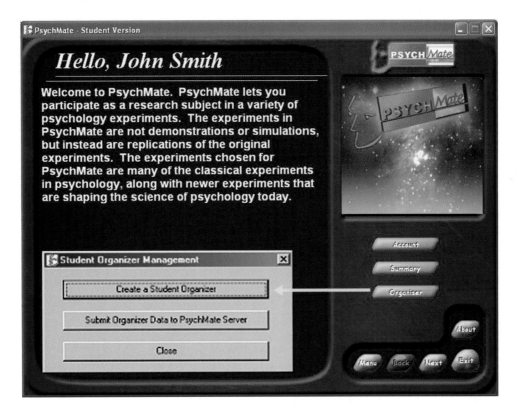

The Student Organizer requires a removable medium to which the data files will be saved until they can be submitted. In the Student Disk Location dialog, specify the location where data files should be stored.

The setup of the Organizer must occur only once if reusing the removable medium (e.g., if you reuse the same floppy disk). Note that the removable medium must be available when you launch PsychMate in order for it to be available from the Student Disk Location dialog. For example, if specifying a memory stick as the file storage location, the memory stick must be connected prior to launching PsychMate.

Log in Using the Student Organizer

To use PsychMate offline (i.e., on a machine not connected to the Internet), launch PsychMate and log in using the Student Organizer.

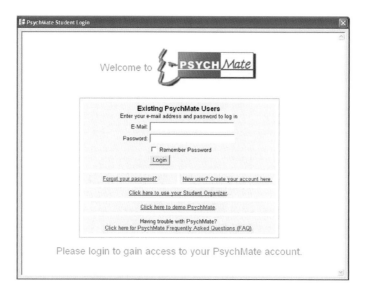

Specify the removable medium to be used for file storage (this would most likely correspond to the medium you specified in the creation of the Student Organizer).

After logging in through the Student Organizer, use the PsychMate experiment launcher to run experiments just as you would as if you were online. When running PsychMate with the Student Organizer, you will perceive no noticeable differences. However, your data files will not be submitted automatically. You will have to perform a separate step to submit the data files from the Student Organizer. Also, you will not have access to your online PsychMate account from the experiment launcher until you reconnect to the Internet.

Submit Data Files from the Student Organizer

After running an experiment using the Student Organizer, you will be notified that the files have been saved to the Organizer and that you must manually submit them.

To submit files saved to the Student Organizer, launch PsychMate using a computer connected to the Internet, and log in using your e-mail address and password. Click the Organizer button to display the Student Organizer Management dialog, and click the button to submit the organizer data.

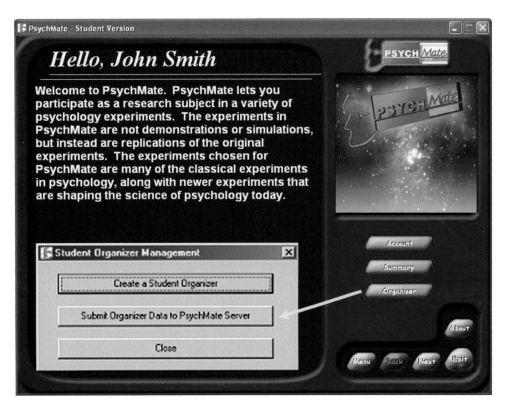

You will once again be prompted to supply the location of the stored data files. After selection of the location, the files will be submitted to your instructor automatically.

General Instructions for Running Experiments

Most of the experiments in this series involve the measure of either accuracy or reaction time as the dependent variable. General instructions are given below for both types of experiments. At the beginning of each experiment, you will be told whether the experiment measures accuracy or reaction time.

Experiments Measuring Accuracy

Accuracy as a dependent variable is usually measured by determining the number of trials of an experiment on which you made a correct response, and then dividing by the total number of trials to yield the proportion correct. Multiplying the proportion correct by 100 yields the percent correct. By comparing accuracy under varying conditions of an experiment, we can gain information about the processes involved in the task.

Please note that experiments that involve accuracy usually are designed so that you will have fairly high error rates. After all, if you were almost always correct in each condition, then there would be little difference in accuracy on which to base an analysis. Note also that in experiments that involve accuracy, you should not try to make fast responses. If you attempt to respond as quickly as possible to these tasks, you likely will have extremely low accuracy.

General Instructions for Running Experiments *(continued)*

Experiments Measuring Reaction Time

Reaction time (hereafter, RT) is a measure of the time elapsed between onset (presentation) of a stimulus and completion of a response (e.g., a key-press). This measure of RT is then used to try to infer something about the nature of the underlying psychological processes involved by comparing the RTs under different conditions. An example (from the exercise "Perceptual Matching") is that it is harder (i.e., longer RT) to decide that two letters seen at the same time have the same name (like "A's") than to decide that two letters are physically the same ("AA" or "aa"). However, if you see one letter two seconds before the other, this effect disappears. This is one piece of evidence that verbal items in short-term memory are stored by sound code, rather than visual imagery, and that it takes about 2 seconds to produce that sound code. Thus, the advantage of physical sameness is lost when you must match the second letter against a memory of the sound of the first letter.

RT is an important measure in psychology, and a powerful one. But, as with experiments using any other methodology, you have to be careful. A number of factors affect RT, in addition to the experimental factors in which we are interested, and some consideration must be given to those. The first and foremost concern in RT research is that you respond as quickly as you can while keeping errors to a minimum. You are to try to react as soon as you can without being sloppy. For most experiments, this means that you should have no more than 10% errors, and usually you should have far fewer. Again, the stress is on speed, but without sacrificing accuracy. Remember, these are not guessing games. Wait until you see the stimulus before you respond!

Do not try to produce the "correct" result. Any effort to be faster in one condition than another will lead to slow, sloppy responding in all conditions. Just do the task as instructed. If your performance is not just like the "average," do not worry. There are large individual differences in overall RT, though most people will show the same general pattern of RTs across various conditions of the experiment.

There are a few things you can do to help maintain good speed and accuracy. For most experiments, you must push a designated key to start each trial. Be sure that you are paying close attention to the task when you press the key to start the next trial. If there is a fixation mark (typically a "+") on the screen that tells you where to look during the trial, make sure that you have that mark in good, clear focus when you start a trial.

Although you could choose to sit and run trial after trial and finish a little sooner, you would do so at the cost of eyestrain and decreased accuracy. For the sake of both your comfort and the accuracy of the data, plan to stop for a few seconds after every few trials (the exact number will depend largely on the type of task). It is possible to sit and stare at the screen for a long time, but you may have difficulty maintaining concentration and your performance will deteriorate. So take a break every 5-10 minutes. Stand up and stretch. Relax your eyes. Not only will you feel better, but your performance will be better also!

While you may not have complete control over your surroundings during testing, you can probably avoid at least some of the worst problems. If you have control over the brightness and contrast of the computer screen, make sure that the stimuli are clear and sharp. A dim screen will make your RTs both slower and less accurate. Also, be sure to eliminate any glare on the screen, since this may partially mask (cover up) the stimuli.

For experiments measuring RT, the computer will report your mean (average) RT for each condition—this is the dependent variable. The mean is used because your RT will vary from trial to trial as a result of many things other than the type of stimulus, although that is the only variable in which we are interested. Momentary changes in degree of attentiveness, clarity of focus, interest or boredom, or many other factors can affect RT. By testing you in many trials of each type, and using the mean of those trials as your score, we can control for all of those variables, since poor attentiveness (or other factors) will occur about equally often for each trial type, and thus the effect will be cancelled out.

PERCEPTION

PERCEPTION

Introduction

A basic issue for psychology, as well as for philosophers down through the ages, is how we come to gain knowledge of the world. Knowledge comes through experience with the world, and that experience is what the study of perception seeks to understand. What we know about the world and the things in it is learned through looking at, listening to, feeling, smelling, and even tasting the world. (Babies seem so inordinately fond of tasting the world because their sense of taste and sense of touch in their mouths are better developed than their other senses.) The act of perception begins with our sense organs such as the eye, the ear, and the vestibular system of the inner ear that helps us balance. These organs are sensitive to different aspects of the external world (and of our own bodies), and translate experience into signals to the brain to indicate what is currently being sensed.

But perception is more than just a passive receiving and interpreting of sensory signals. Perception is also an *activity* that we engage in. Not only do we actively move our eyes to gain new information, but we also move our bodies in order to use our senses most effectively. We move so that we can look around things when we want to know what is behind them, and we climb hills to see what is on the other side. Perception is thus an activity that we control (though imperfectly). We can select which parts of the world we perceive by moving in the world, but we also can restrict attention to only part of what we could currently perceive (for example, paying the most attention to a single instrument while listening to an orchestra). Perceiving things also involves knowing what they are—in short, recognizing them. So memory plays a role in perception, as well.

Various aspects of perception, how we actively use perception, and how memory and perception are related are explored in the experiments and exercises that follow.

1.1 The Filling-In of Blind Spots: Induced Scotomas

Abstract

Blind spots in vision, which are known as *scotomas*, provide an interesting demonstration of how the brain fills in gaps in perception. That process of "filling in" has been shown to be a fairly complex one. In the demonstrations accompanying this chapter, a number of aspects of this filling-in process are illustrated. Both the natural scotoma, which occurs where the optic nerve exits from the eye, and temporary, *induced* scotomas are illustrated.

*I*t is fairly well known (especially among students of psychology) that there is a blind spot in vision (formally, a *scotoma*—pronounced SKUH-TOE-MUH).[1] This blind spot is caused by the fact that, at the *optic disk*, there are no sensory neurons to turn light into neural impulses. (The optic disk is the location in each eye where the optic nerve exits from the eyeball and the blood vessels serving the retina enter and exit.) The natural scotoma is not small. It is about 6 degrees[2] wide, 8 degrees tall, and is centered approximately 15 degrees from straight-ahead in vision—about the size of your hand, with the fingers flexed, at arm's length.

Why do we not notice this scotoma? There are three general explanations. One is that the scotoma falls on opposite sides of the two eyes, thus an image on the blind spot of one eye is not on the blind spot of the other. But if you cover one eye, you still don't notice anything missing. There are, then, some other things going on. A second reason we don't usually notice the natural scotoma is simply that our visual acuity at

15 degrees from the fovea (the central part of vision) is remarkably poor. You can easily demonstrate the poor acuity in peripheral vision by looking at the plus sign below. When you do so, can you read the word?

+   **word**

Of course, you know what the word is, but can you actually see it? At comfortable reading distance, most people cannot. The spacing used here centers the word at about 5 degrees from the fixation point (i.e., where you focus on the plus sign). The third, and perhaps most interesting, explanation is that our brains actually fill in the blind spot with whatever colors or textures surround it. In the demonstrations accompanying this chapter, the filling-in of the natural scotoma with color is illustrated.

In this chapter, the emphasis is on *induced* scotomas—these are scotomas that are produced on demand. Ramachandran and Gregory (1991) reported a series of studies on the filling-

---

[1] The first recorded description of the natural scotoma came in 1668, when Mariotte showed that, by looking off to the side of an object in monocular (one-eyed) vision, the object can be made to disappear. The existence of this blind spot soon became known to King Charles II of France, who amused himself by "beheading" members of his court with it (Walls, 1954).

[2] The size of an object in vision, or of a portion of the visual field, such as the blind spot, is usually specified in *degrees of visual angle*. See Chapter 1.6, *Selective Attention and Response Competition*, for details of the calculation. At a distance of 20 feet, the natural scotoma is thus about 25" wide, 33" tall, and centered 63" from straight ahead.

in of these induced scotomas, and the computer-based demonstrations accompanying this chapter are taken from their article, as well as from Ramachandran (1992) and Ramachandran (1993a & b). A lengthy review of the filling-in process in vision, with a number of commentaries, is Pessoa, L., Thompson, and Noe (1998).

Ramachandran and Gregory (1991) began their studies with the knowledge that patients with discrete damage to either the retina or the primary visual cortex report that the resulting scotoma is filled in by the surrounding background. "If the patient gazes at a companion seen against a background of wallpaper, the companion's head may disappear but the gap gets 'filled in' by the surrounding wallpaper" (p. 699). Note that an object that is covered by the scotoma disappears, and the scotoma is filled in with the surrounding texture, just as occurs in the natural scotoma at the optic disk. Ramachandran and Gregory were interested in finding a way to produce such scotomas without injury. Previous research pointed the way.

One fact of sensory psychophysiology is that stimuli which do not change usually "disappear" from consciousness. Thus, if you wear a ring most of the time, you are seldom aware of it. Similarly, a steady background noise (such as the buzz of fluorescent lights or the steady hum of a computer's fan) quickly will be ignored. This process is termed *habituation*. But why, then, does the visual world not disappear when we gaze at an unmoving object? The answer lies in the fact that our eyes are continually moving. In addition to the relatively large, voluntary eye movements, there are several types of small eye movements that we are unable to suppress voluntarily. These movements are known as *physiological nystagmus*.

• To see an excellent demonstration of these small eye movements, look at the small black dot in the middle of Figure 1.1.1. Stare at it for several seconds, then look at the white dot nearby. You will see a light after-image projected onto the black squares. Observe this after-image for a few moments, and you will notice that it moves a bit and also that you cannot control this movement. The movement of the after-image is due to the small eye movements that make up physiological nystagmus.[3]

To test physiological nystagmus as an explanation of the lack of habituation in vision, Riggs, Ratliff, Cornsweet, and Cornsweet (1953) performed an experiment on stabilized images, in which they made a small contact lens with a stalk extending from it on which a small mirror was mounted. By projecting a visual stimulus using a system of mirrors, they could compensate for movements of the eye so that the resulting image would remain on the same part of the retina, thereby compensating for the small movements due to nystagmus. The result was rather dramatic. Within a few seconds, the stabilized image disappeared. Thus, the reason we usually do not experience habituation in vision is due to the fact that the image on the retina is constantly changing as a result of physiological nystagmus.

It turns out, though, that it is possible to get some visual objects to disappear, without the necessity of a system of mirrors or a contact with a stalk on it (which must have been remarkably uncomfortable—just imagine blinking!). You cannot hold your eye still enough to make objects in foveal vision disappear. (The *fovea* is the part of vision that corresponds to straight-ahead and which is highly favored—both the

---

[3] The small grey patches that you observe at the intersections of the white lines are illusory. If you stare directly at an intersection, the grey patch disappears. This effect was first reported by the 19th-century sensory physiologist Hermann (1870). An explanation for it only became possible with the discovery of the on-center, off-surround receptive fields in the visual cortex by Hubel and Weisel (1961). That explanation is beyond the scope of this chapter. See Jung and Spillman (1970) and Frisby (1980).

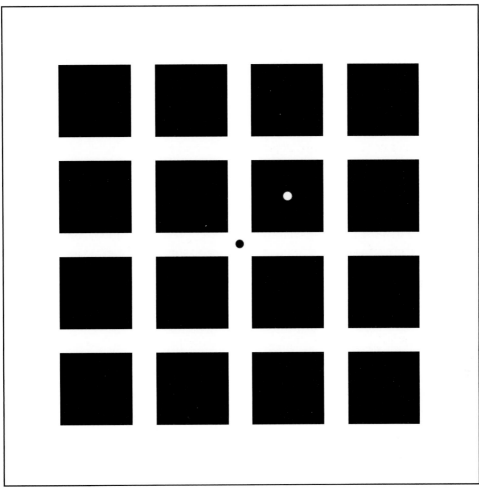

FIGURE 1.1.1 – *Demonstration of physiological nystagmus*

retina and the visual cortex devote most of their neural resources to processing foveal vision.) Objects in peripheral vision are not seen clearly, because visual acuity drops rapidly as an image moves from foveal to peripheral vision. Usually, we are blissfully ignorant of this, because we keep our *eyes* (and heads) moving.

Because a visual image that is a few degrees from the fovea is hard to see clearly, its edges are not sharp, and so the effects of physiological nystagmus are greatly muted—the slight movements are not sufficient to keep habituation from occurring. It is this phenomenon that provided Ramachandran and Gregory (1991) with a method of temporarily inducing scotomas in normal, non-injured persons. It turns out to be rather simple. If you stare at a fixation mark, a discrete stimulus (such as a small grey patch) that is located a few degrees from the fovea will disappear. Since this does not involve the natural scotoma at the optic disk, the viewing can be binocular—i.e., you need not close one eye.

When you run the experiment accompanying this chapter, you will get to experience the series of demonstrations that Ramachandran and Gregory (1991) explored. **NOTE**: You should complete the computerized demonstrations of the filling-in process before you continue reading, because it is helpful that you not be guided by expectation as you report how the blind spot is filled in.

Discussion

Demonstration 1

This is the basic demonstration of the filling-in process with an induced scotoma. Ramachandran and Gregory (1991) reported that the average time for their subjects to report that the grey patch had disappeared was 5 seconds. The scotoma is filled with the same twinkling as the surrounding area. A question raised by Ramachandran and Gregory was whether the filling-in is an active process: "Does this filling-in process involve creating an actual neural representation of the 'twinkle' in the brain areas to which the grey square projects, or does it involve merely ignoring the absence of information?" (p. 700). They concluded that the process is an active creation of a representation, since the twinkling seems to fill in from the edges inward.

Demonstration 2

The next question that Ramachandran and Gregory (1991) raised was whether color and motion are filled in separately, or whether the filling-in is a unitary process. Note that different parts of the visual cortex respond to different aspects of the stimulus. Some parts process color, but not movement, and vice versa. It may be that the filling-in process takes place separately in each of these brain areas, rather than resulting from some higher-level process. To test this, they created the display you saw in Demonstration 2—a pink background behind the twinkling black dots, with black squares moving across the grey patch. Thus, two things could fill in: the twinkling (movement) and the color. Their subjects reported that the pink color filled in the grey patch, but that it was a couple of seconds later before the moving boxes were replaced by the twinkling, suggesting that the filling-in occurred separately for motion and color.

Demonstration 3

Ramachandran and Gregory (1991) next considered the importance of the border region in the filling-in process. In this demonstration, you pressed a key to indicate when the grey patch had been filled in. The screen was then changed to display a slightly smaller grey patch "inside" the previous one. Since the region corresponding to the smaller square has been filled in with twinkling already, there may be no need to start the filling-in again when the smaller patch appears. But, in fact, the smaller grey patch becomes visible and, after a few seconds, is also filled in. They concluded that this indicated that the fading of contours is an essential part of the whole process of filling-in.

Demonstration 4

The next demonstration concerned the question of the depth of suppression within the scotoma. What happens if a small part of the area of the scotoma is changed? Will that change be noticed? For this demonstration, when you indicated that the grey patch had disappeared, a small red spot was displayed in the center of the grey patch. Ramachandran and Gregory reported that all of their subjects reported seeing the red spot, but surrounded by the twinkling. Clearly, there is not a complete suppression of input from the area of the grey patch.

Demonstration 5

How long does the filling-in last? Ramachandran and Gregory (1991) explored this question by waiting until the grey patch disappeared and was filled by the surrounding twinkling, and then switched the screen from a twinkle to a homogeneous grey. Their subjects reported that the twinkling continued inside the scotoma for several seconds, suggesting that the neural representation of the twinkling persists for several seconds.

Questions

1. For each of their experiments, Ramachandran and Gregory (1991) report data from naïve subjects—that is, subjects who did not know the hypothesis being tested. Why was it important to use naïve subjects?

References

Frisby, J. P. (1980). *Seeing: Illusion, brain, and mind.* Oxford, England: Oxford University Press.

Hermann, L. (1870). Eine Erscheinung simultanen Contrastes [An experiment on simultaneous contrast]. *Pflüger's Archiv für die Gesamte Physiologie, 3*, 13-15.

Hubel, D. H., & Weisel, T. N. (1961). Integrative action in the cat's lateral geniculate body. *Journal of Physiology, 155*, 385-398.

Jung, R., & Spillman, L. (1970). Receptive-field estimation and perceptual integration in human vision. In F. A. Young & D. B. Lindsey (Eds.), *Early experience and visual information processing in perceptual and reading disorders* (pp. 181-197). Washington, DC: National Academy of Sciences.

Pessoa, L., Thompson, E., & Noe, A. (1998). Finding out about filling-in: A guide to perceptual completion for visual science and the philosophy of perception. *Behavioral & Brain Sciences, 21*, 723-802.

Ramachandran, V. S. (1992, May). Blind spots. *Scientific American, 266*, 86-91.

Ramachandran, V. S. (1993a). Filling in gaps in perception: Part I. *Current Directions in Psychological Science, 1*, 199-205.

Ramachandran, V. S. (1993b). Filling in gaps in perception: Part II. Scotomas and phantom limbs. *Current Directions in Psychological Science, 2*, 56-65.

Ramachandran, V. S., & Gregory, R. L. (1991). Perceptual filling in of artificially induced scotomas in human vision. *Nature, 350*, 699-702.

Riggs, L. A., Ratliff, F., Cornsweet, J.C., & Cornsweet, T. N. (1953). The disappearance of steadily fixated visual test objects. *Journal of the Optical Society of America, 43*, 495-501.

Verheijen, F. J. (1961). A simple after image method demonstrating the involuntary multidirectional eye movements during fixation. *Optica Acta, 8*, 309-311.

Walls, G. L. (1954). The filling-in process. *American Journal of Optometry, 31*, 329-341.

1.2 Signal Detection

Abstract

Signal Detection Theory is concerned with solving a problem from classical psychophysics, namely, that persons asked to detect a signal (e.g., a faulty part coming off an assembly line) are influenced by more than just how well they can see or hear (i.e., their sensitivity). Their *willingness* to report a signal (i.e., their bias) is also important. Traditional measures of sensory thresholds confound bias and sensitivity, while signal detection theory permits us to measure (and/or manipulate) them separately. In the four experiments in the exercise accompanying this chapter, the intensity of the signal and the intensity of the "noise" are shown to affect sensitivity, while the probability of a signal and the rewards and punishments associated with particular types of responses are shown to affect bias. The applicability of signal detection theory to a wide variety of human endeavors is also demonstrated. Graphing of data onto Receiver Operating Characteristic (ROC) curves is part of the exercise.

One of the earliest concerns for psychology was the measurement of *thresholds* for various senses. This is a very basic question for the study of perception—how intense must a light be before I can see it? And how much brighter must a light get before I can detect the change in brightness? The *absolute threshold* was defined as the smallest stimulus intensity that can be detected 50% of the time, while the *difference threshold* was the smallest change in stimulus intensity that can be detected 50% of the time. Techniques for measuring these thresholds were devised by Gustav Fechner (1856/1966); they mark the beginning of a scientific approach to measuring perception.

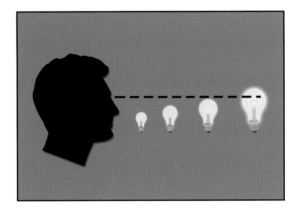

One way to measure the absolute threshold for light is to present a very dim light, and then increase the intensity of the light gradually until the subject can just detect its presence. You could also start with a fairly bright light and decrease the intensity until the subject reported that it was no longer visible. By taking an average of these two intensities, you could arrive at a good estimate of the absolute threshold for that person. Of course, the same basic procedure could be used to measure how intense a sound must be before you can hear it or to measure the acuity of any other sense.

An example of the use of absolute thresholds is the dark-adaptation curve, which is obtained by measuring a subject's absolute threshold for light every few minutes after they enter a totally darkened room. As you know from personal experience, your ability to see in a dark room improves considerably when you have been in the room for a while. A more familiar example is the common eye test, where you see letters of diminishing size and must try to read them. Your absolute threshold for letter recognition is being measured. If your threshold is higher than

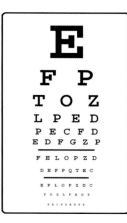

average, you will likely be buying some glasses or contact lenses.

There are some problems with this approach, which is called "classical" psychophysics. A major limitation to this approach is that it confounds sensitivity and bias. This means that the usual measure of a threshold is measuring both sensitivity and bias, and you cannot be sure how much each is influencing the score. *Sensitivity* refers to the actual functioning of your sense organs and nervous system—this is what psychologists (and optometrists) usually are interested in measuring. *Bias* refers to how willing you are to report that you detect a stimulus. Bias can alter our measure of sensitivity using classical psychophysical procedures to measure thresholds

because these procedures measure both sensitivity and bias. The basic reason for this is that there is always some degree of "noise" present, either in the environment or in your nervous system.

Here is an example of noise in your nervous system. You have probably had the experience at some time of being in a totally dark place—a photographic darkroom or a cave with no lights. What do you see? You don't see total blackness, but rather you see occasional points of light, vague gray shapes, and the like. The basic reason for this is that neurons (brain cells) "fire" at some background rate even when they are not being stimulated at all. The "physiological gray" that you see in a totally darkened room is due to that occasional, random firing of neurons in the visual system—noise. Of course, noise can occur in the environment as well. An example would be trying to find a traffic signal light at night on a street that has lots of bright, flashing neon signs. The same traffic signal would be easy to see at an intersection in a

residential neighborhood where there were few other lights, and thus less noise.

You can see, then, that you might occasionally "detect" a faint light in a totally darkened room even when it is not actually present, due to the background noise created by your own nervous system. Or you might not see a traffic light because of visual noise in the environment. The consequences of the latter could range from a traffic ticket to a serious accident.

Signal detection theory (Swets, Tanner, & Birdsall, 1961) is a psychophysical method of separating sensitivity and bias in any kind of task where a person must detect a signal against a background of noise. That signal might be the radar echo of a plane which an air traffic controller must be able to detect against the noise on a radar screen due to rain and other atmospheric "noise." It might involve detecting misprinted words in a book—proofreading—in which case the noise is all the other words on the page. Detecting a tumor on an X-ray is another example of signal detection, where the noise is the X-ray shadows produced by various body organs and tissues. As you can see, signal detection theory deals with issues that directly affect our everyday lives.

Obviously, the sensitivity of your eye (or of a radar scope) has an effect on how well you can perform in a signal detection task. The level of noise against which you are trying to detect a signal also can affect performance. Bias plays a part as well. Under some circumstances (discussed in more detail below), you are more *willing* to report detecting a signal—it depends upon the consequences of being right or wrong.

There are four versions of the signal detection task in the program. Your instructor will tell you which versions you are to complete. The four versions are intended to illustrate (a) variables that affect bias but not sensitivity and (b) variables that affect sensitivity but not bias.

Methodological Considerations

The Receiver Operating Characteristic and Calculation of d' and C

As noted above, sensitivity and bias can be measured separately, using signal detection theory. What follows is a brief explanation of how these are calculated and of how the data from signal detection experiments are graphed in a Receiver Operating Characteristic (ROC) curve.

The four possible outcomes in signal detection are listed below. Figure 1.2.1 illustrates how these four outcomes are determined.

- **hit**—reporting a signal when it is present

- **miss**—failing to report a signal when it is present

- **false alarm**—reporting a signal when it is not present

- **correct rejection**—correctly reporting that no signal is present

		State of the World	
		Noise Only	**Noise + Signal**
Decision	"Yes"	False Alarm	Hit
	"No"	Correct Rejection	Miss

FIGURE **1.2.1** – *Four possible outcomes in signal detection*

Note that if we know the number of trials on which a signal was present or not, the miss and correct rejection rates are completely redundant, since they can be determined if we know the hit rate and false alarm rate. For example, if there were 100 trials where a signal was present, and a subject had 90 hits, we know that he or she also had 10 misses. For this reason, signal detection analysis is based on hits and false alarms only.

The measures of sensitivity and bias are symbolized as **d'** (pronounced DEE-PRIME) and **C**, respec-

p	z	p	z	p	z	p	z	p	z
0.9999*	3.72								
0.99	2.33	0.89	1.23	0.79	0.81	0.69	0.50	0.59	0.23
0.98	2.05	0.88	1.18	0.78	0.77	0.68	0.48	0.58	0.20
0.97	1.88	0.87	1.13	0.77	0.74	0.67	0.44	0.57	0.18
0.96	1.75	0.86	1.08	0.76	0.71	0.66	0.41	0.56	0.15
0.95	1.64	0.85	1.04	0.75	0.67	0.65	0.39	0.55	0.13
0.94	1.55	0.84	0.99	0.74	0.64	0.64	0.36	0.54	0.10
0.93	1.48	0.83	0.95	0.73	0.61	0.63	0.33	0.53	0.08
0.92	1.41	0.82	0.92	0.72	0.58	0.62	0.31	0.52	0.05
0.91	1.34	0.81	0.88	0.71	0.55	0.61	0.28	0.51	0.03
0.90	1.28	**0.80**	0.84	**0.70**	0.52	**0.60**	0.25	**0.50**	0.00
0.49	-0.03	0.39	-0.28	0.29	-0.55	0.19	-0.88	0.09	-1.34
0.48	-0.05	0.38	-0.31	0.28	-0.58	0.18	-0.92	0.08	-1.41
0.47	-0.08	0.37	-0.33	0.27	-0.61	0.17	-0.95	0.07	-1.48
0.46	-0.10	0.36	-0.36	0.26	-0.64	0.16	-0.99	0.06	-1.55
0.45	-0.13	0.35	-0.39	0.25	-0.67	0.15	-1.04	0.05	-1.64
0.44	-0.15	0.34	-0.41	0.24	-0.71	0.14	-1.08	0.04	-1.75
0.43	-0.18	0.33	-0.44	0.23	-0.74	0.13	-1.13	0.03	-1.88
0.42	-0.20	0.32	-0.48	0.22	-0.77	0.12	-1.18	0.02	-2.05
0.41	-0.23	0.31	-0.50	0.21	-0.81	0.11	-1.23	0.01	-2.33
0.40	-0.25	**0.30**	-0.52	**0.20**	-0.84	**0.10**	-1.28	0.0001*	-3.72
*** Use these values when p = 1.00 or p = 0.00**									

TABLE 1.2.1 – *Table of values of z for selected values of "p."*

tively. The calculations of d' and C are quite straightforward, requiring only that you have a table of values of z (the unit normal distribution) with the area below each value of z. A table of selected values is shown in Table 1.2.1. The proportion of hits and false alarms for each condition is reported to you at the end of the experiment. Use the proportion of hits and false alarms to calculate d' and C, and check your calculation with the values displayed on the table. Your instructor may also give you the values for other members of the class who served as subjects in different versions of the experiment. Note that d' and C are calculated for individual subjects **only**. To get an average d' or C, they should first be calculated for each subject individually, and then averaged.

The ROC Curve

A graphical way of representing sensitivity and bias simultaneously is the Receiver Operating Characteristic (ROC—pronounced AR-OH-SEE) "curve." This is constructed by plotting one point on the ROC graph for each condition of a manipulation. Suppose that for one condition your hit rate (proportion of hits) was 0.70 and your false-alarm rate (proportion of false alarms) was 0.10. You would plot that point by finding where the lines for "Probability of a hit" of 0.70 and "Probability of a false alarm" of 0.10 intersect. The further a point is from the bold diagonal (i.e., the closer to the upper-left corner), the greater the sensitivity—i.e., many signals were correctly detected, but few false alarms occurred. In the case of the point just plotted, d' = 1.80, indicating good sensitivity. Note, however, that the point plotted is to the left of the thin diagonal line. This indicates a slight bias toward responding "No"—false alarms occurred somewhat less often than they would have if no bias were present. In fact, the value of C is 0.38 (C = 0 indicates no bias).

If we now varied some condition of the experiment (any of the four manipulations that make up the versions of this experiment), we could plot a series of points that make up an ROC curve. For example, if we varied the probability of a signal (which affects bias only), we would expect to find those points falling along a curve such as one in Figure 1.2.2, representing changes in bias while sensitivity remained constant. On the other hand, if we varied a condition like the intensity of the noise (which affects sensitivity but not bias), we would expect to find the points differing in their distance from the diagonal line (where sensitivity is zero), but the points should not differ in their location along the curved line (showing their similar bias).

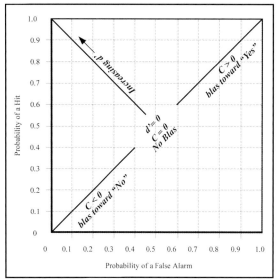

FIGURE 1.2.3 – ROC graph

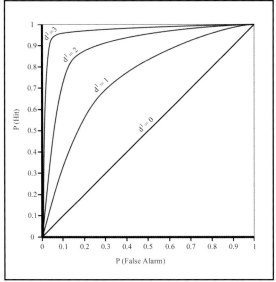

FIGURE 1.2.2 – Typical ROC curves illustrating d'

Another view of the ROC space is shown in Figure 1.2.3, indicating differences of d' and C. A larger copy of this graph can be printed from your disk. Your instructor may ask you to print this table and plot your data on it. You should

plot the points representing probabilities of hits and false alarms for each of the two blocks of trials in the version of the task that you completed in a brief lab. A more complete experiment would, of course, map out more than just two points on the ROC curve, but the number of trials needed to do so is greater than easily can be accommodated. Do sensitivity and/or bias seem to differ between the two conditions? The Discussion section below presents expected outcomes for each version. You should then calculate values of d' and C to determine the actual levels of bias and sensitivity.

Calculation of d'

The calculation of d' (the measure of sensitivity) requires that you look up the z-scores associated with the probability of a hit and the probability of a false alarm. (See Table 1.2.1.) The probability of hits and false alarms are the same as the proportion of hits and false alarms reported to you. The formula for d' is as follows:

d' = [z for p(hit)] – [z for p(false alarm)]

To illustrate, suppose that, for an individual subject, the proportion of hits was 0.70 and the proportion of false alarms was 0.10. Looking up 0.70 (under "p") in the table, we find a corresponding value of z = 0.52. Looking up 0.10 in the table in the same way, we find $z = -1.28$. Applying the formula, we have the following calculation and result.

$$d' = z_{(0.70)} - z_{(0.10)}$$
$$= [0.52] - [-1.28]$$
$$= \mathbf{1.80}$$

Note that a positive d' indicates that sensitivity was at better than a chance level, and the higher the d', the greater the sensitivity. If the proportion of hits and false alarms is equal, however, d' will be zero, indicating that performance was at a chance level. Also, d' can be negative, though only when the proportion of false alarms exceeds the proportion of hits. In this case, sensitivity is at a level worse than merely guessing.

Note also that if you had no false alarms (p = 0) and/or a 100% hit rate (p = 1), the true value of z would be infinity. To permit a reasonable calculation in these cases, we choose instead to use the value of z associated with p of .0001 or .9999, as noted in Table 1.2.1.

Calculation of C
The calculation of C (the measure of bias) requires the same information as when calculating d', but arranged in a different order. The formula for C is as follows:

C = 0.5 [z for p(hit) + z for p(false alarm)]

To illustrate, assume that we have the same values as in the discussion of the calculation of d'—namely, p(hit) = 0.70 and p(false alarm) = 0.10. Applying the formula, we have the following calculation and result.

$$C = 0.5[z_{(0.70)} + z_{(0.10)}]$$
$$= 0.5[0.52 + (-1.28)]$$
$$= \mathbf{-0.38}$$

This indicates a bias toward responding "No," whether or not a signal is present. Note that,

when calculating C, the following conclusions may be drawn:

- A value of C < 0 indicates a bias toward responding "No," whether or not a signal is present.

- A value of C > 0 indicates a bias toward responding "Yes," whether or not a signal is present.

- If C = 0, then no bias is present.

The data illustrated thus would have come from a subject whose sensitivity was pretty good, but whose hit rate was lower than it might have been, partly due to a bias toward reporting that no signal was present.

NOTE: You will need to round the values of p(hit) and p(false alarm) in order to use Table 1.2.1. Your calculations based on this table may differ from those reported at the end of the experiment since those are not rounded. Most statistics textbooks contain more extensive tables that will allow you to make more accurate calculations.

Discussion
The four versions of this experiment are designed to illustrate four general types of variables that affect signal detection. Two of these (the

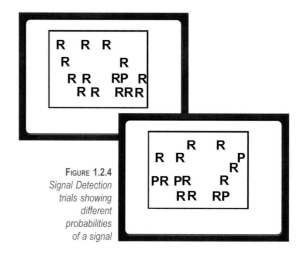

FIGURE 1.2.4
Signal Detection trials showing different probabilities of a signal

probability of a signal and the payoffs) should affect bias but not sensitivity, while the others (intensity of the signal and intensity of the noise) should affect sensitivity but not bias.

Variables Affecting Bias

Version I: Manipulation of the probability of a signal. Note that, for this part of the experiment on signal detection, there are values of both p(hit) and p(false alarm) for two different probabilities of a signal. The expected outcome is that bias (rather than sensitivity) will be affected, with a positive bias (C > 0) occurring when the probability of a signal is 0.80 and, conversely, a negative bias (C < 0) occurring when the probability of a signal is only 0.20. When a signal occurs on most trials, subjects begin to expect it, providing a bias toward responding "Yes." On the other hand, when the signal is relatively rare, subjects begin to expect that there will not be a signal, resulting in a bias toward responding "No." Thus, the value of C (bias) should differ between the two probability conditions, but d' (sensitivity) should not.

Version II: Manipulation of payoffs. In this version of the experiment, the probability of a signal is 50%, but the number of "points" won or lost by the subject is manipulated. In one block of trials, the "payoff" is to win five points for each hit and lose only one point for each false alarm. Ideally, this should result in a bias toward responding "Yes" (C > 0), since the payoff for a hit is large, but the penalty for a false alarm is low. Indeed, if the penalty for a false alarm is low enough, a strategy of just ignoring that penalty and always responding "Yes" might seem reasonable. In effect, you would not even have to bother to look! In the other block of this manipulation, the payoffs are reversed: win one point for a hit, but lose five points for a false alarm. With false alarms so costly, the subjects are expected to respond "Yes" only when they are absolutely certain that the signal was present. This should result in a bias toward responding "No" (C < 0). Again, the value of C

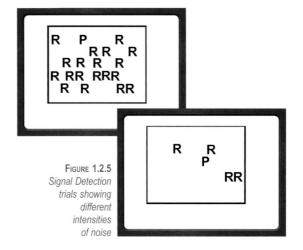

FIGURE 1.2.5
Signal Detection trials showing different intensities of noise

(bias) should differ between the two payoff conditions, but d' (sensitivity) should not.

Variables Affecting Sensitivity

Version III: Manipulation of intensity of the signal. In this version of the experiment, the intensity of the signal is manipulated by changing the number of times the target letter "P" occurs in the display: either once or four times. It is expected that it will be easier to spot a "P" if there are a lot of them present than if there is only one. Because this manipulation makes the signal easier to see, it should affect sensitivity, but not bias, with sensitivity being greater (i.e., d' will be larger) when the more "intense" signal is present. Since the target appears on 50% of the trials and no explicit payoffs are presented, C should be near 0 for both blocks of trials. (Individual subjects actually may show a bias toward "Yes" or "No," based on implicit payoffs and their own expectations about what is "good" performance. In this case, C may be greater or less than 0, but the bias should still be about the same in each block of trials.)

Version IV: Manipulation of the intensity of the noise. In this version, intensity of the noise is manipulated by varying the number of the letter "R" (the noise) displayed on the screen: either four or nineteen. When only four noise letters are on the screen, it is expected that determining whether or not a "P" was present should be relatively easy. On the other hand, when there are nineteen "R's" on the screen, a "P" will be more likely to "disappear" into the background of noise. This manipulation affects the ability of the subject to see the target and thus should affect sensitivity but not bias, with d' being larger (reflecting greater sensitivity) when there is less noise. Since the target appears on 50% of the trials and no explicit payoffs are presented, C should be near 0 for both blocks of trials. (As in the manipulation of signal intensity, individual subjects may actually show a bias toward "Yes" or "No," based on implicit payoffs and their own expectations about what is "good" performance. In this case, C may be greater or less than 0, but the bias should still be about the same in each block of trials.)

• • • • • • • • • • • • • • • • • • • •
Expected Running Time = 45 minutes
• • • • • • • • • • • • • • • • • • • •

Questions

1. What are the dependent and independent variables in these experiments? What are some important controls?

2. What are the results? What effect does each independent variable have on bias and on sensitivity?

3. A real-world signal detection task is decision-making by a jury in a criminal case. What would be a hit? A false alarm? What might bias the jury in favor of a guilty verdict or in favor of acquittal? How might you improve the sensitivity of the jury?

Extension Experiments

1. Devise other signal-detection tasks, along with ways to manipulate both sensitivity and bias. The search task used in the experiment on automaticity (Chapter 2.8, *Automatic versus Controlled Processing*) could be studied using signal-detection measures.

References

Commons, M. L., Nevin, J. A., & Davison, M. C. (Eds.). (1991). *Signal detection: mechanisms, models, and applications.* Hillsdale, NJ: Lawrence Erlbaum.

Fechner, G. (1966). *Elements of psychophysics* (H. E. Adler, Trans.). New York: Holt, Rinehart and Winston. (Original work published 1856)

Gescheider, G. A. (1997). *Psychophysics: The Fundamentals* (3rd ed.). Mahwah, NJ: L. A. Erlbaum Associates.

Swets, J., Tanner, W., & Birdsall, T. (1961). Decision processes in perception. *Psychological Review, 68,* 301-340.

Wickens, C. D. (1992). *Engineering psychology and human performance.* New York: HarperCollins.

1.3 Rotation of Mental Images

Abstract

Psychology had an early concern for mental imagery, but problems with that research led to the virtual abandonment of the study of imagery. More recently, researchers have found ways to measure certain aspects of imagery. One successful technique uses "rotation" of mental images. A person is shown two shapes and must decide whether or not they are the same (regardless of rotation). One shape is sometimes rotated with respect to the other, and people report that they make the judgment by rotating their image of one shape to determine whether it matches the other. If peoples' reports are accurate, it should take longer to rotate the image when the stimulus is rotated farther from vertical. Shepard and his colleagues (e.g., Cooper & Shepard, 1973) have done a number of experiments of this type, and have found that images do seem to be rotated, and at a steady, measurable speed. The exercise accompanying this chapter has students perform one of two versions of this task to measure the speed of rotation of mental images.

*H*ow many windows are in your family home? Take a moment to answer this question before you continue. In order to answer the question, you probably constructed an image of each room in your house or of the outside of your house viewed from various directions and then counted the number of windows you "saw." That's an example of a mental image. Other examples might include imagining a friend's face or picturing to yourself which buildings you have to walk past to go to the library.

The study of mental imagery illustrates an interesting challenge for the science of psychology-namely, how to study internal mental processes that are not open to direct observation. Note that I cannot directly observe your mental images, nor can you observe mine. But through careful experimentation, it is possible not only to make legitimate inferences about images, but also to actually measure some aspects of them.

Because of the difficulty of studying mental images, such study fell from favor during much of the 20th century. But new techniques emerged that brought it back in a very prominent way. The modern study of images comes from two general lines of research. Paivio (1963; see Paivio, 1995, for a review) showed that concrete nouns (names of actual objects, such as "boat" or "pencil") are recalled better than abstract nouns (such as "beauty" or "justice") in a wide variety of contexts. He interpreted this concreteness effect in terms of a dual-code theory of memory: We can store concrete nouns, both in terms of the word itself and in terms of an image of the object, whereas it is hard to form images of abstract nouns. Because concrete nouns have two representations, we are more likely to retain a good retrieval cue.

The second line of research that brought imagery back to the mainstream of psychology was the work of Shepard and his colleagues (Shepard & Metzler, 1971; Shepard & Feng, 1972; Cooper & Shepard, 1973) on transformations of mental images. The discovery of quantitative relationships regarding how reaction times change as a stimulus is altered has proved to be a very powerful tool in understanding the underlying mechanisms for many cognitive operations. The experiments accompanying this chapter illustrate this approach to studying internal processes in psychology.

Methods for Studying Mental Imagery

If mental images are in some ways analogous to direct perceptions of objects, then it follows that mental images should follow some of the same rules that govern perception of physical objects. For example, if I showed you a picture of someone and asked you who it was, but I handed you the picture upside-down, you probably would have to turn the picture right-side-up in order to recognize the face. The operation of rotating the picture would require some measurable amount of time. Does manipulation of mental images operate in a similar fashion?

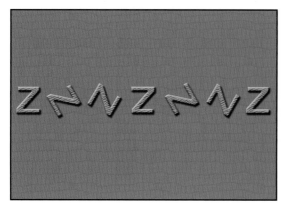

FIGURE 1.3.1

Behavioral Analysis

A series of studies suggests that they do. Cooper and Shepard (1973) briefly presented subjects with pictures of letters that were rotated left or right in varying degrees between right-side-up and up-side-down (see Figure 1.3.1). The letters also varied in that some were mirror images of actual letters. The subject's task was to report

whether the letter was normal or mirror-image. The main question was whether subjects would take longer to make that judgment when the letters were rotated further from vertical. The results showed that the farther the letter was rotated, the longer it took for a subject to make the judgment about whether the letter was normal or mirror-image.

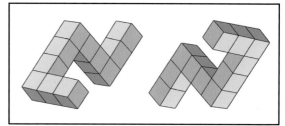

FIGURE **1.3.2** – *Example 2D figures similar to those used by Shepard and Metzler*

Shepard and Metzler (1971) did a similar experiment, except that they presented two figures at once, and subjects had to decide whether or not the two figures were the same (see Figure 1.3.2).

The figures varied in that one was rotated with respect to the other. Again, the greater the rotation, the longer it took subjects to identify two figures as the same or different. The

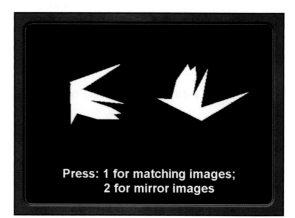

FIGURE **1.3.3** – *Example trial from the Rotation of Mental Images experiment*

experiment in which you will participate is similar to the Shepard and Metzler (1971) experiment, except that two-dimensional (2D) geometric forms are used (see Figure 1.3.3).

Psychophysiological Analysis

An issue of considerable interest to both cognitive scientists and neuroscientists is whether the production of mental images uses any of the brain mechanisms used during actual perception. That is, are some of the same parts of the brain that are used when we actually see an object also used when imagining that same object? Some evidence suggests that this is true. Using PET scans, Kosslyn et al. (1993) showed similar patterns of activation of the cerebral cortex during both perceptual and imagery versions of the same task.

A similar result was reported by Le Bihan, Turner, Zeffiro, Cuenod, Jezzard, and Bonnerot (1993) using functional Magnetic Resonance Imaging (fMRI). They showed an increase in activation of the visual cortex, but not of the non-visual cortex, during both perception and imagery (though the activation was slightly less with imagery). Kosslyn and Sussman (1995) reviewed other evidence for the intimate role of imagery in everyday perception.

Georgopulous, Lurito, Petrides, Schwartz, and Massey (1989) studied activation of single neurons in the motor cortex of a monkey trained to perform a version of a mental rotation task. As the monkey prepared to move its arm in a certain way, there were changes in activation of neurons along a trajectory, as would be expected if there was an anticipation of moving the arm through a series of locations.

Additional Findings

Sex differences in the mental rotation task are another fascinating development. Studies consistently find rather large differences in reaction time for mental rotation tasks, favoring

males. For the version of the task used in the experiment accompanying this chapter, the difference is usually about 200 ms. This difference in mental rotation is one of the largest sex differences found in cognitive tasks (Hyde & McKinley, 1997). The cause of the sex difference in mental rotation is not known, though there has been a lot of speculation about both biological and psychological causes (Caplan, Crawford, Hyde, & Richardson, 1996; Halpern, 2000). Research on an analogous task suggests that the difference may be reduced or eliminated by practice (Kass, Ahlers, & Dugger, 1998).

The Imagery Debate

Although many researchers accept that mental images exist and that they are depictive, rather than descriptive, others have challenged that point of view. Kosslyn (1994) argued that the issue of whether there are depictions (images) or descriptions that represent our knowledge of spatial/visual objects had been settled in favor of the existence of images. Essentially, the claim is that mental images involve the same brain mechanisms that are used in actual perception. Pylyshyn has raised doubts about this interpretation. Though the debate is too wide-ranging to be covered here, the principle arguments and counter-arguments were summarized by Pylyshyn (2002, 2003). Pylyshyn's (2002) Mental imagery: In search of a theory was published in Behavioral and Brain Sciences, which is a journal with which the student of psychology should be acquainted. The journal publishes lead articles on various areas of research, with invited commentaries by other researchers in the field, and the lead author's reply to them. Kosslyn, Thompson, and Gaddis (2002) are among those who replied to Pylyshyn's lead article. (The lead article and all of the commentaries and replies are available in PDF format on Zenon Pylyshyn's web site at *www.uccs.rutgers.edu/faculty/pylyshyn.html*.)

Methodological Considerations

There have been two general types of presentations used in studies of mental rotation. Cooper and Shepard (1973) presented single pictures, with subjects comparing them to a stored representation of an upright object, such as a letter. Shepard and Metzler (1971) presented two stimuli at a time, with one rotated relative to the other, as in the experiment accompanying this chapter. Note that this permits the use of arbitrary, abstract stimuli for which there is no defined "right-side-up." This has the advantage of not relying on subjects' memories; however, it also presents a disadvantage in that it is harder to determine which figure is being rotated-perhaps the subject rotates both at once.

. . . .
Expected Running Time = 18 minutes
. . . .

Questions

1. What are the dependent and independent variables in this experiment? What are some important controls?

2. Can we rotate images in more than the two dimensions used in this experiment? Shepard and Metzler (1971) performed such an experiment, and you should refer to their article.

3. What is the speed of rotation of the shapes? Calculate this in degrees per second. Was the speed constant? Compare your results to Shepard and Metzler's (1971) findings with "picture-plane" pairs. If there is a difference, how might it have been influenced by the nature of the shapes used? Cooper (1975) also compared a number of different images. This experiment used two of her shapes.

4. How clear are your mental images? Discuss this with your classmates. You may find that some people claim that they "see" their images almost as clearly as if they were actually looking at the objects. Others will report that they have only rather vague images. These reports are like the introspection used by early psychologists. What sorts of problems are there in interpreting these reports?

Extension Experiments

Because this experiment involves the presentation of bitmapped image files, it is possible for you to make many modifications to the stimulus materials using the existing program. In order to do this, you will need to have your stimuli stored as .bmp files. If you use a graphics program to make the stimulus files, simply save them as .bmp files. If you choose to draw your stimuli freehand or to copy them from another source, use a scanner to import them into a graphics program where you can adjust the size and save the result as a .bmp file. Note that you will need to make copies of the stimuli in all necessary rotations. Most graphics programs enable you to rotate an image easily by a specified amount.

Advanced Questions

1. Is the speed of rotation dependent on the specific shapes used? (Note that, in this experiment, the data were averaged across shapes, but the data as to what shape was used on each trial was stored by the computer and could be subject to analysis.) Cooper (1975) compared a number of different shapes. The two used in this experiment were her Forms B and D.

2. What are the results for non-visual presentation? Specifically, what happens if the shapes are presented haptically (i.e., by touch)? See Carpenter and Eisenberg (1978).

3. Another task that has been used to study the manipulation of mental images is mental paper-folding, in which a subject is shown a diagram of a box that has been unfolded into a flat surface. Two edges are marked, and the subject must decide whether those edges would meet if the object were folded into a box again. For this task, it seems that people must make a series of discrete manipulations of the mental image, rather than a continuous change such as rotation. Shepard and Feng (1972) did an experiment using this task, finding that there was an increase in reaction time as the number of "folds" required was increased. Stimuli such as they used can be drawn easily on paper. Because of the time required to do this task, a stopwatch can be used to record the reaction times with sufficient accuracy.

References

Caplan, P. A., Crawford, M., Hyde, J. S., & Richardson J. T. E. (Eds.). (1997). *Gender differences in human cognition.* New York: Oxford University Press.

Carpenter, P. A., & Eisenberg, P. (1978). Mental rotation and the frame of reference in blind and sighted individuals. *Perception and Psychophysics, 23,* 117-124.

Cooper, L. A. (1975). Mental rotation of random two-dimensional shapes. *Cognitive Psychology, 7,* 20-43.

Cooper, L. A., & Shepard, R. N. (1973). Chronometric studies of the rotation of mental images. In W. G. Chase (Ed.), *Visual information processing.* New York: Academic Press.

Halpern, D. F. (2000). *Sex differences in cognitive abilities* (3rd ed.). Hillsdale, NJ: Lawrence Erlbaum Associates.

Hyde, J. S., & McKinley, N. M. (1997). Gender differences in cognition: Results from meta-analysis. In P. A. Caplan, M. Crawford, J. S. Hyde, & J. T. E. Richardson (Eds.), *Gender differences in human cognition* (pp. 30-51). New York: Oxford University Press.

Kass, S. J., Ahlers, R. H., & Dugger, M. (1998). Eliminating gender differences through practice in an applied visual spatial task. *Human Performance, 11,* 337-349.

Kosslyn, S. (1980). *Image and mind.* Cambridge, MA: Harvard University Press.

References *(continued)*

Kosslyn, S. (1994). *Image and Brain: The resolution of the imagery debate.* Cambridge, MA: MIT Press.

Kosslyn, S., Alpert, N., Thompson, W., Maljkovic, V., Weise, S., Chabris, C., et al. (1993). Visual mental imagery activates topographically organized visual cortex: PET investigations. *Journal of Cognitive Neuroscience, 5,* 263-287.

Kosslyn, S., & Sussman, A. (1995). Roles of imagery in perception: Or, there is no such thing as immaculate perception. In M. S. Gazzaniga (Ed.), *The cognitive neurosciences* (pp. 1035-1042). Cambridge, MA: MIT Press.

Kosslyn, S., Thompson, W., & Ganis, G. (2002). Mental imagery doesn't work like that. *Behavioral and Brain Sciences, 25,* 198-200.

Le Bihan, D., Turner, R., Zeffiro, T. A., Cuenod, C. A., Jezzard, P., & Bonnerot, V. (1993). Activation of human primary visual cortex during visual recall: A magnetic resonance imaging study. *Proceedings of the National Academy of Sciences USA, 90,* 11802-11805.

Paivio, A. (1963). Learning of adjective-noun associates as a function of adjective-noun word order and noun abstractness. *Canadian Journal of Psychology, 17,* 370-379.

Paivio, A. (1971). *Imagery and verbal processes.* New York: Holt, Rinehart & Winston.

Paivio, A. (1995). Imagery and memory. In M. S. Gazzaniga (Ed.), *The cognitive neurosciences* (pp. 977-986). Cambridge, MA: MIT Press.

Pylyshyn, Z. W. (1973). What the mind's eye tells the mind's brain: A critique of mental imagery. *Psychological Bulletin, 80,* 1-24.

Pylyshyn, Z. (2002). Mental imagery: In search of a theory. *Behavioral and Brain Sciences, 25,* 157-237.

Pylyshyn, Z. (2003). Return of the mental image: Are there really pictures in the head? *Trends in Cognitive Science, 7,* 113-118.

Shepard, R. N., & Feng, C. A. (1972). A chronometric study of mental paper folding. *Cognitive Psychology, 3,* 228-243.

Shepard, R. N., & Metzler, J. (1971). Mental rotation of three-dimensional objects. *Science, 171,* 701-703.

1.4 Perceptual Matching

• •

Abstract

In the exercise accompanying this chapter, letters are compared, and subjects must indicate whether they are the same or different. Two letters are considered to be the "same" if they are physically the same (e.g., "A" and "A") or if they have the same letter name but differ in physical appearance (e.g., "A" and "a"). Comparisons of interest concern name-match vs. physical-match, as well as the time interval between presentation of the first and second letters. The experiment repeats one by Posner, Boies, Eichelman, and Taylor (1969). While the results of this experiment were initially thought to indicate the use of a visual code, with the stimuli then being recoded phonetically (representing the sound of the letter name), later research has suggested that this is not the case. Other models of the data are considered. The letter-matching task has become a standard task for comparing various special populations, and research on those issues is presented.

• •

A basic question concerning perception and memory is how we compare two stimuli to determine whether they are the same. If you are asked to compare two visual stimuli that are both visible at the same time, you need only examine them visually to determine whether or not they are the same—you don't need to name the stimuli in order to do this. On the other hand, if only one stimulus is visible at a time, the first must be remembered for comparison to the second.

The experiment accompanying this chapter replicates (with minor changes) Posner, Boies, Eichelman, and Taylor's (1969) Experiment 1, which examines how information presented visually is encoded in short-term memory (STM). (Note that short-term memory is also known as working memory.) The experiment uses a letter-matching task in which subjects see two letters presented visually on a computer screen, as shown in Figure 1.4.1. They must decide, as quickly as possible, whether the two letters are the same (e.g., "A"/"A" or "B"/"b") or whether they are different (e.g., "A"/"B" or "B"/"a"). On some trials, both letters are presented at the same time. On other trials, one letter is presented either one or two seconds before the other.

Posner and Keele (1967) reported that a physical match (e.g., "A"/"A" or "b"/"b") was faster than a name match (e.g., "A"/"a" or "b"/ "B") by about 90 ms if both were presented simultaneously, but that difference disappeared when there was a delay of 1.5 seconds between presentation of the two letters. Posner et al. (1969) replicated that finding. Their interpretation was that when both letters are seen at the same time, subjects can respond most easily to a physical match. The response to a name match is slowed because the letters must be switched to

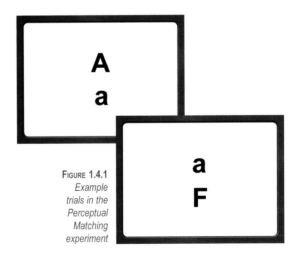

FIGURE 1.4.1
Example trials in the Perceptual Matching experiment

a phonetic (sound) representation. When there is a delay, subjects have time to switch to a phonetic representation (e.g., "BEE" instead of "B"). When the second letter appears, it must be switched to a name code in order to make the comparison, whether the second letter is a physical match or a name match. Thus, the difference between name matches and physical matches is reduced to zero if enough time elapses to permit the first letter to be switched to a phonetic representation.

There is considerable evidence that, in some cases, short-term memory for visual stimuli is based on a sound or name code. In Baddelay's (1986) *working memory* model, this is called the *phonological loop*. It sometimes is referred to as the *articulatory loop*, also. (See Figure 1.4.2.) For example, if visually shown the letter "b" and asked to rehearse it, we usually remember the sound "BEE" rather than a visual representation of the letter "b." Evidence for the use of this name code in short-term memory comes from work by Sperling (1963), who found that errors in recall in a task involving brief visual presentation of sets of letters were usually the result of acoustic confusions. For example, subjects who had seen an "F" were more likely to incorrectly recall an "S" (which sounds like *ef*) rather than an "E" (which *looks like* an "F"). This finding has been replicated and extended by Conrad (1964).

But the interpretation of Posner et al.'s (1979) results has been challenged. Kroll and Parks (1979) showed a continued advantage for physical matches over delays as long as 12 seconds. Carrasco, Kinchla, and Figueroa (1988) also presented data challenging the existence of a phonetic representation. Besner, Coltheart, and Davelaar (1984) argued for an abstract representation of letter identities that is neither visual nor phonological. Marquer and Pereira (2002) present evidence for a variety of strategies that subjects might use in this task.

Boles and Eveland (1983) and Boles (1992) have provided perhaps the best evidence that phonetic representation is not used in mixed-case (e.g. "A"/"a") letter-matching. Using a variant of the Posner letter-matching task (which apparently was first introduced by Thorson, Hochhaus, and Stanners, 1976), they presented *same* pairs that were either physical or name matches, but their *different* pairs were either phonetically similar (e.g., "A"/"j") or not (e.g., "A"/"z"). They found no difference in RT between the two types of different pairs, whether the letters were presented simultaneously or successively, despite the clear findings of acoustic confusions in the work of Sperling (1961) and Conrad (1964) noted above. They argue that the phonetic representation is thus ruled out.

Moreover, Boles (1992) argued for some kind of visual matching, based on experiments with pairs of letters whose opposite cases resemble each other (such as "Q"/"g", where "Q" resembles "G" and "g" resembles "q"). In this case, RTs are increased for such pairs, relative to pairs where the case of one does not resemble the case of

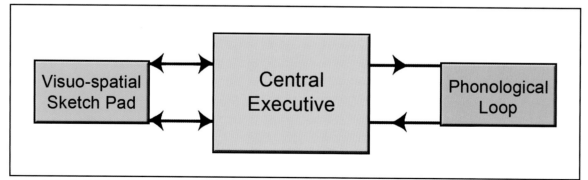

FIGURE 1.4.2 – *Baddelay's working memory model, illustrating the phonological or articulatory loop*

the other (such as "A"/"b"). They accounted for their results with the *fast-generation model.* That model proposes that we automatically generate the opposite case representation when we see a letter. For different pairs where the letters resemble the opposite cases, a confusion results. For example, on seeing "Q"/"g," we generate "q" (the opposite case of "Q") and also "G" (the opposite case of "g"). We then compare the generated representations to the actual stimulus representations. The resulting confusions of visually similar representations slow the RT. The existence of visual confusions in the absence of phonological confusions thus reinforces the claims by others that the original results of Posner et al. (1969) are not, as claimed, based on conversion to a phonological representation.

Other Uses of the Letter-Matching Task

Whatever the ultimate outcome of the theoretical debates concerning the letter-matching task, such robust findings of a faster response to physical matches than to name matches has found its way into other literatures. For example, Kerr, Calogero, Vitiello, and Prinz (1992) explored changes in letter-matching performance in normal-aging persons, in Alzheimer's patients, and in persons with major depression. They found that major depression had little effect on performance, compared to normals of about the same age. While normal aging led to overall slower performance, the difference between name matches and physical matches increased, also. The Alzheimer's patients showed a similar slowing relative to aged normals. Reuter-Lorenz, Stanczak, and Miller (1999) also report on bihemispheric processing in older and younger subjects in letter-matching tasks.

A fascinating finding (Eviatar & Zaidel, 1993) is that overall RT for letter-matching tasks is faster when the letters are presented bilaterally—i.e., one on the right and one on the left. Due to the nature of the pathways from the eyes to the visual cortex, it turns out that each letter is presented initially to a single hemisphere of the brain. (The visual signals from the left side of each eye are sent to the left hemisphere, whereas signals from the right side of each eye are sent to the right hemisphere.) Hagelthorn, Brown, Amano, and Asarnow (2000) have explored the development of this bilateral advantage with age. They conclude that it is based on maturation of the corpus callosum (the large brain structure that is the main relay of signals between the two hemispheres) and a resulting improvement in the ability to integrate information across the midline.

Methodological Considerations

The stimuli and ordering of presentation are nearly identical to those of Posner et al. (1969).

Interstimulus interval (ISI) is blocked, with the order of the blocks being randomized for each subject. The issue of blocking is considered in several of the *PsychMate Student Guide* chapters (see, in particular, Chapter 5.1, *Reaction Time Procedures*). The essential issue is that if all the trials were randomized across ISIs, subjects might treat the trials as being all alike—for example, if a delay sometimes occurs, they may always prepare for a delay. In that case, any changes in processing that occur due to the different ISIs may well be masked.

Expected Running Time = 30 minutes

Questions

1. What are the dependent and independent variables for this experiment? What are some important controls?

2. What are the results? Does the RT advantage for physical matches over name matches decrease with increasing ISI? If so, there should be a significant interaction between ISI and type of match.

3. In what ways did this experiment differ from that of Posner et al.'s (1969) Experiment 1? Do these differences seem to have had any effect on the results?

Extension Experiments

1. Boles (1992) presents a series of variants on the Posner et al. (1969) task that dispute the phonological-representation theory of why physical matches are slower than name matches at short ISIs. A number of those would be relatively easy to explore.

References

Baddelay, A. D. (1986). *Working memory.* Oxford: Oxford University Press.

Besner, D., Coltheart, M., & Davelaar, E. (1984). Basic processes in reading: Computation of abstract letter identities. *Canadian Journal of Psychology, 38,* 126-134.

Boles, D. B. (1992). Fast visual generation: Its nature and chronometrics. *Perception and Psychophysics, 51,* 239-246.

Boles, D. B., & Eveland, D. C. (1983). Visual and phonetic codes and the process of generation in letter matching. *Journal of Experimental Psychology: Human Perception and Performance, 9,* 657-674.

Carrasco, M., Kinchla, R., & Figueroa, J. G. (1988) Visual letter-matching and the time course of visual and acoustic codes. *Acta Psychologica, 69,* 1-17.

Conrad, R. (1964). Acoustic confusions in immediate memory. *British Journal of Psychology, 1964,* 75-84.

Eviatar, Z., & Zaidel, E. (1992). Letter matching in the hemispheres: Speed-accuracy trade-offs. *Neuropsychologia, 30,* 699-710.

Hagelthorn, K. M., Brown, W. S., Amano, S., & Asarnow, R. (2000). Normal development of bilateral field advantage and evoked potential interhemispheric transmission time. *Developmental Neuropsychology, 18,* 11-31.

Kerr, B., Calogero, M., Vitiello, M.V., & Prinz, P. N. (1992). Letter matching: Effects of age, Alzheimer's disease, and major depression. *Journal of Clinical and Experimental Neuropsychology, 14,* 478-498.

Kroll, N. E., & Parks, T. E. (1978). Interference with short-term visual memory produced by concurrent central processing. *Journal of Experimental Psychology: Human Learning and Memory, 4,* 111-120.

Marquer, J., & Pereira, M. (2002). "Know the method your subject is using…" and "Never average over methods": An application of Newell's admonition to letter-matching. *Cognitive Science Quarterly, 2*, 141-162.

Posner, M. I., Boies, S. J., Eichelman, H. W., & Taylor, R. L. (1969). Retention of visual and name codes of single letters. *Journal of Experimental Psychology Monographs*, 79 (1, Pt. 2).

Posner, M. I., & Boies, S. J. (1971). Components of attention. *Psychological Review, 87*, 391-405.

Posner, M. I., & Keele, S. W. (1967). Decay of visual information from a single letter. *Science, 158*, 137-139.

Reuter-Lorenz, O. A., Stanczak, L., & Miller, A. C. (1999). Neural recruitment and cognitive aging: Two hemispheres are better than one, especially as you age. *Psychological Science, 10*, 494-500.

Sperling, G. (1963). A model for visual memory tasks. *Human Factors, 5*, 19-31.

Thorson, G., Hochhaus, L., & Stanners, R. F. (1976). Temporal changes in visual and acoustic codes in a letter-matching task. *Perception & Psychophysics, 19*, 346-348.

1.5 Attentional Interference and the Stroop Effect

Abstract

The *Stroop effect* refers to the very robust finding that persons asked to *name* the colors in which letters are displayed are much slower to do so if the letters form the names of other colors (e.g., BLUE printed in red ink or RED printed in blue ink) than if they form the name of the color in which they are displayed (e.g., BLUE printed in blue ink or RED printed in red ink) or if the letters do not form words (e.g., XXXX or XXXXXX). This slowing in the time to name the colors works only in one direction. Subjects asked to *read* the words are *not* slowed when a word does not match the color in which it is displayed. Since the initial publication of these findings (Stroop, 1935), there has been an enormous amount of research done to try to find the reason for this slowing. There now seems to be reasonable agreement that the Stroop effect is the result of both (a) the automatic nature of reading and (b) our inability to inhibit this automatic process, such that we cannot inhibit an at least partial response of saying the word, which then interferes with the ability to name the color of the letters.

*I*n 1935, J. Ridley Stroop published a paper in the *Journal of Experimental Psychology* that became one of the most-cited papers in psychology.[4] Stroop's Experiment 2 is the most direct demonstration of the Stroop effect. He had his subjects name out loud the colors in which either solid squares of color or words were printed. When the subjects named the color in which words were printed, the words named other colors. The difference in time to name the colors of 100 squares or 100 words was dramatic. Naming the colors of the squares took, on average, 63.3 seconds, while naming the colors of words that named other colors took an average of 110.3 seconds—a 74% increase. Stroop's Experiment 1 demonstrated an important related phenomenon—there is no interference in *reading* words (as opposed to *naming the colors* in which they are printed), whether the words were printed in colors that did not match (e.g., RED printed in blue ink) or printed in black. The mean times to read the 100 color names for this experiment were 41 seconds for the words in black and 43.4 seconds for those in

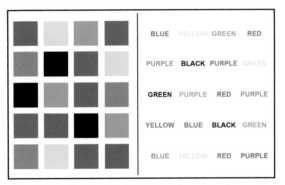

FIGURE **1.5.1** – *The Stroop task illustrated a tremendous increase in the time to name the print colors for words versus solid squares.*

a different color—a negligible slowing of less than 6% for words printed in other colors.

This slowing in color-naming when the letters formed the names of other colors is known as the *Stroop effect* and has been the basis for a huge number of studies in psychology. In his 1991 review of the literature, MacLeod noted that there were over 700 published studies, most coming after the earlier reviews by Jensen and Rohwer (1966) and Dyer (1976). A search of PsycINFO found 152 articles under the index

---

[4] For a brief biography of Stroop, see MacLeod (1992).

term "Stroop effect" between January, 2000, and June, 2003. Why this fascination? The Stroop effect is one of the easiest phenomena in psychology to replicate, but its causes have been rather resistant to explanation.

Theories of the Stroop Effect

In his 1991 review (indispensable reading for anyone beginning research on the Stroop effect), MacLeod noted that Stroop was building on a considerable literature before him, though none had posed the problem as well as he had in his 1935 article. James McKeen Cattell (who was to become among the most prominent of early American psychologists) reported in 1886, in his doctoral work with Wilhelm Wundt (founder of the first formal laboratory and academic department of psychology), that reading the word "red" out loud was faster than saying "red" in response to a patch of red color, and he gave a distinctly modern explanation: "This is because, in the case of words and letters, the association between the idea and the name has taken place so often that the process has become automatic, whereas in the case of colors … we must by a voluntary effort choose the name" (Cattell, 1886, p. 65, cited in MacLeod, 1991).

MacLeod, in his 1991 review of the Stroop literature, presented a list of 18 empirical results in regard to the Stroop effect that he argues must be accounted for by any theory of the Stroop effect. He also reviewed the extant theories of the Stroop effect. Here, we can do no more than sketch these theories and note some related studies.

One theory is the *relative speed of processing* theory. In this theory, words are read faster than colors are named. The result is that two potential responses compete for the production of the final response of a spoken word or a key-press. MacLeod notes that this view, with some elaboration, can account for 15 of the 18 "critical findings" from his review of the literature. However, he rejects this theory because a number of studies that directly manipulated the speed of

processing, or that previewed the allegedly slower dimension, failed to produce the expected results of reversing the direction of the interference.

Another theory—perhaps the most widely accepted in some form—invokes the notion of *automaticity.* (See Chapter 2.8, *Automatic versus Controlled Processing,* and Chapter 3.5, *Automaticity and Stereotyping.*) On this account, reading is automatic, but color-naming is not. Indeed, Posner and Snyder (1975), in one of the first of the modern discussions of automaticity, used the automatic nature of reading as one of their primary examples of an automatic process. The assumption of this theory is that we very strongly associate words with their spoken responses. Indeed, it is hard to look at letters that form a word and not to, at least, *subvocalize* the word. (*Subvocalization* refers to saying a word to yourself, rather than out loud.) On the other hand, as you look around a room at objects of various colors, do you find yourself automatically saying "red" or "green"? Probably not, unless you are deliberately attempting to name colors. This account, then, proposes a failure of selective attention in the sense that you can ignore the colors while naming the words (Stroop's Experiment 1, 1935), but you cannot name the colors and ignore the words, because reading words is automatic.

MacLeod and Dunbar (1988) argued that automaticity, to be regarded properly, should be seen as a continuum, not as an all-or-none issue. Evidence for this continuum comes from studies of the development of automaticity in children as they learn to read. (It should be obvious that an illiterate person would not show the Stroop effect.) Schiller (1966) showed an increase in the Stroop effect, from a minimal effect in Grade 1 to a maximal effect in Grade 3, with some decline thereafter (presumably reflecting the increased automaticity of reading). In a study designed to address the same sort of approach, MacLeod and Dunbar had subjects learn to make a color-word response to an arbitrary shape. Their subjects had practice at saying "pink" when they saw a given shape. (Three other color-shape combinations were also learned.) After varying amounts of practice, subjects were asked to respond by naming the color of a shape as it was presented, where the color either did or did not match the color-name assigned to that shape. As subjects became more and more automatic at saying "pink" in response to the assigned shape, Stroop interference increased. Thus, for children learning to read and for adults learning an arbitrary color-shape association, the Stroop effect emerges with increased automaticity of naming the word or shape.

Response competition is a concept that some-times has been included in explanations of the Stroop effect. Both the relative-speed and automaticity theories can make use of the response-competition concept, which assumes that motor responses (whether vocal or key-press) receive at least partial priming as the evidence for which response to make accumulates after the stimulus is presented (C. W. Eriksen & Schultz, 1979). The existence of such response competi-tion has been confirmed in a psychophysiological study by Eriksen, Coles, Morris, and O'Hara (1985), as well as behaviorally by St. James (1990). Both of those studies examined response competition in the *flankers task* (C. W. Eriksen, 1995), in which subjects must make a speeded response to indicate which of two letters was presented. On some trials, a letter may be flanked either by repetitions of itself (congruent trials) or by the opposite target letter (incongruent trials). Massive slowing in RT (and increase in error rates) occurs with incongruent trials. Eriksen (1995) drew the obvious parallel to the Stroop effect. Psychophysiological studies of the Stroop effect, using EEG and fMRI, have found clear evidence of response competition in Stroop interference (see below).

We should mention a challenge to the automatic-ity theory from Besner, Stolz, and Boutilier (1997). They showed that the Stroop effect is reduced (though usually not completely eliminated) if only a single letter of the color-word is in color

(e.g., GREEN where "G" is printed in green ink). Their research has been replicated several times (Brown, Joneleit, Robinson, & Brown, 2002; Danziger, Estevez, Mari-Beffa, 2002; Monahan, 2001), and the basic finding is in little doubt, though Marmurek (2003) failed to find the effect with a vocal Stroop task. We would suggest, however, that they were premature in declaring the automaticity explanation of the Stroop effect to be a "myth." Instead, it seems more reasonable to interpret this kind of result as demonstrating a *boundary condition* for the automaticity of reading. The boundary conditions of a phenom-enon describe the range of conditions under which a phenomenon can occur. With only a single letter colored, subjects may be able to focus attention on that letter and avoid evoking the usual automatic response of reading.

MacLeod also reviewed Logan's (1980) theory, which treats the Stroop effect as arising from the accumulation of evidence across time, and a parallel distributed-processing model (Cohen, Dunbar, & McClelland, 1990). Both of these theories attempt to more fully specify the mecha-nisms underlying a new theory that is essentially like the automaticity-plus-response-competition theory.

Other Approaches to the Stroop Effect

Some authors have taken an *individual-differ-ences* approach to the Stroop effect. Both Kane and Engle (2003) and Long and Sprat (2002) have shown correlations between working memory capacity (presumed to be related to the degree of executive control available to inhibit task-irrelevant information) and various aspects of Stroop interference.

Though the relationship was noted by MacLeod (1991), Dishon-Berkovitz and Algom (2000) and Sabri, Melera, and Algom (2001) have tied a number of issues concerning the Stroop effect to Garner's work on integrality of dimensions, or situations in which different aspects of a complex stimulus may be seen as integral or not (e.g., Garner & Felfoldy, 1970).

Psychophysiological Studies of the Stroop Effect

A number of studies have examined the Stroop effect using various procedures for integrating the behavioral data with psychophysiological recordings. In one of the earliest such studies, Duncan-Johnson and Kopell (1981) reported that most of the Stroop interference was related to changes in the late components of the event-related brain potential[5], and they argued for a central role of response competition in the Stroop effect. More recently, in another event-related brain-potential study, Atkinson, Drysdale, and Fulham (2003) also argued for a response-stage effect of Stroop interference. Mead, Mayer, Bobholz, Woodley, Cunningham, Hammeke,& Rao (2002) reached a similar conclusion in an fMRI study of the Stroop effect.

The Emotional Stroop Task

An interesting use of the basic idea of Stroop-like interference has been developed in what is usually called the Emotional Stroop Task (EST). In the EST, subjects are asked to name the color in which words are presented. Unlike the usual Stroop task, in which the words are congruent, neutral, or incongruent color-words, the EST compares RT to emotion-laden words or neutral words. For example, Watts, McKenna, Sharrock, and Trezise (1986), using subjects who were phobic to spiders, showed that those persons showed a distinct slowing in RT to name the colors of letters when the letters formed words that were related to spiders, such as *crawl* and *hairy*. The same subjects did not show interference when the words were related to general anxiety (as opposed to phobic-related anxiety), such as *fear* and *death*. The interference effect was reduced following desensitization treatments for phobia. Williams, Mathews, and MacLeod (1996) review the rather large literature showing an emotional Stroop effect in anxiety and depressive disorders. The emotional Stroop effect also has been shown for gambling-related words in subjects who exhibit impaired control over gambling (Boyer & Dickerson, 2003). Erblich, Montgomery, Valdimarsdottir, Cloitre, & Bovbjerg (2003) showed an emotional Stroop effect for cancer-related words in women with a known family history of breast cancer.

Methodological Considerations

In the experiments accompanying this chapter, we present three versions of the Stroop task. One, the *multi-item version*, is an essential replication of Stroop's (1935) Experiment 2, except that the neutral condition uses rows of "X's" instead of a colored square, and there is a congruent condition, in which the color name matches the color in which the word is presented (e.g., RED printed in red ink). (See MacLeod, 1991, p. 174, for a discussion of congruency effects.) Also, there are only 24 words in each set, instead of the 100 that Stroop used.

It should also be noted that there is careful counterbalancing across the lists. Each set of congruent, incongruent, and neutral lists is constructed in the following manner. For each of the 24 positions, a color is chosen randomly. The correct response is to name that color. In the congruent condition, the word displayed is the name of the color. Thus, if the color red was chosen, the word "RED" would

---

[5] Event-related brain potentials are changes in the electrical activity of the brain, as measured by an electroencephalogram, that follow the presentation of a stimulus (the "event"). "Late" components are those changes occurring relatively late in the processing of the stimulus—closer in time to the response, and therefore assumed to reflect response preparation, rather than stimulus interpretation.

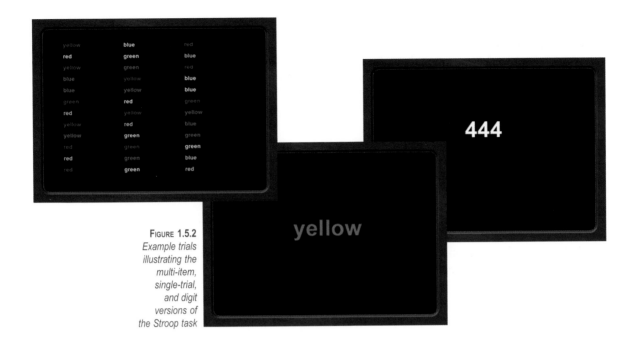

FIGURE 1.5.2
Example trials
illustrating the
multi-item,
single-trial,
and digit
versions of
the Stroop task

appear in red. For the incongruent condition, the word displayed is chosen randomly from the other color names. If the color red was chosen, the word presented would be chosen randomly from the words "BLUE," "GREEN," or "YELLOW." Finally, for the neutral condition, the number of X's displayed is chosen randomly from the possible number of letters making up the other color names. If the color chosen is red, the number of "X's" is chosen randomly to be either 4, 5, or 6. This selection is necessary because each of the four color names used is distinctive in the number of letters, making a possible confound in the neutral condition—if the number of "X's" matched the number of letters in the color name (e.g., there were always three "X's" and the color was red), then the number of letters would also indicate the correct response.

A second version is a *single-trial Stroop* (MacLeod & Dunbar, 1988). In this version, RT is measured for individual trials. On each trial, the subject sees a word (or row of "X's") and must make a speeded response to indicate the color in which it is presented. In this version, congruent, incongruent, and neutral trials occur equally often, but are intermixed in a random order. Subjects respond by making key presses to indicate the colors. Four colors are used, to make it fairly easy to remember the association between colors and keys.

The third version is included to demonstrate that the Stroop effect occurs in settings other than color-naming. In this version, subjects see a row of either digits or plus signs ("+") and must indicate how many digits or plus signs there were. The digits can be either congruent to the number of digits (e.g., "333" or "4444") or incongruent to the number of digits (e.g., "222" or "1111"). This version was apparently first suggested by Windes (1968; see Dyer, 1973). The version presented in PsychMate is a single-trial version. An interesting version of the digit-Stroop (Ischebeck, 2003) examined response times to naming digits ("9") versus reading the names of digits ("Nine"), using a version of the B. A. Eriksen and C. W. Eriksen (1974) flankers task.

How can we quantify Stroop interference (or possible facilitation when the color and word match)? Stroop interference is measured by the difference between the mean response times for the incongruent and neutral conditions, divided by the mean for the neutral condition to express the interference as a proportion. To change this to a percentage, multiply the proportion by 100.[6] In similar fashion, Stroop facilitation is measured by the difference between the congruent mean and the neutral mean, divided by the neutral mean. If subjects are faster for congruent stimuli (e.g., RED printed in red ink) than for neutral stimuli (e.g., "XXX"), they will have a positive Stroop facilitation.

If you compare the Stroop interference across the multi-item and single-trial versions, typically you will find much more interference in the multi-item version. We discuss this further in the Extension Experiments section below. Salo, Henik, & Robertson (2001) discuss this difference in light of the clinical application of the Stroop task, noting the inconsistency in clinical versions and their possible impact on interpretation of the results.

· ·
Expected Running Time = 18 minutes
· ·

Questions

1. What are the dependent and independent variables for this experiment? What are some important controls?

2. What was the result? Did the Stroop effect occur in your data?

3. Logan and Zbrodoff (1998) reported an interesting variant of the Stroop task in which their subjects *typed* the name of the color. What were their results?

Extension Experiments

1. If you have subjects complete both the single-trial and multi-item versions of the Stroop effect, you should compare the levels of Stroop interference. In most cases, the interference will approach 100% for the multi-item version, but will be far less for the single-trial version. This difference is most likely due to the fact that the automatic response to seeing a word is to subvocalize it. We have not automatized a key-press response. Because the key-press response is only partially controlled by the subvocalized response, it produces a weaker interference. (See Logan & Zbrodoff, 1998, p. 988.)

   Note that there is a prediction from this hypothesis that you could test. If you give subjects large amounts of practice in responding to words with key-presses, you should increase Stroop interference when a key-press is made in response to a color. To do this, you would repeatedly present the four color words and have the subject press the red key for the word "RED" (in a neutral color), thus increasing the automaticity of the response to reading the word.

2. The reliability of the Stroop effect has been the subject of some research (see MacLeod, 1991, p. 166, for a discussion and references). One measure of reliability is test-retest reliability, which is simply the correlation between the test score on an initial test and the scores for the same subjects on a later administration of the same test. You could measure the Stroop interference (see the Methodological Considerations, above) on two occasions and compute the reliability.

3. See Extension Experiment 1 in Chapter 2.5, *Executive Control, Planning, and the Tower of London*.

---

[6] For example, if the RT for the incongruent condition was 800 ms, and the RT for the neutral condition was 600 ms, the interference would be $((800-600)/600)*100 = 33\%$. For the multi-item version, the response times will be in seconds, but the calculation is the same.

References

Atkinson, C., Drysdale, K., & Fulham, W. R. (2003). Event-related potentials to Stroop and reverse Stroop stimuli. *International Journal of Psychophysiology, 47,* 1-21.

Besner, D., Stolz, J. A., & Boutilier, C. (1997). The Stroop effect and the myth of automaticity. *Psychonomic Bulletin and Review, 4,* 221-225.

Boyer, M., & Dickerson, M. (2003). Attentional bias and addictive behaviour: Automaticity in a gambling-specific modified Stroop task. *Addiction, 98,* 61-70.

Brown, T. L., Joneleit, K., Robinson, C., & Brown, C. (2002). Automaticity in reading and the Stroop task: Testing the limits of involuntary word processing. *American Journal of Psychology, 115,* 515-543.

Cohen, J. D., Dunbar, K., & McClelland, J. L. (1990). On the control of automatic processes: A parallel distributed processing account of the Stroop effect. *Psychological Review, 97,* 332-361.

Danziger, S., Estevez, A., & Mari-Beffa, P. (2002). Stroop interference effects in partially colored Stroop words. *Psychonomic Bulletin & Review, 9,* 536-541.

Dishon-Berkovitz, M., & Algom, D. (2000). The Stroop effect: It is not the robust phenomenon that you have thought it to be. *Memory and Cognition, 28,* 1437-1449.

Duncan-Johnson, C. C., & Kopell, B. S. (1981). The Stroop effect: Brain potentials localize the source of the interference. *Science, 214,* 938-940.

Dyer, F. (1973). The Stroop phenomenon and its use in the study of perceptual, cognitive, and response processes. *Memory and Cognition, 1,* 106-120.

Erblich, J., Montgomery, G., Valdimarsdottir, H., Cloitre, M., & Bovbjerg, D. (2003). Biased cognitive processing of cancer-related information among women with family histories of breast cancer: Evidence from a cancer Stroop task. *Health Psychology, 22,* 235-244.

Eriksen, B. A., & Eriksen, C. W. (1974). Effects of noise letters upon the identification of a target letter in a nonsearch task. *Perception and Psychophysics, 16,* 143-149.

Eriksen, C. W. (1995). The flankers task and response competition: A useful tool for investigating a wide variety of cognitive problems. *Visual Cognition, 2,* 101-118.

Eriksen, C. W., Coles, M. G. H., Morris, L. R., & O'Hara, W. P. (1985). An electromyographic examination of response competition. *Bulletin of the Psychonomic Society, 23,* 165-168.

Eriksen, C. W., & Schultz, D. W. (1979). Information processing in visual search: A continuous flow conception and experimental results. *Perception and Psychophysics, 25,* 249-263.

Garner, W. R., & Felfody, G. L. (1970). Integrality of stimulus dimensions in various types of information processing. *Cognitive Psychology, 1,* 225-241.

Ischebeck, A. (2003). Differences between digit naming and number word reading in a flanker task. *Memory and Cognition, 31,* 529-537.

Jensen, A., & Rohwer, W., Jr. (1966). The Stroop color-word test: A review. *Acta Psychologica, 24,* 398-408.

Kane, M., & Engle, R. (2003). Working-memory capacity and the control of attention: The contributions of goal neglect, response competition, and task set to Stroop interference. *Journal of Experimental Psychology: General, 132,* 47-70.

Logan, G. D. (1980). Attention and automaticity in Stroop and priming tasks: Theory and data. *Cognitive Psychology, 12,* 523-553.

References *(continued)*

Logan, G. D., & Zbrodoff, N. J. (1998). Stroop-like interference: Congruity effects in color naming with typewritten responses. *Journal of Experimental Psychology: Human Perception and Performance, 24*, 978-992.

Long, D. L., & Sprat, C. S. (2002). Working memory and Stroop interference: An individual differences investigation. *Memory and Cognition, 30*, 294-301.

MacLeod, C. M. (1991). Half a century of research on the Stroop effect: An integrative review. *Psychological Bulletin, 109*, 163-203.

MacLeod, C. M. (1992). The Stroop task: The "gold standard" of attentional measures. *Journal of Experimental Psychology: General, 121*, 12-14.

MacLeod, C. M., & Dunbar, K. (1988). Training and Stroop-like interference: Evidence for a continuum of automaticity. *Journal of Experimental Psychology: Learning, Memory, and Cognition, 14*, 126-135.

Marmurek, H. H. (2003). Coloring only a single letter does not eliminate color-word interference in a vocal-response Stroop task: automaticity revealed. *Journal of General Psychology, 130*, 207-224.

Mead, L., Mayer, A., Bobholz, J., Woodley, S., Cunningham, J., Hammeke, T., et al. (2002). Neural basis of the stroop interference task: Response competition or selective attention? *Journal of the International Neuropsychological Society, 8*, 735-742.

Monahan, J. S. (2001). Coloring single Stroop elements: Reducing automaticity or slowing color processing? *Journal of General Psychology, 128*, 98-112.

Posner, M. I., & Snyder, C. R. R. (1975). Attention and cognitive control. In R. L. Solso (Ed.), *Information processing and cognition: The Loyola symposium* (pp. 55-85). Hillsdale, NJ: Lawrence Erlbaum Associates.

Sabri, M., Melara, R. D., & Algom, D. (2001). A confluence of contexts: Asymmetric versus global failures of selective attention in Stroop dimensions. *Journal of Experimental Psychology: Human Perception and Performance, 27*, 515-537.

St. James, J. D. (1990). Observations on the micro-structure of response competition. Perception and Psychophysics, 48, 517-524.

Salo, R., Henik, A., &, Robertson, L. (2001). Interpreting Stroop interference: An analysis of differences between tasks. *Neuropsychology, 15*, 462-471.

Schiller, P. H. (1966). Developmental study of color-word interference. *Journal of Experimental Psychology, 72*, 105-108.

Stroop, J. R. (1935). Studies of interference in serial verbal reactions. *Journal of Experimental Psychology, 18*, 643-662.

Watts, F., McKenna, F., Sharrock, R., & Trezise, L. (1986). Color-naming of phobia-related words. *British Journal of Psychology, 77*, 97-108.

Williams, J., Mathews, A., & MacLeod, C. (1996). The emotional Stroop task and psychopathology. *Psychological Bulletin, 120*, 3-24.

Windes, J. D. (1968). Reaction time for numerical coding and naming of numerals. *Journal of Experimental Psychology, 78*, 318-322.

1.6 Selective Attention and Response Competition

Abstract

Selective attention involves focusing on one aspect of the environment while excluding other interfering stimuli. One way to measure the success of selective attention is through the use of experimental conditions that produce response competition—a slowing in the correct response due to "priming" of the incorrect response. As the conflicting stimuli are moved farther from the target, their influence should be diminished if subjects can successfully restrict attention solely to the target. This provides a measure of the area to which visual selective attention can be focused.

Selective attention refers to a focusing of attention on some perceptual inputs to the exclusion of others. Selective attention can operate in several ways. One is to select the perceptual modality attended to—when attending to visual material, you are less sensitive to auditory inputs. An example you may be familiar with is being so intent upon a book you are reading or studying that someone else has a hard time getting your attention by calling your name—you were selectively attending to the book. Another way that you can selectively attend is to try to attend to one dimension of a single stimulus, while trying to ignore other dimensions. An example would be naming the color in which a word is printed while ignoring the word. This type of selective attention is the focus of Chapter 1.5, *Attentional Interference and the Stroop Effect.* Figure 1.6.1 illustrates the Stroop Effect. Finally, you can selectively

BLUE	YELLOW	GREEN	RED
PURPLE	BLACK	PURPLE	GREEN
GREEN	PURPLE	RED	PURPLE
YELLOW	BLUE	BLACK	GREEN
BLUE	YELLOW	RED	PURPLE

FIGURE **1.6.1** – *An illustration of the Stroop Effect; note the difficulty of naming the colors when the letters spell the name of another color.*

choose one physical location to attend to while trying not to attend to other locations. That type of selective attention is the focus of the experiment accompanying this chapter.

One way that we very easily attend selectively to one location in the visual environment is simply to change where our eyes are pointing. If we wish to attend to a page of print, rather than to the images on a television screen, we point our eyes at the printed page instead of the television. Indeed, we do this sort of selective atten-

tion so easily that we are hardly aware of changing eye position (or head position). But can we focus attention selectively within a single fixation? That is, can we decide which part of the visual array to attend to without moving our eyes? And, if so, on how small an area can we choose to focus attention?

B. A. Eriksen and C. W. Eriksen (1974) suggested a simple procedure for answering these questions. A single target letter appeared in a known location, and subjects had to press a lever either left or right to indicate which letter they saw. On some trials the target letter was flanked on the left and right by one of several types of noise letters. Sometimes there were compatible noise letters that were simply repetitions of the target letter. Sometimes there were "neutral" noise letters that never appeared as targets. Finally, sometimes the noise letters were letters that called for the opposite response as the target letter. This "incompatible" noise led to a marked increase in reaction time, since subjects did not seem to be able to ignore it if the noise letters were right next to the target letter.

This slowing is referred to as *response competition*, since it seems that the target and noise letters are each priming a response, which slows the execution of the correct response. This shows a failure of selective attention—subjects could not focus their attention on the targets and ignore the noise letters. But what would happen as the noise letters are moved farther away from the target? Note that the target letter always occurred in the same location. If subjects can selectively attend to only part of the visual array, it is to their advantage to do so in this experiment, to try to avoid the slowing in reaction time caused by incompatible noise. Suppose that subjects could restrict their attention to an area of one degree of visual angle (see below for a discussion of visual angle). In that case, incompatible noise only a half degree from the target should produce a slowing in reaction time, while noise farther than a degree away should successfully be

ignored and, hence, should produce no change. Thus, Eriksen and Eriksen argued, we can use the degree of response competition to measure the size of the selective attentional focus—the area to which we can restrict attention. That area is determined by seeing how far away the flanking noise letters must be moved before they produce an increase in reaction time.

In this replication of Eriksen & Eriksen's experiment, we make use of the response competition produced when two competing responses are both triggered. The task involves identifying which of two letters appears above a fixation mark. On some trials, the opposite target letter will appear to the left and right of the target letter. By varying the distance from the target to the conflicting letters, we can determine how far away those letters must be before the response competition effect disappears. This will give us a measure of the degree to which visual attention can be focused voluntarily.

Recent Uses of the Flanker Paradigm

C. W. Eriksen (1995) discussed both the development of the flanker task and a variety of applications. Because the flanker task has been so well studied, and because it replicates extremely reliably, it has become a tool for studying other issues besides the size of focused attention.

Zeef, Sonke, Kok, Buiten, and Kenemans (1996) used the flanker task to investigate changes with age in selective attention, reporting that incompatible flankers produced more interference in their older subjects compared to the younger, but only when the flankers were close to the target letters.

Priming of responses to one stimulus by another is the subject of the experiment with the lexical decision task (see Chapter 2.1, *Lexical Decisions*) . The flanker task has also been used to study the nature of priming, where the prime matched either the target or a flanker. Stadler and Hogan (1996) presented a variant of the flanker task in which a stimulus that was to be ignored on one trial had to be attended on the next. In that situation, the second presentation leads to a longer RT, due to negative priming. By varying timing and other features of the task, they were able to investigate theories of the nature of priming effects.

Fuentes and Humphreys (1996) have also used a priming version of the flankers task to study unilateral visual neglect, a condition arising in some brain-injured patients who ignore, or

neglect, stimuli in half of the visual field. Their studies indicate that, despite conscious neglect, ignored stimuli still activated internal representations, but negative priming seems to require the involvement of conscious attention.

Paquet (2001) has reviewed the literature and reports experiments on the issue of the spatial relationship between flankers and targets in the flankers task. Sanders and Lamers (2002) also report recent studies using the flankers task.

Methodological Considerations

The letters "S" and "H were chosen as target letters because they have virtually no feature overlap. In other words, they are easily distinguishable from each other. The letters "P" and "Q" were chosen as neutral noise letters because they do not share any resemblance with the target letters. Though response competition is maximal when the flankers are themselves target letters, flankers that share features with the target letters will also produce some response competition. The four flanker types and three spacings are all mixed in a single block of trials. Note that if the spacings were presented in separate blocks, subjects might use different strategies in regard to selective attention, rather than simply trying to focus attention as tightly as possible on each trial.

In this experiment, it is necessary to control, or at least to measure, the distance from the subject's eye to the screen in order to accurately specify the size of the displays and how far away the flanking letters are located.

Measurement of Visual Angle

Since the main issue of this experiment is how far away the incompatible noise has to be before the response conflict effect disappears (indicating that you can selectively attend to the target, and ignore the noise), it is important to report that distance correctly in the write-up of the experiment. The size of a display, or the distance between elements in a display, is usually reported in degrees of visual angle. This measure assures that the size of the object and its distance from the viewer are taken into account—a 1-inch object at 2 feet subtends the same visual angle as a 2-inch object at 4 feet. Thus, comparisons across experiments are easier—they are all reported in degrees of visual angle.

How do you determine degrees of visual angle? To do so, you must know the size of the display and the distance from the display to the viewer's eye. That presents a problem when using a computer screen, unless subjects use a chin-rest, or otherwise restrict their head placement. B. A. Eriksen and C. W. Eriksen (1974) used a viewing hood to control distance to the stimulus. That consisted of a face-mask-shaped opening through which the subject viewed the stimuli, so that they had to put their faces up to the mask to see the stimuli.

In doing this experiment, you should avoid shifting closer to and farther from the screen during the experiment. Measure the distance from your eyes to the center of the screen. (For most published experiments, care must be taken to ensure that this distance is known within very close tolerances.) Also, measure the distance of the flanking noise letter from the target for each of the three spacings.

Methodological Considerations *(continued)*

Measure this from the centers of the letters. At the end of the experiment you will be given the opportunity to make these measurements. Given the size of the display and the distance from the display to the viewer, you can solve for visual angle using the law of cosines. With a calculator with inverse trigonometric functions, you can solve the following equation:

visual angle = inverse tangent (W/D)

This can be approximated by:

visual angle in degrees = 57.3W/D

where *W = width of object*, *D = distance from object to viewer*, and *W* and *D* are expressed in the same units.

For example, a character that is 5 millimeters high at a distance of 500 mm has a visual angle of inverse tangent (5/500) = 0.5719º. That object would be said to *subtend* 0.5719º. [**NOTE:** If you use the approximation (57.3 x 5/500), you get 0.573º.]

Expected running time = 24 minutes

For complete balancing of the experimental design, there are trials designated as Flanker Type = None (no flanking letters) that are 1, 3, and 8 spaces away from the target letter. These conditions are really all the same—there is no flanker. This actually provides a useful check on the experiment, sometimes called a marker variable. Note that the mean RT for these three conditions should be very close to the same, since they are the same condition. If these three means differ a lot, the reliability of the experiment is in doubt. Fortunately, for this experiment, the three means are usually within about 10 ms of each other.

Questions

1. What are the dependent and independent variables for this experiment? What are some important controls?

2. What is your estimate of the width of the attentional field at its narrowest focus?

3. Does this estimate agree with that of Eriksen and Eriksen (1974)?

FIGURE **1.6.2** – *A representation of the measurement of visual angle; the red lines illustrate the height of the computer screen in terms of visual angle.*

Extension Experiments

1. You have estimated the size of the attentional field when the subjects are trying to restrict it to a minimum and have all the time they need to do so (since the target was always in the same place). This operation of restricting attention can be assumed to take some time to occur. How might you estimate the time required to restrict attention? See Eriksen and St. James (1986). While their experiment was fairly complex, the basic idea is to vary the position of the target, with a precue appearing at various times before the target to indicate its location.

2. How would you measure how long interference due to response competition lasts as a function of the stimulus onset asynchrony (SOA) of the target and distractors?

3. What would be the effect of flanking letters that are visually similar to the target letters, but not identical (Eriksen & Eriksen, 1974)?

4. What other stimuli would produce response competition? Kopp, Rist, and Mattler (1996) used arrows pointing to left and right as the central stimuli, with responses made by the corresponding hand. Flankers were either arrows pointing the same or the opposite way, with boxes as the neutral stimuli. Note that this relates to a large literature on stimulus-response compatibility.

References

Coles, M. G. H., Gratton, G., Bashore, T. R., Eriksen, C. W., & Donchin, E. (1985). A psychophysiological investigation of the continuous flow model of human information processing. *Journal of Experimental Psychology: Human Perception and Performance, 11*, 529-553.

Eriksen, B. A., & Eriksen, C. W. (1974). Effects of noise letters upon the identification of a target letter in a nonsearch task. *Perception and Psychophysics, 16*, 143-149.

Eriksen, C. W. (1995). The flankers task and response competition: A useful tool for investigating a wide variety of cognitive problems. *Visual Cognition, 2*, 101-118.

Eriksen, C. W., & St. James, J. D. (1986). Visual attention within and around the field of focal attention: A zoom lens model. *Perception and Psychophysics, 40*, 225-240.

Fuentes, L., & Humphreys, G. (1996). On the processing of "extinguished" stimuli in unilateral visual neglect: An approach using negative priming. *Cognitive Neuropsychology, 13*, 11-136.

Kopp, B., Rist, F., & Mattler, U. (1996). N200 in the flanker task as a neurobehavioral tool for investigating executive control. *Psychophysiology, 33*, 282-294.

Paquet, L. (2001). Eliminating flankers effects and negative priming in the flankers task: Evidence for early selection. *Psychonomic Bulletin and Review, 8*, 301-306.

Sanders, A. F., & Lamers, J. M. (2002). The Eriksen flanker effect revisited. *Acta Psychologica, 109*, 41-56.

Stadler, M. A., & Hogan, M. E. (1996). Varieties of positive and negative priming. *Psychonomic Bulletin & Review, 3*, 87-90.

Zeef, E., Sonke, C., Kok, A., Buiten, M., & Kenemans, J. (1996). Perceptual factors affecting age-related differences in focused attention: Performance and psychophysiological analyses. *Psychophysiology, 33*, 555-565.

1.7 Iconic Memory

- -

Abstract

Visual information no longer present in the environment persists briefly in the "sensory register" or icon following its disappearance. One limitation to the study of the icon is its very brief duration. As people begin reporting the contents of the icon, it is already disappearing. Sperling (1960) invented the partial-report technique to overcome this difficulty, and he was able to show that the icon has a large capacity and measure its duration. This classic experiment is repeated in this exercise.

- -

*E*arly work on reading (e.g., Erdman and Dodge, 1898) had been concerned with how much information could be acquired at a single fixation in reading. The typical finding from briefly presenting a set of letters and having the subject report as many letters as possible was that the perceptual span was 4 to 5 letters. One problem with these findings was that it is possible that the information in a brief display decays rapidly, and that the 4 to 5 letters reported was not the limit of how much was *perceived*, but rather was the limit of how much could be *reported* before the perceptual impression vanished. To get a feeling for this sort of visual display, think of when you have seen a lightening flash on a dark night.

Such a flash gives you a very brief exposure to a visual stimulus. If you were asked to describe what you had seen (assuming you weren't familiar with the scene and you were just recalling from memory), you probably would omit many objects and details. But you probably would have the feeling of having seen a very rich visual display during the lightening flash. Such is the topic of the experiment on the icon—how much can you see in a brief visual display, and how long does that visual information last after the display is turned off?

How can we get around the problem of the older studies of perceptual span—that subjects' reports might be limited by a rapid decay of the visual

persistence rather than by a severe limit to its size? Sperling (1960) devised a method. He reasoned that the visual persistence (later called the icon) decayed too rapidly for subjects to report all they had seen. But suppose we tell them after they see the display to report only a part of it? If a person could report most of a randomly selected part of the display on one trial, and most of another part on another trial, this would suggest that they had seen much more than they could report.

Sperling's test was much like the older studies—he presented a 3x3 or 3x4 matrix of letters, flashed for 50 ms. But rather than just using the *whole-report* method of previous studies (report as much as you can of the whole display), he used a new *partial-report* method. In his study, subjects saw the display of letters, then heard a

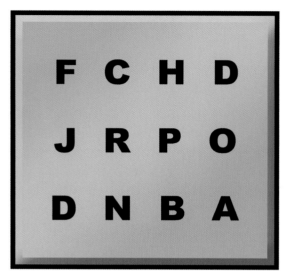

FIGURE **1.7.1** – *A 3x4 matrix similar to that presented by Sterling.*

tone that was either high-pitched, low-pitched, or in between. The high-pitched tone indicated "report the top line of the display," with the medium and low tones signaling the report of the middle and bottom lines, respectively.

What Sperling found was that subjects could report about 80% of the letters on a line if the tone was sounded just before the letters were presented. That drops only slightly—to about 75%—when the tone immediately follows the letters. However, if the tone is delayed by only a half second, subjects can report only about 50% of each line, which corresponds to the 4 to 5 letters previously estimated as the span of a visual impression. Sperling's experiment showed quite conclusively that the limit in report of letters from a brief visual display was due to a rapid decay of the visual trace, rather than to a severe limit on the amount of visual information stored. Neisser (1967) in his *Cognitive Psychology* (the first textbook of the then newly-emerging area of cognitive psychology) chose the term *icon* to refer to the brief persistence of information from a visual display after the display is no longer present.[7] Other terms used for the same phenomenon are the

precategorical visual store, preperceptual visual store, the visual sensory register, visual sensory memory, iconic memory, and sensory information storage—take your pick.

Sperling (1960) showed that the duration of the icon could be increased to several seconds if subjects were dark-adapted for some time prior to the experiment and the stimuli were bright enough. On the other hand, if the field where the image is shown is brighter than the image, either before or after the presentation of the image, the duration of the icon is diminished.

Sperling's demonstration of the icon came at a time when information-processing models were beginning to come to the forefront of psychological theorizing. Only two years earlier, Peterson and Peterson (1959) had demonstrated rapid (less than 20-second) forgetting of small amounts of information, inaugurating the study of what soon became known as short-term memory (see Chapter 2.2, *Scanning Short-Term Memory* for later conceptualizations of this brief memory). These two experiments brought on a rush of research to try to explore the properties of iconic memory and short-term memory.

Later investigators, such as Averbach and Coriell (1961) and Eriksen and Collins (1967) studied the icon further, confirming that it has a duration of about 250 ms and a storage capacity of at least 9 items. (There are many problems with estimating the upper limit to iconic capacity, and it is probably much greater than 9 items— indeed, it is probably a near-complete image of what was seen.) These researchers also examined how iconic storage is integrated across time. Averbach and Coriell did an experiment essentially the same as Sperling's, but asked subjects to report a single letter that was cued immediately after the array disappeared (see Figure 1.7.2). The cue they used was a circle that

---

[7] He named the brief persistence of an auditory stimulus the *echo*. Eriksen and Johnson (1964) estimated the duration of this auditory persistence at 3-4 seconds, but with some detection even at 10.5 seconds.

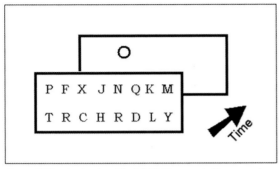

FIGURE **1.7.2** – *Averbach and Coriell (1963) presented two rows of letters briefly, then presented a circle around one letter to cue the subject to report that letter. If the circle follows the letters with the right timing, it effectively blocks out the iconic memory for that letter.*

appeared surrounding the area where the letter has just been seen. Under this circumstance, the circle actually serves to wipe out the icon—reporting of the cued letter was at a near-zero accuracy. Eriksen and Collins, on the other hand, demonstrated that, under some circumstances, two successive images can be integrated together, as shown in Figure 1.7.3. They presented two seemingly random dot patterns, one after the other. If a subject saw the two images superimposed, they would see that the "random" dots actually form letters. The question Eriksen and Collins posed was whether subjects could combine the two images if they saw one right after the other. They found that subjects could easily read the letters if the second set of dots immediately followed the first. When they were delayed by 100 ms or more, however, they usually saw two random dot patterns—no integration of the icons occurred.

> "As the reader can verify for himself [sic], the two dot patterns are not such that they can be cognitized and/or remembered in such a manner as to yield the contained nonsense syllable. The nonsense syllable would seem to be capable of being perceived only if the two halves are perceived as psychologically simultaneous or the perceptual trace [icon] of the first half is still present when the second stimulus half occurs" (p. 477).

"How much is an icon worth?"

Few areas of psychology are without their disputation. Haber (1983, 1985) has argued that, though the icon surely exists, it is irrelevant to real-world perception. "Brief discrete flashes have a visual persistence. But normal perception is not made up of brief discrete flashes, singly or in combination" (1983, p. 3). Because our heads and eyes are in near-constant motion, the icon cannot serve as a storage of information, according to Haber. "The notion of an icon as a brief storage of information persisting after stimulus termination cannot possibly be useful in any typical visual information-processing task except reading in a lightening storm" (1983, p. 1).

Loftus (see Haber, 1983) replied that "humans need to acquire some, and discard the rest, or the total environmental information impinging on the sense organs. A logical way to meet this need would be to provide a large-capacity, raw-information storage buffer, in conjunction with a selective filter capable of extracting the relevant information from the bugger...The icon, along with a selective-attention mechanism, precisely fits this specification" (p. 28).

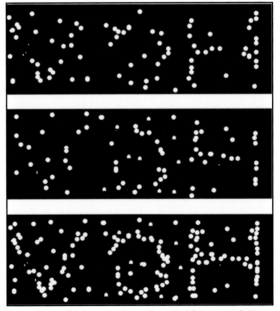

FIGURE **1.7.3** – *This image replicates figure 1 of Eriksen and Collins (1967).*

The question that forms the heading for this section was the title of an article by Loftus, Johnson, and Shimamura (1985) that attempted to measure the perceptual advantage of having an iconic memory. They showed subjects brief presentations of sets of pictures and then tested them on recognition. The comparison of most interest was that between (a) pictures that were followed by a pattern mask that was intended to wipe out the icon and (b) pictures followed by a blank screen, permitting an icon. They concluded that the icon was the equivalent of about 100 ms of extra exposure to the physical picture.

Recent work on the icon

Becker, Pashler, and Anstis (2000) have explored the role of iconic memory in change blindness experiments, such as the one replicated in Chapter 1.8, *Change Blindness*. They found the typical change blindness—or inability to detect changes in a visual scene—if there was a brief, blank interstimulus interval (ISI) between the two scenes. However, if a visual cue marking the location of the change was inserted during the ISI, change detection improved. They interpreted this to suggest that the first scene is actually represented in detail, but the second scene effectively obliterates the iconic memory of the first one, unless attention is shifted to the location of the change.

Methodological Considerations

A major consideration for this experiment is the quality of the stimulus displays. You should adjust the brightness and contrast on the computer monitor to give the sharpest image possible. You will be shown a display at the beginning of the experiment that gives you an opportunity to make those adjustments. If at all possible, reduce the ambient lighting of the room to a minimum. In other words, turn out the lights!

At the beginning of the experiment, you will also be given a few trials of practice at recognizing the three tones used to signal which line to report during the partial-report trials.

Because the task involved is a difficult one, a large amount of practice (120 trials) will be given before you begin the 120 trials of the actual experiment. All practice trials will involve partial report with no delay between presentation of the letters and the tone to indicate which line to report. After the practice trials, each subject will be tested in four blocks of 30 trials each. On each trial, there will be a 100 ms presentation of a matrix of letters consisting of three rows of four letters each, with the 12 letters randomly chosen from the 21 consonants. One block of trials will require whole report—there will be no tone, and you must try to report as many letters as you can from anywhere in the display. The other three blocks of trials will differ in the delay between the letters and the onset of the tone indicating the line to be recalled. Delays will be 0, 150, and 500 ms. The order of the four blocks will be counterbalanced across subjects. A high-pitched tone will signal report of the top line of the display, with medium- and low-pitched tones signaling reports of the middle and bottom lines, respectively.

After each trial, you will be cued to enter as many of the letters from the appropriate row as you can. If you are not familiar with the keyboard, you might want to write the letters down immediately after each trial. You can then take your time entering them when cued. If possible, execute this experiment in a dimly lighted room (not as bright as a normal classroom, but enough light to see by).

For this experiment, unlike most of the experiments in PsychMate, you need to carefully adjust the brightness and contrast on your computer display to get as bright and sharp an image as possible. That is because this experiment uses brief displays of 100 ms. Displays like this—those that do not permit you to scan the stimulus, but basically give you a "snapshot" of it—are called *data-limited* displays. Most of the experiments replicated in PsychMate do not use data-limited displays—the stimuli either remain on the screen until the subject responds, or they are of a sufficiently long duration that subjects have plenty of time to scan them. The experiment on *Signal Detection* is one that uses a data-limited display—if subjects could examine the stimuli for as long as they want, performance would be perfect. There are a number of technical difficulties that arise with such data-limited displays. If you do experimentation with displays of less than 150 ms or so, you should consult Schneider, Eschman, and Zuccolotto's (2002) Chapter 3 on critical timing of displays within E-Prime, which is the application used to create and run the experiments in PsychMate.

Questions

1. What is the dependent variable in this experiment? What is the independent variable? What are some important control variables? What sort of counterbalancing is used in this experiment?

2. According to your data, what is the duration of the icon? Does the capacity seem to be greater than the 4 to 5 letters (33 - 42% recall) usually found in whole-report procedures? Do your results agree with Sperling's?

3. What was the technique used by Eriksen and Collins (1967) to measure the duration of the icon? Do their results agree with Sperling's?

Advanced Questions

1. Suppose you wanted to determine the upper limit of capacity of the icon. Could you simply extend this experiment to a 4 x 4 or 5 x 5 matrix of letters? What procedural problems might you encounter in doing so? [Hint: Miller (1956) discusses the issue of absolute judgment and the number of distinguishable tones. See his Figure 1 and discussion on page 84.]

2. If the icon is a visual persistence of information after the actual objects being perceived are no longer present, can we extract usable information from the icon? That is, do we actually *use* the icon in normal perception? Loftus, Johnson, and Shimamura (1985) attempted to measure how much an icon is "worth."

3. Are there phenomena equivalent to the icon for other sensory modalities? Describe their characteristics.

Extension Experiments

1. This experiment employed different delays before the signal of which line to report. Does it matter whether the delays are the same for a whole block of trials (*blocked*) or whether they change from trial to trial (*random*)?

2. Sperling found that the icon's duration was partly dependent on the adaptive state of the subjects' eyes. Does the icon last longer if the eye is dark-adapted?

References

Averbach, E., & Coriell, A. S. (1961). Short-term memory in vision. *Bell System Technical Journal, 40,* 309-328.

Becker, M. W., Pashler, H., Anstis, S. M. (2000). The role of iconic memory in change-detection tasks. *Perception, 29,* 273-286.

Coltheart, M. (1983). Iconic memory. *Philosophical Transactions of the Royal Society, London B, 302I,* 283-294.

Eriksen, C. W., & Collins, J. F. (1967). Some temporal characteristics of visual pattern perception. *Journal of Experimental Psychology, 74,* 476-484.

Eriksen, C. W., & Johnson, H. J. (1964). Storage and decay characteristics of nonattended auditory stimuli. *Journal of Experimental Psychology, 68,* 28-36.

Erdman, B., & Dodge, R. (1998) [Psychological studies on reading.] Halle: M. Niemeyer. Cited in R. Woodworth & H. Schlossberg *Experimental psychology.* New York: Holt.

Haber, R. N. (1983). The impending demise of the icon: A critique of the concept of iconic storage in processing visual information. [including replies.] *Behavioral and Brain Sciences, 6,* 1-54.

Loftus, G. R., Johnson, C. A., & Shimamura, A. P. (1985). How much is an icon worth? *Journal of Experimental Psychology: Human Perception and Performance, 11,* 1-13.

Miller, G. A. (1956). The magical number seven, plus or minus two: Some limits on our capacity for processing information. *Psychological Review, 63,* 81-97.

Neisser, U. (1967). *Cognitive psychology.* New York: Appleton-Century-Crofts.

Sakitt, B. (1976). Iconic memory. *Psychological Review, 83,* 257-276.

Schneider, W., Eschman, A., & Zuccolotto, A. (2002). *E-Prime user's guide.* Pittsburgh, PA: Psychology Software Tools.

Sperling, G. (1960). The information available in brief visual presentations. *Psychological Monographs, 74* (Whole number 11).

1.8 Change Blindness

· ·

Abstract

Recent research on the ability of human observers to detect change in visual scenes has found that one of the most striking features of change detection is how poorly it works. The inability to detect change turns out to be a ubiquitous finding that challenges a long-held assumption that we integrate the information from successive visual fixations to form a rich representation of the visual scene before us. That *change blindness* is the focus of this chapter and the accompanying experiment.

· ·

Our subjective experience suggests that we have a near-complete and highly accurate representation of the visual scene before us. However, there is a severe limitation to the input to visual experience. Visual acuity is good only in a small area straight ahead, where the image is focused on a part of the retina called the *fovea* (see Figure 1.8.1). The fovea is only about 2° of visual angle[8] across. At a distance of 20 feet, that would be an area with a diameter of about 8.5 inches. Visual acuity drops rapidly as the

image moves outside the fovea, with visual acuity at 5° from straight ahead typically no better than 20/300—in other words, the smallest letter you could see 5° from straight ahead could be seen in foveal vision from 300 feet away! We overcome this problem to some degree by frequently re-orienting our focus. Figure 1.8.2 illustrates the small size of foveal vision and the difficulty of not automatically redirecting our gaze in order to see an object clearly. We make saccadic eye movements about three times per second (Buswell, 1920; Rayner, 1998). *Saccades* are the rapid eye movements (up to 500°/s) from one fixation to another.[9] *Fixations* are the periods when our eyes are relatively still. Note that there is no pick-up of visual information during a saccade, as the speed of the eye movement blurs any input beyond recognition.

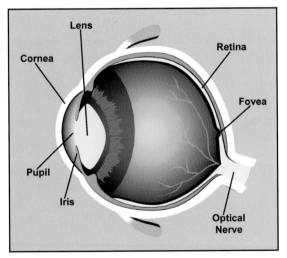

FIGURE **1.8.1** – *The parts of the eye, including the fovea.*

alshfirocpsntm**x**

FIGURE **1.8.2** – *A demonstration of visual acuity. Concentrate on the "x" in bold at the end of the line of letters and try to name the letters to the left of it, **without moving your eye**. Note that you can recognize only a few of them. This illustrates the limited visual acuity outside the fovea. Note how difficult it is to keep from "cheating" by looking at the letters.*

---

[8] See Chapter 1.6, *Selective Attention and Response Competition*, for a discussion of measurement in degrees of visual angle.

[9] In scene perception, we typically make about three saccades per second, averaging 5°, with each saccade lasting 40-50 ms and fixations averaging 330 ms (Rayner, 1998).

Our subjective experience is that we have a near-complete experience of the visual scene before us, despite the fact that we see only a tiny part of the world on each fixation. A long-standing hypothesis to explain this has been that we have some form of visual buffer that stores the input from successive fixations to form a high-resolution image of the scene before us (see Henderson and Hollingworth, 1999, for a review). If this hypothesis is correct, however, we should be able to detect changes in the scene with relative ease. In fact, we are remarkably poor at detecting change. The literature reviewed below, and the accompanying replication of Rensink, O'Regan, and Clark's (1997) Experiment 1, suggest that—as Henderson and Hollingworth (1999) put it—the visual system "does not create a composite representation by overlaying images from consecutive fixations" (p. 442).

A growing body of work on the issue of the conditions under which humans detect change in a visual scene has confirmed the great difficulty that we have in this task. This phenomenon has come to be known as *change blindness*.[10] Like many apparently new findings, it had been anticipated. Rensink reviews earlier research from the 1950's through the 1980's. For example, McConkie and Zola (1979) addressed the issue of whether information perceived on successive fixations during reading is integrated to form a larger percept. Their subjects read text on a cathode ray tube monitor which permitted very fast changes in the visual display, contingent on eye movements.[11] The text they read was in alternating upper- and lower-case letters, as shown in Figure 1.8.3. Their eye movements were monitored with an eye-tracking apparatus which could detect when a saccade took place. During some saccades, the letters were all shifted from upper- to lower-case or vice versa.

Eye movement patterns were completely unaffected and subjects were completely unaware of the changes.

Fixation 1:

     *

ThE SuBjEcT rEaD tExT pReSeNtEd LiKe ThIs.

Fixation 2:

            *

tHe sUbJeCt ReAd TeXt PrEsEnTeD lIkE tHiS.

FIGURE 1.8.3 – *Stimuli like those of McConkie and Zola (1979). The asterisks mark the locations of two possible successive fixations. During the saccade between the fixations, the case of the letters was changed.*

One major difference between the earlier work and the experiments that form the major basis for this discussion is their reliance on changes during saccades (see Bridgeman, van der Heijden, & Velichkovsky, 1994) and how we construct an apparently stable view of the world, despite the fact that our eyes are jumping from one part of the scene to another.

But the poor ability to detect changes across saccades generalizes to a much wider variety of viewing conditions. Several researchers, working with somewhat different paradigms, reported at about the same time experiments that suggest that the poor ability to detect changes occurs when a scene is disrupted by a saccade (as discussed above), a flicker (Rensink, O'Regan, & Clark, 1997), or a camera cut in a film (Levin & Simons, 1997).

Levin and Simons (1997) have shown several striking examples of change blindness in brief video clips. You might want to watch their videos

---

[10] The interested student should consult Rensink's (2002) review, which covers far more of the methodological and theoretical issues than this brief presentation.

[11] In reading, we typically make about four saccades per second, with each shifting the eye on average about 2° (about 8 letters), and lasting just 30 ms, with fixations averaging 225 ms (Rayner, 1998).

before reading the descriptions below. You can view each of these movie clips online by accessing the following Internet address:

http://viscog.beckman.uiuc.edu

(They are listed under "Change Blindness Examples.") The three mentioned are "Changes across cuts in a motion picture," "A person change video," and "A subject in a real-world person change event."

Three of Levin and Simons' demonstrations are described here. They showed a brief film ("Changes across cuts...") to 10 observers. There were nine changes, each of which occurred during a "cut" in the film, when the point of view shifted and then returned. There were thus 90 opportunities for change detection. Only one subject detected one change! When instructed to watch for changes, the same observers, on average, still detected only two changes each. The changes were such things as a woman wearing a scarf which is no longer there when the camera cuts away for a few seconds and then returns. Another change is the color of a plate sitting in front of the woman, and so on. There were other similar types of changes, which are known in the movie business as *continuity errors*—see Levin and Simons (2000).

In another brief movie clip ("A person change video"), viewers see a man get up from a desk and walk directly toward the camera. The camera angle then changes and you see him emerging from his office to answer a telephone on the wall of the hallway. Virtually no one noticed that the actor changed from one cut to the next, though when you know it happens, it is quite obvious! And, in an effort to see whether changes in the actor would be noticed in a real-world setting ("...real-world person change

event"), they stopped strangers on their campus, ostensibly to ask for directions. As they were talking to the stranger, two workmen carrying a door rudely barged between them with the door facing toward the subject, momentarily blocking the subject's view of the person asking directions. This was a setup, of course, and the person who had asked directions actually grabbed the door and walked away holding the door while one of the people who had been carrying the door remained and continued the conversation. Half of their subjects failed to detect the change in a person right there in front of them (Simons & Levin, 1998).

A different approach to change blindness has been pursued by Rensink and his colleagues.[12] Rensink, O'Regan, and Clark (1997) developed one of the most widely used experimental paradigms for studying change blindness. In their experiments, subjects completed a series of trials of change blindness. Each trial consisted of a three-second warning screen, then a one-second blank grey screen. Two versions of a picture were then shown repeatedly for up to 60 seconds, until the subject spotted the difference. One version of the picture was presented twice for 240 ms each time, followed by an 80-ms grey screen, then the second version of the picture was presented twice for the same amounts of time. Subjects continued to watch the alternating images until they detected the difference. Rensink et al.'s Experiment 1 is replicated in the experiment accompanying this chapter. Their other two experiments explored slight variations of the basic technique, which made little difference in the outcome.

Rensink, O'Regan, and Clark (2000) further explored the basic paradigm. In one experiment, they increased the viewing time of the first

---

[12] Many of the publications by Rensink and his colleagues are available in full-text versions at **http://www.psych.ubc.ca/~rensink/publications/index.html**.

FIGURE **1.8.4** – *Sequence of two images containing a marginal-interest change similar to those presented by Rensink et al. Did you notice the change in the lamp on the table in the background?*

presentation of the first picture to eight seconds. This manipulation was a check on the possibility that people simply never formed a memory of the scene durable enough to survive the flickers between versions. Central-interest changes were still detected with about half as many presentations as marginal-interest changes. In another of their experiments, they varied the duration of the blank grey screen between presentation of the scenes, using durations of 40, 80, 160, and 320 ms. Central-interest changes were still detected far faster than marginal-interest changes, and change blindness clearly occurred at all durations, though the overall speed of detection was faster with the 40-ms flicker. (Figure 1.8.4 shows an example of a marginal-interest change.)

They suggest that this may be due to the fact that, at these brief inter-stimulus intervals, the two scenes show *temporal integration*—two events close enough together in time are seen as simultaneous. The color and luminance of the blank screens was manipulated in another experiment and had no effect. Finally, they replaced the 80-ms grey field with a set of six small "mudsplashes," or black-and-white textured rectangles that were superimposed on the picture, but—importantly—did not appear over the position where the change occurred. Thus, there was no blank screen between presentations at the point of the change. In this condition, there was no difference between central- and marginal-interest change detection times, though change blindness was very much in evidence.

O'Regan, Rensink, and Clark (1999), reviewing these experiments (especially those with "mudsplashes"), noted that "this phenomenon is potentially important in driving, surveillance, or navigation, as dangerous events occurring in full view can go unnoticed if they coincide with small, apparently innocuous disturbances" (p. 34). They summarized their findings as follows.

These results indicate that humans' internal representation of the visual field is much sparser than the subjective experience of 'seeing' suggests. Only the parts of the environment that observers attend to and encode as interesting are available for making comparisons....

If only attended parts of the environment are represented in the brain, how can we have the impression of such richness and completeness in the visual world outside us? The answer might be that the visual world acts as an external memory. We have the impression of simultaneously seeing everything, because any portion of the visual field that awakens our interest is immediately available for scrutiny through an unconscious flick of the eye or attention. However, those parts of the scene that are not being currently processed (and in some sense are not 'seen') nevertheless constitute a background or setting that enlivens our visual experience (p.34).

The work reviewed above does not control for eye movements during scanning of scenes. Recent studies of scene changes during saccades have also found poor change detection.

Henderson and Hollingworth (1999) made changes in a scene contingent on saccades going toward or away from critical areas of the scene. Objects in the scene were  either rotated or deleted during the chosen saccades. Change detection was extremely poor, except when the saccade was moving toward the target object, when it was quite good—detection of the deletion of an object when the saccade moved toward that location was 90%. They suggest that it is focal attention toward an object that leads to this high level of change detection. Currie, McConkie, Carlson-Radvansky, and Irwin (2000) also studied changes during saccades, with similar results—good detection of object change when the object was the target of a saccade. When we note that saccades are frequently made toward objects that attract our

attention, these results mesh nicely with the other studies of change blindness. We usually are blind to changes in areas of the visual scene that are not of central interest or that otherwise do not attract the focus of attention.

Note that versions of this change blindness experiment occur on many coin-operated game machines found in taverns, such as the Force2004™ PhotoHunt™. These present two pictures side by side and take advantage of touch-screen technology to have the player touch the screen at the places where the two pictures differ. The amusement of the game is in the difficulty of detecting the changes. Though somewhat different, a staple of children's puzzle books over the last century has been pictures with either hidden figures to be detected (the *Where's Waldo?* books by Martin Handford are a modern version) or "What's wrong with this picture?" puzzles. Both provide amusement by the difficulty of finding the hidden figures or missing parts or other types of things "wrong."

FIGURE **1.8.5** – *Can you identify the five differences between the leprechaun on the left and the one on the right? (Answers follow References section.)*

Methodological Considerations

Rensink et al. (1997) classified their pictures according to whether the change was in an area or object of central interest or marginal interest. To determine this, they had five naïve observers describe one version of each scene. A change was classified as being of central interest if three or more of the observers mentioned the object or area. An example is a picture of Notre Dame Cathedral that shifts position relative to the foreground. Almost anyone describing the picture would mention the cathedral. A change was classified as being of marginal interest if none of the observers mentioned it. An example of marginal interest is a picture of a harbor scene with a reflection in the water that is present in one version and absent in the other. Asked to describe the picture, you probably would not mention the reflection. Note, however, that even the marginal-interest changes are completely obvious and hard to ignore once they are detected.

Rensink et al. (1997) had subjects verbally report the nature of the change after indicating that they had detected it, which gave them a check on accuracy which is lacking in the PsychMate version. That precludes a subject just guessing, but obviously requires that an experimenter record whether the detection was correct or not. That check is difficult to implement in a format in which student subjects test themselves. However, the rate of error in Rensink et al.'s experiment was only 1.7%, so this seems unlikely to introduce any major difference.

Questions

1. What are the dependent and independent variables for this experiment? What are some important controls?

2. Do your results agree with those of Rensink, O'Regan, and Clark's (1997) Experiment 1?

3. What did Rensink, O'Regan, and Clark (1977) find in their Experiment 1 when they did not have a blank screen between the presentations of the pictures? Why was this an important control condition?

Extension Experiments

You can create your own change-blindness experiments easily, even without using a computer to test your subjects. Use photo-manipulation software such as Adobe Photoshop™ to create two versions of the same photograph. Present them to your subjects by putting the two photographs back to back in a clear report cover. Have your subjects look at one and then turn the cover over to see the other, doing this over and over until they detect the change. The dependent variable would be the number of times the cover was turned over before the change was detected. You could also record the time needed to detect the change.

References

Bridgeman, B., van der Heijden, A. H., & Velichkovsky, B. M. (1994). A theory of visual stability across saccadic eye movements. *Behavioral and Brain Sciences, 17,* 247-292.

Buswell, G. T. (1920). *An experimental study of the eye-voice span in reading.* Chicago: University of Chicago.

Henderson, J. M., & Hollingworth, A. (1999). The role of fixation position in detecting scene changes across saccades. *Psychological Science, 10,* 438-443.

Levin, D. T., & Simons, D. J. (1997). Failure to detect changes to attended objects in motion pictures. *Psychonomic Bulletin and Review, 4,* 501-506.

Levin, D. T., & Simons, D. J. (2000). Perceiving stability in a changing world: Combining shots and integrating views in motion pictures and the real world. *Media Psychology, 2,* 357-380.

McConkie, G. W., & Zola, D. (1997). Is visual information integrated across successive fixations in reading? *Perception and Psychophysics, 25,* 221-224.

Mitroff, S. R., Simons, D. J., & Franconeri, S. L. (2002). The siren song of implicit change detection. *Journal of Experimental Psychology: Human Perception and Performance, 28,* 798-815.

O'Regan, J. K., Rensink, R. A., & Clark, J. J. (1999). Change blindness as a result of "mudsplashes." *Nature, 398,* 34.

Rayner, K. (1998). Eye movements in reading and information processing: 20 years of research. *Psychological Bulletin, 124,* 372-422.

Rensink, R. A., O'Regan, J. K., & Clark, J. J. (1997). To see or not to see: The need for attention to perceive changes in scenes. *Psychological Science, 8,* 368-373.

Rensink, R. A., O'Regan, J. K., & Clark, J. J. (2000). On the failure to detect changes in scenes across brief interruptions. *Visual Cognition, 7,* 127-145.

Simons, D. J., & Levin, D. T. (1998). Failure to detect changes to people during a real-world interaction. *Psychonomic Bulletin and Review, 5,* 644-649.

Answers from page 1-51: (1) the buckle on his hat; (2) the dimple in his chin; (3) the number of tails on his coat; (4) the direction of his cane; and (5) the buckle on his shoe.

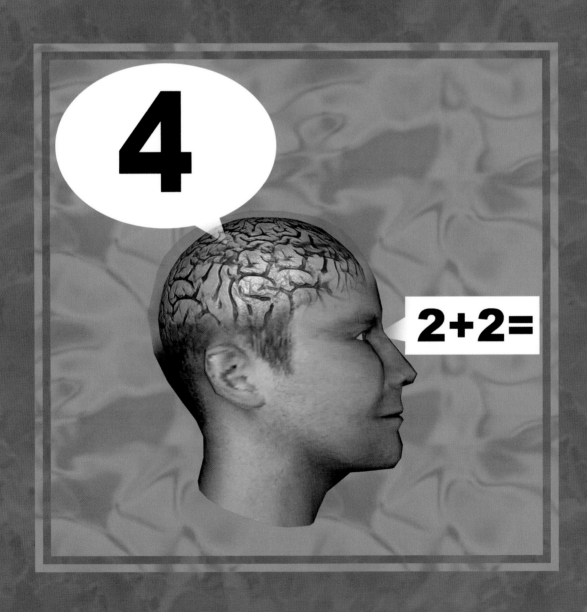

COGNITION

Introduction

Cognition is thinking, and thinking is central to psychology. Thinking is made up of many processes, and the study of cognition is the study of those many different processes that make up thinking—including memory, problem-solving, language, imagery, and reading. Psychologists have devised a number of useful approaches to the study of cognition. Researchers can use external measures to identify the components of cognitive processes. Two of the most important such measures have been (1) the study of *errors* in memory or problem-solving and (2) the study of *reaction time*, or the time needed to perform a cognitive task. These methods have become standard for cognitive psychology, yielding many insights into how cognition works. The study of errors under varying conditions of an experiment can help us study the role of imagery in problem-solving, the role of organization in memory, or the best way to rehearse material that we need to remember for a long time. By comparing the time needed to make decisions under varying conditions, we can explore how people search through short-term memory, how networks of memories are organized, or how automatic cognitive skills are developed.

In this section, a number of experiments and exercises explore many of the approaches psychology uses to study the nature of cognition.

2.1 Lexical Decisions

Abstract

A number of models of the organization of knowledge in memory treat memory as a network of specific memories connected together by links. Most of these models assume that when we remember something, we "activate" that location in memory, and that this activation spreads down the links between that location and others to which it is linked. In the experiment accompanying this chapter, the lexical-decision task of Meyer and Schvaneveldt (1971) is replicated. Subjects must make judgments about whether or not a string of letters is a common word. Generally, a word is more quickly identified as such if it follows a related word (e.g., "BUTTER" following "BREAD") than if it follows an unrelated word (e.g., "DOCTOR" following "BREAD"). This result is interpreted as supporting what are known as "spreading activation" models of memory organization.

*E*arly psychological studies of memory were principally concerned with the recall or recognition of recently learned material. The material to be learned often consisted of nonsense syllables, such as "DAQ," which were assumed to have little previous meaning associated with them. But much of our memory involves things we have learned long ago, have recalled frequently, and which have meaning. In fact, we don't usually think about reading or writing or talking as being memory tasks, but that is just what they are—at least in part. Using or recognizing a word requires the use of memory, albeit usually very familiar memory.

A conceptualization of memory for words and facts that has been studied widely by cognitive psychologists treats memory as a network of associated ideas. Each location in this network—known as a *node*—represents, for example, a word and its meaning or perhaps a basic fact or proposition. Each node is connected to other nodes by *links*, which are often depicted as specifying the relationship between the nodes. Thus, "BIRD" and "FEATHERS" are connected by a link that specifies that "BIRDS *have* FEATHERS," while "BIRD" and "CANARY" are connected by a link that specifies that "a CANARY *is a* BIRD." A large class of such models has been developed (see Anderson & Lebiere, 1998). These models

of what is usually called *semantic* memory (i.e., memory for word meanings and general information) assume that items in long-term memory vary from moment to moment in how easily they are available to working memory.

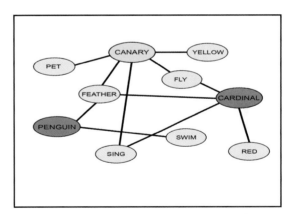

FIGURE 2.1.1 – Example network linking associated ideas or facts

A standard approach for analyzing the relative ease with which items in semantic memory become available to working memory involves the concept of *spreading activation* (see Figure 2.1.1). When we encounter a word, for example, we activate the associated node in semantic memory. This activation is assumed to *spread* to "nearby" nodes, thus partially activating them. This partial activation then makes the other nodes more likely to be accessed by working memory, thereby making that access faster. An experiment by Meyer and Schvaneveldt (1971) was important in establishing this notion of spreading activation. They performed a reaction-time experiment using a *lexical-decision* task. A lexical decision involves deciding whether or not a string of letters is a word. In their experiment, Meyer and Schvaneveldt presented their subjects with two letter-strings at once, and subjects had to indicate as quickly as possible whether both were words. Their finding, which provides strong support for the notion of spreading activation, was that if both letter-strings formed words, subjects were much faster when the words were related. For example, if the top word were "NURSE," you would be faster at deciding that the bottom string of letters was a word if it were "DOCTOR" than if it were "BUTTER."

Given a network-based model of memory, if two words are close together in the network, "activating" one by recognizing it may result in the activation spreading to other, nearby words. For example, if seeing "NURSE" leads to partial activation of words close to it in the network, then "DOCTOR" should receive such activation. Now when "DOCTOR" is seen, it requires less time to recognize, because it already is partially activated. Seeing "NURSE" would not activate a word farther away in the network, such as "BUTTER," and so the time to recognize it would

not be affected. Reaction time, then, becomes a sensitive measure of the degree of association between two words or concepts.

In Figure 2.1.2, we represent parts of the networks that are likely to exist relative to "NURSE" and "BUTTER." Note that the node for "DOCTOR" is linked to the node for "NURSE," whereas the node for "BUTTER" is not. (Of course, now having read this, you might add a new link between "NURSE" and "BUTTER"!)

While spreading activation has been an influential theoretical approach to memory, Ratcliff and McCoon (1995) have proposed a compound-cue model as a competitor to the classical spreading-activation model.

Other Considerations in Regard to Spreading Activation

The concept of spreading activation is related to a number of other lines of research. One such research area is the study of categorization by Rosch (1975). (See Chapter 2.3, *Typicality in Categorization*, for a related PsychMate experiment.) One of the tasks she used to demonstrate categorical structure was the sentence-verification task, in which subjects must indicate the correctness of sentences such as "A hammer is a tool." Here, reading the word "HAMMER" leads to a priming of the word "TOOL."

Another research area that involves the notion of spreading activation is that of automaticity of stereotyping. (See Chapter 3.5, *Automaticity and Stereotyping*, for a related PsychMate experiment based on that of Blair and Banaji, 1996.) This research suggests that seeing a word that is considered to be stereotypically masculine (e.g., "CIGAR") or feminine (e.g., "COSMETICS") leads to the activation of a stereotype, such that subjects are faster at classifying the sex of a name as being male following a masculine prime and female following a feminine prime.

An interesting demonstration of spreading activation is in an experiment on producing false memories. Roediger and McDermott (2000) showed that if you present a series of words such

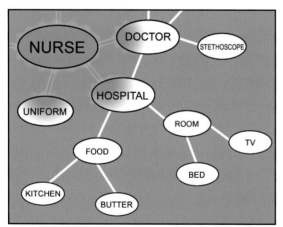

FIGURE 2.1.2 – *Example network in which NURSE and BUTTER are likely to exist. Activation of NURSE partially activates related nodes, but this activation does not affect BUTTER, which is not directly related to NURSE.*

as "WAKE," "DROWSY," "BED," etc., and then ask for recall of the list, many subjects will recall "SLEEP," even though that word was not presented. One interpretation of this false "memory" is that all of the words on the list relate to *sleep*, hence activation spread from each of the words to "SLEEP," thereby giving it a high level of activation and thus leading to a false recall.

Methodological Considerations

In this experiment, subjects are presented with two letter-strings, one appearing a few lines above the other (see Figure 2.1.3). The task is to press one key if *both* letter-strings form words and to press another key, otherwise (i.e., if either or both letter-strings are nonwords). Trials on which both strings form words make up 50 of the 98 trials. Within those trials, half consist of two unrelated words, while half consist of two related words.

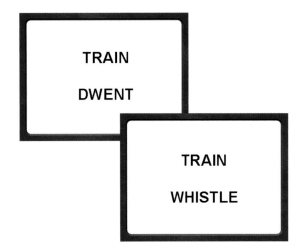

FIGURE *2.1.3* – Example trials from the Lexical Decisions experiment illustrating a word paired with a non-word and a pairing of two related words

Of the 48 trials where one or both letter-strings are nonwords, 16 each (in random order) are word above nonword, nonword above word, or both nonwords. Note that the trials in which there is a nonword present are largely uninteresting, theoretically. It is only the comparison of "word/related-word" to "word/unrelated-word" pairs that matters. However, the other trials are necessary to make the experiment work.

An issue for research using nonwords concerns how those are constructed. For this experiment, nonwords were constructed by using common words, but replacing one or two letters to form a nonword letter-string that is orthographically similar (i.e., using visually similar letters) to a real word. These are formally known as *orthographically normal* nonwords. *Orthography* refers to spelling according to accepted usage, so an orthographically normal nonword is one that could be a word, but isn't. For example, if you start with a word like "BRAKE," but change the "K" to a "T," you get "BRATE," which could be an English word, but clearly is not. On the other hand, a string of letters like "QZILG" simply could not be a word in English. Orthographically normal nonwords are harder to distinguish from real words than are nonnormal letters-strings like "QZILG," thereby making the lexical-decision task more difficult.

· ·
Expected Running Time = 14 minutes
· ·

Questions

1. What are the dependent and independent variables in this experiment? What are some important controls?

2. What are the results of this experiment? Specifically, is there any difference in the speed of the lexical decision for "word/related-word" and "word/unrelated-word" letter-string pairs?

3. What was the result of Meyer and Schvaneveldt's (1971) Experiment 1? Note especially the RT for the word/nonword pair. How do Meyer and Schvaneveldt account for the extreme slowing in this condition? (See their Discussion, p. 231.) Relate this to the experiment on response competition by B. A. Eriksen and C. W. Eriksen (1974).

Extension Experiments

1. Does activation grow continuously or by discrete jumps? Yantis and Meyer (1988) addressed this at length.

2. Meyer and his colleagues have used *pairs* of words/nonwords in various formats. Suppose that the experiment consisted of *single* trials, with each involving a word/nonword judgment. Would "NURSE" be responded to faster if preceded by "DOCTOR" in this case? Perhaps more interestingly, would the facilitation in responding drop off if there were another trial in between? Would this depend on the nature of that trial (i.e., whether word or nonword)? Does the facilitation drop with time, even if no other word intervenes? Chwilla and Kolk (2002) investigated two- and three-step priming.

3. Do opposite words (antonyms) prime each other (e.g., "HOT"/"COLD")? How would you discriminate the positive and negative priming effects?

References

Anderson, J. R., & Lebiere, C. (1998). *The atomic components of thought.* Mahwah, NJ: Erlbaum.

Blair, I., & Banaji, M. (1996). Automatic and controlled processes in stereotype priming. *Journal of Personality and Social Psychology, 70,* 1142-1163.

Chwilla, D. J., & Kolk, H. H. (2002). Three-step priming in lexical decision. *Memory and Cognition, 30,* 217-225.

Eriksen, B. A., & Eriksen, C. W. (1974). Effects of noise letters upon the identification of a target letter in a nonsearch task. *Perception and Psychophysics, 16,* 143-149.

Meyer, D. E., & Schvaneveldt, R. W. (1971). Facilitation in recognizing pairs of words: Evidence of a dependence upon retrieval operations. *Journal of Experimental Psychology, 90,* 227-234.

Meyer, D. E., Schvaneveldt, R. W., & Ruddy, M. G. (1975). Loci of contextual effects on visual word recognition. In P. M. A. Rabbit & S. Dornic (Eds.), *Attention and performance V.* London: Academic Press.

Ratcliff, R., & McKoon, G. (1995). Sequential effects in lexical decision: Tests of compound-cue retrieval theory. *Journal of Experimental Psychology: Learning, Memory, & Cognition, 21,* 1380-1388.

Roediger, H. L., & McDermott, K. B. (2000). Tricks of memory. *Current Directions in Psychological Science, 9,* 123-127.

Rosch, E. (1975). Cognitive representations of semantic categories. *Journal of Experimental Psychology: General, 104,* 192-233.

Yantis, S., & Meyer, D. E. (1988) Dynamics of activation in semantic and episodic memory. *Journal of Experimental Psychology: General, 117,* 130-147.

2.2 Scanning Short-Term Memory

Abstract

Sternberg (1966) proposed a method of studying how people search short-term memory (STM) to determine whether certain information is present. The experiment accompanying this chapter replicates his to determine (a) whether we search STM *serially* (i.e., one item at a time) or in *parallel* (i.e., all at once) and (b) whether the search is *self-terminating* (i.e., it stops when the item is located) or *exhaustive* (i.e., it must continue through the entire contents of STM). This experiment illustrates reaction-time methodology, the study of internal cognitive processes, and the testing of alternative hypotheses. In addition, the typical finding of exhaustive search illustrates the limitations of generalizing from intuitions, as opposed to formal testing of hypotheses.

In the late 1950's, experiments by Brown (1958) and Peterson and Peterson (1959) spurred a major interest in the study of what came to be called *short-term memory* (STM—though, more recently, many psychologists have preferred the term *working memory*[13]). A question that arose was the nature of the process of searching STM. Suppose you are given a set of numbers to remember, and you are permitted to rehearse them by saying them over and over to yourself. At various times, you are given a number and must decide whether it is one of the numbers you were first given. In order to do this, you must somehow search the items you are rehearsing in STM in order to decide whether the test item is among them. The experiment described below uses just such a task to examine the nature of the search process in STM.

Sternberg (1966, 1969) developed a procedure that he argued permits a test of two questions about the nature of the search of STM. The first question was whether the contents of STM are searched all at once (*parallel* search) or one item after another (*serial* search). The second question concerned whether the search stops when the search target is found (*self-terminating* search) or whether all items in STM must be compared to the search target (*exhaustive* search). After a description of the task Sternberg used to study searching of STM, we will return to these two questions and the sorts of predictions about experimental results that come from them.

Sternberg's task was a simple one. The subject is given a list of one to six digits, called the *memory set*, which he or she is permitted to rehearse. A few seconds later, the subject sees a single digit (called the *probe* digit) and must indicate, by pressing one of two buttons, whether or not that probe digit is a member of the memory set. The dependent variable is reaction time (RT), or how long it takes the subject to make a decision and press the appropriate button. As in most RT experiments, subjects are instructed to press the button as quickly as possible without making many errors (typically 5% or less). The independent variable is the size of the memory set (1-6 digits), which varies from trial to trial. On half of the trials, the probe is a member of the memory set (known as *positive* trials) and on half it is not (*negative* trials).

---

[13] There is considerable controversy over the proper conceptualization of the brief storage of information in memory. Anderson (2000) reviews much of that controversy. Searches in PsycINFO for short-term memory and for working memory will reveal the depth of the difficulties, which are beyond the scope of this review.

Serial vs. Parallel Search

Sternberg's first question was whether subjects search the whole memory set at once, or whether they must search through the memory set one item at a time. An analogy might help to make this distinction clearer. Suppose you had to visually search a short shelf of books for a particular book. You might, for example, have all your textbooks together in one place. If you are looking for your calculus textbook, you might just glance at the whole set of books at once and be able to tell whether the calculus book was among them (e.g., the calculus book has a distinctive color). This would be a parallel search. But suppose the books were several volumes of an encyclopedia—all the same size and color, but *not* in the correct order—and you had to decide whether the E-G volume was among them. Now you would likely have to look at each book, in turn, to make a decision. This would be a serial search.

Getting back to searching of STM, how can we tell which sort of search people actually do? Sternberg reasoned as follows: If you search serially, then the more items there are to search, the longer it should take. That is, RT should increase as the memory set size increases. On the other hand, if you can search all the items at once, it should not matter how many there are—RT should be the same for any memory set size (up to the capacity of STM). The test is now a simple one—does RT increase with memory set size (indicating serial search) or not (indicating parallel search)?

Self-Terminating vs. Exhaustive Search

The second question Sternberg's experiment was designed to answer was whether the search through STM (assuming it is a serial search) *stops* when a match is found between the probe and an item in the memory set (self-terminating search), or whether it must continue through the whole memory set (exhaustive search). Again, an analogy to a small shelf of books might be useful. Suppose you have several volumes of an encyclopedia on a shelf, and you must decide whether the E-G volume is among them. You have to search one volume at a time, looking at the letters on the cover. If the E-G volume *is* on the shelf, you will probably quit looking when you have found it. But if the E-G volume is *not* on the shelf, you must search through all of the books before you can be sure it is not there. An important point to note is that you *must* do an exhaustive search if the book you are looking for is not on the shelf—the only way you can know it is not there is to look at each book.

What, then, are the predictions for search of STM? We know that you *must* do an exhaustive search if the probe is negative. That is, the only way you can be sure the probe is *not* in the memory set is to compare it to *all* members of the set. For a positive probe, on the other hand, you might be able to do a self-terminating search and stop searching when you find a match between the probe and an item in the memory set. What happens, then, as we increase memory set size? Since we are assuming that the search is serial, the RT will increase as memory set size increases. We already know that the search must be exhaustive for negative probes. So if you do an exhaustive search on *all* trials, then the increase in RT as memory set size increases should be the same for both positive and negative probes.

What would happen if you used a self-terminating search? Suppose the memory set size was 3 digits. On a third of the trials, the probe would

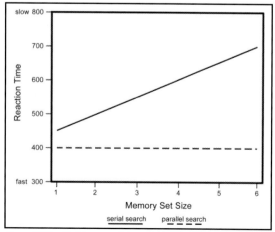

FIGURE **2.2.1** – *Serial vs. parallel search*

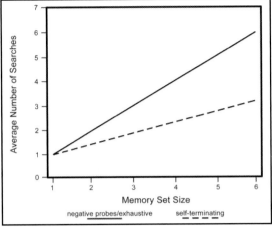

FIGURE 2.2.2 – *Exhaustive vs. self-terminating search*

match the first digit, and the search would end. On another third of the trials, the probe would match the second digit to which it was compared and the search would end. On the remaining third of the trials, a match would not be found until comparison to the third digit. Thus, on average you would have to make only two comparisons, instead of the three required for an exhaustive search. The average number of comparisons required for exhaustive and self-terminating searches is shown in Figure 2.2.2.

If we assume that each comparison takes the same amount of time, and if the search is self-terminating, then RT for positive probes will increase with memory set size only half as fast as RT for negative probes. If the search is exhaustive, on the other hand, RT will increase the same for both negative and positive probes as memory set size increases.

At this point, you should think about the questions raised and the predictions made about RT and memory set size. Think about the task as described above, and try to decide for yourself what you think the result will be. Will RT increase as memory set size increases, suggesting a serial search? If it does, will RT increase more for negative probes than for positive ones, indicating a self-terminating search? Or will it increase the same amount for positive probes as for negative probes, indicating an exhaustive search? Why would you continue searching when you have found what you are looking for?

What conclusion do you reach with regard to whether the search of STM is serial or parallel? Sternberg found that RT did increase with memory set size. For his subjects, each additional item in STM added about 38 ms to the RT, and he concluded that the search of STM is serial—one item at a time, rather than all at once.

Assuming that you also found an increase in RT with increases in memory set size, you should now address the second question—is the search self-terminating or exhaustive? Sternberg argued that exhaustive search is indicated if the slopes of the lines for positive and negative probes are the same. He found that the slopes (which represent increases in RT as memory set size is increased) were nearly identical for positive and negative probes, indicating an exhaustive search.

How can it make sense to do an exhaustive search? After all, if you are looking for a book in the library, you stop (one would hope!) when you find it. But Sternberg argued that an exhaustive search actually does make sense, if we assume that making a comparison between the probe and an item in STM is a separate step from making a decision about whether the comparison produced a match. If this is the case, and if a decision takes a relatively long time, then it is actually faster to do all of the comparisons first, and then make only a single decision.

Other Considerations in the Sternberg Paradigm

Despite Sternberg's interpretation of his data as indicating a serial, exhaustive search, his logic has not gone unchallenged. Baddeley (1976, pp. 146-147) notes some competing models of the search process which suggest that a parallel search can lead to increasing RT as memory set size increases—the very finding that Sternberg used to support a serial search. How could that happen? If you think of a parallel search as examining all items at the same time, perhaps there is some limit to the resolving power of the search. That is, searching six items all at once may lead to each item getting less of whatever resources are used for the search, whereas if one item were searched, that item would get all of the resources. Such a model would also predict longer RT for larger memory sets. There are, however, other arguments for a serial search. Schneider and Shiffrin (1977) found that when subjects had extensive experience searching for target letters from a single memory set, they obtained flat functions relating memory set size to RT—in other words, parallel processing. This suggests that the search is initially serial, but can become parallel with extensive practice searching for the same targets. (See Chapter 2.8, *Automatic vs. Controlled Processing*.) More recently, Garavan (1998) has reported data suggesting that only a single "object" can be held in "working memory" at a time. For a thorough discussion of the logic of distinguishing serial and parallel processes in general, see Townsend (1990).

Whatever the final conclusions regarding Sternberg's (1966) model, it had an enormous impact on the development of cognitive psychology (Anderson, 2000). It clearly illustrated the *information-processing* approach to cognition, which treats cognitive processes as a series of transformations of information between the initial registration of a stimulus and our response to the stimulus. It also captured the highly symbolic nature of representations of information in memory.

Recent Contributions

A major development in ideas concerning short-term memory is the working memory (WM) model of Baddeley and his colleagues (see Baddeley, 1976). This model proposes that working memory consists of three components: a central executive and two slave systems. The slave systems consist of (1) a phonological loop, used for rehearsing auditory information, and (2) the visuospatial sketchpad, for rehearsing via visual imagery. Raichle (1993) has provided neurophysiological support for these slave systems, showing that different parts of the brain are active in the Sternberg task (which requires rehearsal via the phonological loop) and in a task that requires remembering the spatial location of targets (presumably using the visuospatial sketchpad). One role of the central executive is to activate the slave systems (rehearsal loops). (See the PsychMate experiment on *Executive Control, Planning, and the Tower of London* in Chapter 2.5.)

Methodological Considerations

An important consideration in Sternberg's experiment was limiting the memory set size to a maximum of six items. Note that if the memory set size increased much beyond six items, it would exceed the capacity of short-term memory and thus fundamentally alter the nature of the task. Even the basic question of the capacity of short-term memory is loaded with considerable theoretical baggage. For many years, the limit seemed well-described by Miller's (1956) classic paper on the "magical number" 7 ☐ 2—the capacity of short-term memory was about seven items, but sometimes a little more or less, which corresponds very well to the digit span. As mentioned in Note 1, there is a rich area of argument about how to conceptualize the brief storage of information. That extends to the issue of capacity limitations. See Cowan (2001) for a lengthy discussion (with commentaries).

· · · · · · · · · · · · · · · · · · ·
Expected Running Time = 40 minutes
· · · · · · · · · · · · · · · · · · ·

Questions

1. What are the dependent and independent variables in this experiment? Is this a within- or between-subjects design? What are some important controls?

2. Does the evidence from this experiment suggest a serial search or a parallel search? Why?

3. Does the evidence from this experiment suggest a self-terminating search or an exhaustive search? Why?

4. Compare your group data to the data reported in Sternberg (1966, Figure 1). Graph the points from Sternberg's figure onto the plot of your group data. Are the overall RTs about the same? If not, what factors could affect the difference?

Extension Experiments

1. How does the comparison process change as a function of the complexity of the material to be searched (e.g., letters, numbers, words, and pictures, as well as single colors or shapes and conjunctions of colors and shapes)? See Teichner and Krebs (1974), Briggs and Johnson (1973), and Fisk and Schneider (1983).

2. How does the comparison process change as a function of degree of practice, and also whether the memory set changes often or not? See Schneider and Shiffrin (1977) and Kristofferson (1972a,b); also see Chapter 2.8, *Automatic vs. Controlled Processing*, in this guide.

3. As you increase the number of items in the memory set (and hence the number of comparisons that must be made), do you expect a shift from exhaustive to self-terminating search? Can subjects be *trained* to make a self-terminating or exhaustive search? See Schneider and Shiffrin (1977, p. 27, 32).

References

Anderson, J. R. (2000). *Cognitive psychology and its implications* (5th ed.). New York: Worth.

Baddeley, A. D. (1976). *The psychology of memory*. New York: Basic Books.

Briggs, G. E., and Johnsen, A. M. (1973). On the nature of central processes in choice reactions. *Memory and Cognition, 1*, 91-100.

Brown, J. A. (1958). Some tests of the decay theory of immediate memory. *Quarterly Journal of Experimental Psychology, 10*, 12-21.

Cowan, N. (2001). The magical number 4 in short-term memory: A reconsideration of mental storage capacity. *Behavioral and Brain Sciences, 24*, 87-185.

Fisk, A. D., & Schneider, W. (1983). Category and word search: Generalizing search principles to complex processing. *Journal of Experimental Psychology: Learning, Memory, and Cognition, 9*, 177-195.

References *(continued)*

Garavan, H. (1998). Serial attention within working memory. *Memory and Cognition, 26*, 263-276.

Kristofferson, M. (1972a). Effects of practice on character classification performance. *Canadian Journal of Psychology, 26*, 54-60.

Kristofferson, M. (1972b). When item recognition and visual search functions are similar. *Perception and Psychophysics, 12*, 379-384

Miller, G. A. (1956). The magical number seven, plus or minus two: Some limits on our capacity for processing information. *Psychological Review, 63*, 81-97.

Peterson, L. R., & Peterson, M. J. (1959). Short-term retention of individual verbal items. *Journal of Experimental Psychology, 58*, 193-198.

Raichle, M. E. (1993). The scratchpad of the mind. *Nature, 363*, 583-584.

Schneider, W., & Shiffrin, R. M. (1977). Controlled and automatic human information processing: I. Detection, search, and attention. *Psychological Review, 84*, 1-66.

Sternberg, S. (1966). High-speed scanning in human memory. *Science, 153*, 652-654.

Sternberg, S. (1969). Memory scanning: Mental processes revealed by reaction-time experiments. *American Scientist, 57*, 421-457.

Teichner, W. H., & Krebs, M. J. (1974). Visual search for simple targets. *Psychological Bulletin, 81*, 15-28.

Townsend, J. T. (1990). Serial vs. parallel processing: Sometimes they look like Tweedledum and Tweedledee but they can (and should) be distinguished. *Psychological Science, 1*, 46-54.

2.3 Typicality in Categorization

Abstract

Categorization is a fundamental issue for psychology. To recognize or name an object is to categorize it. A major assumption of the "classical theory" of categorization holds that categories are defined by the shared properties of their members. That is, all members of a category have some shared features that define the category. Studies by Rosch and her colleagues provide a challenge to that account by demonstrating that categories have structure—that is, not all members of a category are equally "good" members. Studies based on production of examples of categories, direct ratings of goodness-of-example, and reaction time to verify sentences such as "A cat is an animal," all demonstrate that some members of a category are "better" than others.

Why should psychologists be concerned with categories? In his book, *Women, Fire, and Dangerous Things*, Lakoff (1987) argues the centrality of categorization for psychology:

> Categorization is not a matter to be taken lightly. There is nothing more basic than categorization to our thought, perception, action, and speech. Every time we see something as a *kind* of thing, for example, a tree, we are categorizing. Whenever we reason about *kinds* of things—chairs, nations, illnesses, emotions, any kind of thing at all—we are employing categories. Whenever we intentionally perform any *kind* of action, say something as mundane as writing with a pencil, hammering with a hammer, or ironing clothes, we are using categories. The particular action we perform on that occasion is a *kind* of motor activity (e.g., writing, hammering, ironing), that is, it is in a particular category of motor actions. They are never done in exactly the same way, yet despite the differences in particular movements, they are all movements of a kind, and we know how to make movements of that kind. And anytime we either produce or understand any utterance of reasonable length, we are employing dozens if not hundreds of categories: categories of speech sounds, of words, of phrases and clauses, as well as conceptual categories.

> Without the ability to categorize, we could not function at all, either in the physical world or in our social and intellectual lives. An understanding of how we categorize is central to any understanding of how we think and function, and therefore central to an understanding of what makes us human. (Lakoff, 1987, p. 5-6).

While categorization is clearly of major importance, it had long been assumed that categories were well understood. Dating back at least to Aristotle, it has been assumed that categories are defined by their shared features. It was assumed that categories are *well-defined*—that is, things are in the same category because they share the *defining features* of that category. The defining features of a category consist of the necessary and sufficient features—that is, the features that are individually necessary, and that, taken together, are sufficient. For instance, the defining features of a triangle are that it is a bounded figure, consisting of three straight sides. Anything that has those features is a triangle. Anything that lacks any one of them is not.

This assumption about categories—that they are defined by the features common to their members—is termed the "classical theory" by Lakoff. (1987). He notes that "this classical theory was not the result of empirical study. It was not even a subject of major debate. It was a philosophical position arrived at on the basis of *a priori* speculation. Over the centuries it simply became part of the background assumptions taken for granted in most scholarly disciplines" (p. 6). But is this classical theory of categorization correct? Work by the philosopher Wittgenstein (1953) began to question it. Wittgenstein tried to find the defining features of a game. You might want to try this for yourself. Can you list the features that all games have in common and that are not shared by non-games? (Consider that this must include chess, football, solitaire, and Old Maid!) Wittgenstein concluded that he could not. The category *game*, at least, does not seem to be a well-defined category.

More recently, experiments by Rosch and her associates (Mervis, Catlin, & Rosch, 1976; Mervis & Rosch, 1981; Rosch, 1973, 1975; Rosch & Mervis, 1975) also have called the classical theory into serious question. Rosch noted that, if the classical theory is correct, then no member of a category has any special status. That is, no member of the category can be a "better" member than another. Consider again the (well-defined) category, *triangle*. If I showed you several triangles, could any one of them be a "better" triangle than another? There seems to be no basis for that to occur. Rosch reasoned that if categories, in fact, have "better" (or even "best") members, then they cannot be well defined—or, at least, it is clear that our minds do not treat them as well-defined.

There was already some work that suggested that, at least for some categories, some members do have a special status. Zadeh (1965) pointed out that some categories have graded membership, such as *tall people*. Whether or not someone is tall is a matter of degree, as well as kind. Presumably, no one would argue that a person four feet tall is "tall." Nor would they argue that a person seven feet tall is not. But is a six-footer "tall?"

Research on color names also suggested that categories might have "best" members. Consider the category *red*. There are many shades of red. Berlin and Kay (1969) showed people a set of color chips, containing some reds, as well as other colors, and ask them to point to an example of *red*. What they discovered was that most people would point to the same example of red, and this same example was chosen by people from all over the world. That best example of red, which they refer to as "focal" red, was essentially a "fire-engine" red. [Some languages do not have a specific word for *red*, and some have only two words for color. In those languages, the two words correspond basically to what artists call the "warm" colors (red, orange, yellow, white) and the "cool" colors (black, blue, green, gray). Berlin and Kay found that if they asked speakers of those languages to point to a "warm" color, they might point to a white, yellow, orange, or red. When they pointed to a red color, though, it was the same focal red chosen by others.]

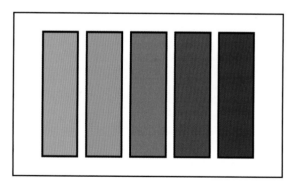

It is worth noting that the "best" red is not determined by culture, but rather by human physiology. The three types of cones in the human eye are maximally sensitive to light in the "red," "green," and "blue" parts of the spectrum. The focal red that Berlin and Kay's subjects chose corresponds to the wavelength of light to which the "red" cones are most sensitive. (There are no cones maximally sensitive to yellow, but neurons that get input from both "red" and "green" cones function as yellow receptors.) The main point is that some members of the color-category *red* are clearly agreed to be better examples than others.

A very different approach that also suggested a special status for some members of a category was taken by Posner and Keele (1968). They created artificial categories by randomly placing nine dots on a 30x30 matrix. They created several such dot patterns (see Figure 2.3.1). Then they created categories of dot patterns by making several distortions of each of the originals. (Basically, they moved each dot a randomly chosen distance in a randomly chosen direction.) The result was that the set of distortions of each dot pattern constituted a category. Their subjects were repeatedly shown a set of the distortions from each category (but not the originals) and were required to sort them into categories. With some practice, subjects became quite accurate. The test was then to ask them to sort the distortions with which they had practice, some new distortions they had never seen before, and the original dot patterns from which the distortions were produced (and which they also had never seen before).

The result was that the originals were sorted as easily as the distortions with which the subjects had practiced, and more easily than the new distortions. Posner and Keele argued that subjects' experience with the various members of a category had led them to abstract a "prototype" or schema of the category that was essentially an average of the individual members. But, of course, the average of the individual members would, in this case, match closely to the original. The main point here is that the original dot patterns were more easily sorted than new members of the category, even though neither the new members nor the originals had been seen before—the original patterns had a

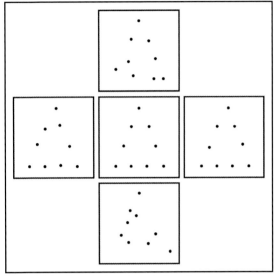

FIGURE 2.3.1 – *Example dot patterns similar to those used by Posner and Keele*

special status by virtue of matching the prototype their subjects had abstracted from experience with the individual distortions.

While there were a number of indications, beginning with Wittgenstein, that all might not be well with the classical theory, it was Rosch and her associates who put together a series of demonstrations of the fact that, for most categories, membership is structured—that is, some members of the category are truly more central, more typical, "better" members than others. Those demonstrations form the basis for the experiment accompanying this chapter. Rosch studied several ways to demonstrate *typicality*, or the fact that some members of a category are more typical ("better") than others.

One technique Rosch devised for exploring typicality effects was simply to ask subjects to indicate on a rating scale how good an example an item was of its category. *Goodness-of-example ratings* turn out to be quite stable. Individual subjects show high agreement, and comparisons of West-coast and East-coast subjects showed high agreement (correlations above 0.92). One of the two experiments accompanying this chapter replicates Rosch's (1975) study of goodness-of-example ratings, using the original lists.

Another technique Rosch (1973) used to test typicality was reaction time to *sentence verification*. In this task, the subject sees a sentence like "A chicken is a bird" and must try to indicate as quickly as possible whether the sentence is true or false. Of course, there are a number of false sentences included as well, to make the experiment work. The question for Rosch was whether words that received high ratings of goodness-of-example would also have the fastest reaction times in sentence verification. They did, indicating that sentence verification also shows the typicality effect. This forms the basis for the second of the experiments accompanying this chapter. Similar effects have been reported by Rips, Shoben, and Smith (1973).

Yet another technique was the *production of examples*. When subjects are asked to name members of various categories, they are far more likely to generate some members than others. Asked to name an animal, for example, people are more likely to name "bear" or "dog" than "rattlesnake" or "sponge." Battig and Montague (1969) provided production norms for a wide variety of categories. Those formed the basis for Rosch's (1975) experimental lists that showed a strong correlation between subject ratings of goodness-of-example and the production of examples.

The three techniques described above agree remarkably. Each of the three demonstrates typicality—some members of a category are more central, more typical, than others. Recall that Rosch argued that, if categories are well-defined, as the classical theory states, then there is simply no

basis for typicality effects. Typicality effects occur in virtually all categories. Therefore, the classical theory must be wrong, at least for most categories.

But if the classical theory is wrong, how are categories defined? One way that category membership arises is through what Wittgenstein called "family resemblance." Consider the children in a large family. Some may not look

much alike at all, but each will share some resemblance to part of the others. A wide range of other possible mechanisms for category formation are discussed by Lakoff (1987). Lakoff also discusses a number of mechanisms that can produce typicality effects (pp. 288-299).

One aspect of category membership and typicality that should be discussed here is that typicality, as reflected through the three techniques Rosch used, is not fixed or permanent. It depends upon experience—both your personal experience and that of your (or other) culture. While a robin is judged highly typical of the category *bird*, and penguin is very low in typicality, one might expect the opposite of someone raised in a culture where penguins are seen everyday and robins are only read about in books.

Methodological Considerations

The two parts of this experiment use the materials developed by Rosch (1975, Experiment 1, Set 3), which are based on the production norms of Battig and Montague (1969). Rosch reported goodness-of-example norms for those words. For this experiment, we used words from her lists (see her Table 1), consisting of items that were either high, medium, or low in ratings of goodness-of-example. (One change was made. We replaced the item "bolt" from the category *carpenter's tool* with "crowbar," as a bolt is hardware, not a tool.) Those words were then used for the two parts of this experiment, which are counterbal-

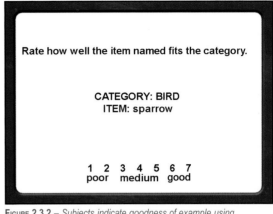

FIGURE **2.3.2** – *Subjects indicate goodness of example using a Likert scale*

anced in order across subjects, based on subject number. In one version, the subject is told the category and shown an item from that category, and must indicate on a 7-point Likert scale their rating of goodness-of-example (see Figure 2.3.2), with 1 representing a poor member of a category and 7 representing a good one. (This reverses Rosch's scale.)

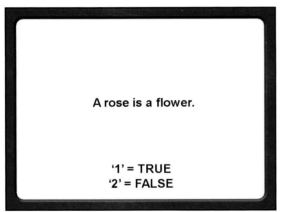

FIGURE **2.3.3** – *Subjects indicate whether or not an item is a member or a category*

In the other version, the subject sees a sentence of the form "A(n) (item) is a (category)." The subject is instructed to indicate as quickly as possible whether the sentence is true or false, and reaction time is measured. (See Figure 2.3.3.) Half of the sentences are false. Those sentences were constructed by using items from other categories, such that the false items accompanying any given category were each taken from a separate category.

Expected Running Time = 16 minutes

Questions

1. In each of these two studies, what are the dependent and independent variables? What are some important controls?

2. Do your results confirm a typicality effect?

3. In her initial lists, Rosch (1975) used the category *toy*. She dropped that category from the rest of her experiments. Why?

References

Banaji, M., & Hardin, C. (1996). Automatic stereotyping. *Psychological Science, 7*, 136-141.

Bargh, J. A. (1994). The four horsemen of automaticity: Awareness, intention, efficiency, and control in social cognition. In R. S. Wyer & T. K. Srull (Eds.), *Handbook of social cognition: Vol. 1. Basic processes* (pp. 1-40). Hillsdale, NJ: Lawrence Erlbaum Associates.

Bargh, J. (1997). The automaticity of everyday life. In R. Wyer (Ed.), *Advances in social cognition: Vol. X. The automaticity of everyday life* (pp. 1-61). Mahwah, NJ: Erlbaum.

Bargh, J., & Ferguson, M. (2000). Beyond behaviorism: On the automaticity of higher mental processes. *Psychological Bulletin, 126*, 925-945.

Bartlett, F. C. (1932). *Remembering: A study in experimental and social psychology.* Cambridge, UK: Cambridge University Press.

Battig, W. F., & Montague, W. E. (1969). Category norms for verbal items in 56 categories: A replication and extension of the Connecticut category norms. *Journal of Experimental Psychology Monograph, 80,* (3, Pt. 2).

Berlin, B., and Kay, P. (1969). *Basic color terms: Their universality and evolution.* Berkeley, CA: University of California Press.

Blair, I., & Banaji, M. (1996). Automatic and controlled processes in stereotype priming. *Journal of Personality and Social Psychology, 70*, 1142-1163.

Fiske, S. T., & Taylor S. E. (1984). *Social cognition* (1st ed.). Reading, MA: Addison-Wesley.

Fiske, S. T., & Taylor S. E. (1991). *Social cognition* (2nd ed.). New York: McGraw-Hill.

Gilbert, D. T., & Hixon, J. G. (1991). The trouble of thinking: Activation and application of stereotypic beliefs. *Journal of Personality and Social Psychology, 60*, 509-517.

Kučera, H., & Francis, W. (1967). *Computational analysis of present-day American English.* Providence, RI: Brown University Press.

Lakoff, G. (1987). *Women, fire, and dangerous things.* Chicago: University of Chicago Press.

Logan, G. (1989). Automaticity and cognitive control. In J. S. Uleman & J. Bargh (Eds.), *Unintended thought* (pp. 52-74). New York: Guilford.

Macrae, C. N., & Bodenhausen, G. V. (2001). Social cognition: Categorical person perception. *British Journal of Psychology, 92*, 239-255.

Macrae, C. N., Bodenhausen, G. V., Milne, A. B., Thorn, T. M. J., & Castelli, L. (1997). On the activation of social stereotypes: The moderating role of processing objectives. *Journal of Experimental Social Psychology, 33*, 471-489.

Macrae, C. N., Milne, A. B., & Bodenhausen, G. V. (1994). Stereotypes as energy-saving devices: A peek inside the cognitive toolbox. *Journal of Personality and Social Psychology, 66*, 37-47.

Meyer, D. E., & Schvaneveldt, R. W. (1971). Facilitation in recognizing pairs of words: Evidence of a dependence upon retrieval operations. *Journal of Experimental Psychology, 90*, 227-234

Mervis, C. B., Catlin, J., & Rosch, E. (1976). Relationships among goodness-of-example, category norms, and word frequency. *Bulletin of the Psychonomic Society, 7*, 283-284.

Mervis, C. B., & Rosch, E. (1981). Categorization of natural objects. *Annual Review of Psychology, 32*, 89-115.

Moskowitz, G., Wasel, W., Goldwitzer, P. W., & Schaal, B. (1999). Preconscious control of stereotype activation through chronic egalitarian goals. *Journal of Personality and Social Psychology, 77*, 167-184.

Neely, J. (1977). Semantic priming and retrieval from lexical memory: Roles of inhibitionless spreading activation and limited-capacity attention. *Journal of Experimental Psychology: General, 106*, 226-254..

Neely, J. (1991.) Semantic priming effects in visual word recognition: A selective review of current findings and theories. In D. Besner & G. Humphreys (Eds.), *Basic research in reading: Visual word recognition* (pp. 264-336). Hillsdale, NJ: Erlbaum.

Oakes, P. J., & Turner, J. C. (1990). Is limited information processing the cause of social stereotyping? In W. Stroebe & M. Hewstone (Eds.), *European review of social psychology* (Vol. 1, pp. 111-135). Chichester, UK: Wiley.

Posner, M. I., & Keele, S. W. (1968). On the genesis of abstract ideas. *Journal of Experimental Psychology, 77*, 353-363.

Rips, L. J., Shoben, E. J., & Smith, E. E. (1973). Semantic distance and the verification of semantic relations. *Journal of Verbal Learning & Verbal Behavior, 12*, 1-20.

Rosch, E. (1975). Cognitive representations of semantic categories. *Journal of Experimental Psychology: General, 104*, 192-233.

Rosch, E. H. (1973). Natural categories. *Cognitive Psychology, 4*, 328-350.

Rosch, E., & Mervis, C. B. (1975). Family resemblances: Studies in the internal structure of categories. *Cognitive Psychology, 7*, 573-605.

Wittgenstein, L. (1953). *Philosophical investigations.* New York: Macmillan

Zadeh, L. (1965). Fuzzy sets. *Information and Control, 8*, 338-353.

2.4 Sentence-Picture Comparison

Abstract

Clark and Chase (1972) proposed a model of how we compare sentences and pictures to determine whether or not a sentence is true of a picture. In the experiment accompanying this chapter, you will replicate one of their experiments, in which a sentence is presented, followed by a picture. Clark and Chase argued that the sentence and picture must be encoded into mental representations of the same type for comparison. According to their model, the sentence and the picture are each converted into propositions and then compared. By varying the sentences in several ways, it is possible to show that their theory provides a good fit to the data. Sentences were phrased either positively or negatively (e.g., "is" or "isn't"), were either true or false in relation to the picture, and used either a marked or an unmarked adjective. Clark and Chase's theory makes some specific predictions about the patterns of reaction times obtained, which are used to test the theory. The additive-factors logic (Sternberg, 1969) can be applied to testing the assumption that there is a series of stages of processing that lead to the decision about whether the sentence is true of the picture.

*I*n the experiment accompanying this chapter, you will replicate a study by Clark and Chase (1972) that examined the process by which one compares a sentence and a picture to determine whether the sentence accurately describes the picture. The sentences are simple ones, such as the following:

The star is above the plus.

The pictures are of the form shown in Figure 2.4.1. For this sentence, of course, the answer would be "true" for the picture on the left and "false" for the picture on the right.

The sentences and pictures vary in a number of ways. The pictures can be either of those shown above, while the sentences can be either true or false, can be either positive or negative ("is" or "isn't"), and can contain either the word "above" or "below." You will be examining the pattern of reaction-time latencies (RTs) for these various conditions to test Clark and Chase's theory of how we do this task.

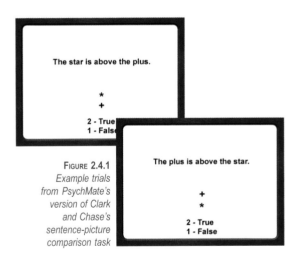

FIGURE 2.4.1
Example trials from PsychMate's version of Clark and Chase's sentence-picture comparison task

In the experiment by Clark and Chase that you are replicating, they were concerned with the process of sentence-picture comparison when the sentence is presented first. (Their model of this process requires some modification when the picture is presented first, but we won't be concerned with that situation.) Clark and Chase postulated four stages in the process of comparing the sentence and the picture. These stages are specified as follows:

- a mental representation of the sentence is formed,

- a mental representation of the picture is formed,

- the representations of the sentence and picture are compared, and

- a response is made.

Figure 2.4.2, taken from Clark and Chase (1972), illustrates the steps of the process in flowchart form.

When **a mental representation of the sentence is formed**, it is assumed that the representation is stored as a set of propositions (a proposition may be thought of as a simple statement). The sentence, "The star *is* above the plus" (or "The plus *is* above the star") requires a single proposition: "STAR ABOVE PLUS." But, the sentence, "The star *isn't* above the plus" requires two propositions: (1) "STAR ABOVE PLUS" and (2) "NOT TRUE." For this reason, a negative sentence will take longer to encode or form a representation than a positive sentence.

According to Clark and Chase's model, "above" and "below" will be treated somewhat differently in the process of forming the mental representation. "Above" is assumed to be the normal ("unmarked") statement, while "below" is the less direct statement, called a *semantically marked* form. The linguistic analysis that leads to this assumption is beyond the scope of this text (*see* Clark, 1971, for a detailed discussion of marking), but the prediction it makes is that the time to encode "below" will be longer than the time to encode "above." To make this distinction more meaningful, think about how you describe such relationships. Which would you find the more natural way to describe the relationship between a ceiling and a floor: *The floor is below the ceiling*, or *The ceiling is above the floor*? Try this with other objects that could be above or below one another, and you will likely find that you are generally more comfortable saying *A is above B* than saying *B is below A*, even though the two sentences mean the same thing.

In the next stage of the process, **a mental representation of the picture is formed**. Clark and Chase assumed that the picture is encoded as a proposition (statement) in such a way that a picture with the star on top will be encoded as "STAR ABOVE PLUS" if the sentence

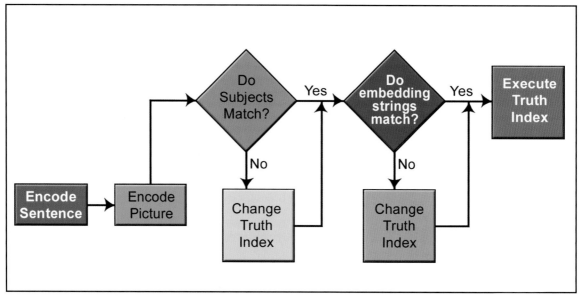

FIGURE **2.4.2** – *Stages of processing in sentence-picture comparison* (Redrawn from Clark & Chase, 1972, Table 1)

had "above" as the relationship, and as "PLUS BELOW STAR" if the sentence had "below" as the relationship.

In the third stage, **the representations of the sentence and picture are compared**, but they cannot be compared simply for surface identity. The propositions for "The star isn't above the plus" are "STAR ABOVE PLUS" and "FALSE." But these propositions are also true of the picture encoded as "PLUS ABOVE STAR." So, this third stage must involve a series of steps in making the comparisons, not just a check for identity of the encoded propositions. These comparisons involve first checking to see whether the subjects of the propositions match, and then checking to see whether there is a "FALSE" proposition for the sentence.

In the final stage, **a response is made**, based on whether the outcome of the previous stages was TRUE or FALSE. This stage is assumed to add a constant amount of time to RT, since either a *true* or *false* response should require the same time to execute.

The exact predictions from this model are quite involved, but, for our purposes, they can be summarized as follows:

- A sentence with "below" will require longer to process than one with "above," resulting in longer RT.

- Negative sentences will take longer than positive ones ("isn't" takes longer to process than "is").

- False sentences will take longer to process than true ones (a mismatch requires extra processing time).

Later Uses of the Sentence-Picture Comparison Task

Clark and Chase's (1972) seemingly simple task has provided fertile ground for research. Much of that research has focused on the use of different strategies for completing the task. Carpenter and Just (1975) proposed a more extensive model of the process of verifying simple sentences against pictures, using Clark and Chase's basic task.

MacLeod, Hunt, and Mathews (1978; see also Mathews, Hunt, and MacLeod, 1980; Neubauer and Freudenthaler, 1994) examined individual differences within the context of Carpenter and Just's (1975) model and reported that a majority of subjects' data was well-fitted by that model, but also that a sizable minority was not. Tests of spatial ability and verbal ability suggested that subjects with high spatial ability were more likely to use a visual-spatial strategy.

A more recent study of strategies in sentence verification used the fMRI to examine differences in brain activation based on instructions to use either a verbal strategy or a visual-spatial strategy (Reichle, Carpenter, & Just, 2000). In the latter, subjects were instructed to "form a mental image of the objects in the sentence and their arrangement" (p. 268), prior to the presentation of the picture. For the verbal strategy, they found an increase in activation in Broca's area[14], which is known to be involved in speech production, with no activation of the superior parietal lobe, which is known to be involved in spatial processing of sensory information. When subjects used the visual-spatial strategy, the pattern reversed, with a distinct increase in superior parietal activation and no

---

[14] In 1861, the French neurologist Broca reported that damage to a specific area of the left frontal lobe produced a characteristic deficit in speech production. Damage to the analogous areas of the right hemisphere did not. Broca correctly concluded that this area, now known as Broca's area, was involved in speech production. See Gardner (1975).

activation of Broca's area. They also reported that subjects with better visual-spatial ability, as measured by a version of the mental rotation task (see Chapter 1.3, *Rotation of Mental Images*), showed even lower activation of the left parietal cortex when using the visual-spatial strategy. (See Figure 2.4.3.)

A search of PsycINFO using the term "sentence picture" will find most of this literature, though you will have to sift through a number of articles unrelated to this line of research.

Methodological Considerations

The experiment accompanying this chapter replicates Clark and Chase's (1972) Experiment 1. In this experiment, subjects see a sentence, followed by a picture. The task is simply to indicate, by pressing the appropriate keys, whether the sentence is a true statement about the picture or a false one. The pictures are of a star (*) and a plus (+), one above the other. There are a total of eight types of trials, combining "true"/"false," "is"/"isn't," and "above"/ "below." There are two sentences of each of these 16 types, and each of those is presented 10 times. Thus, there are 20 trials of each type.

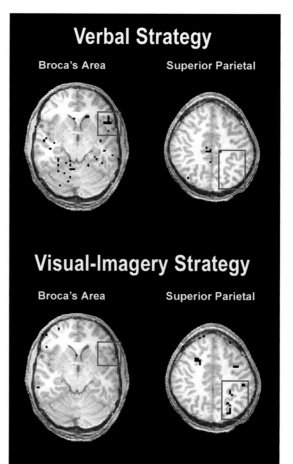

FIGURE **2.4.3** – *Functional MRI (fMRI) image of verbal versus visual strategy effect on Broca's region and superior parietal activity (from Reichle et al., 2000)*

An examination of the literature on this task shows that many variations have been tried, including whether the sentence and picture were presented at the same time, as well as the duration of the *inter-stimulus interval* (ISI). With an ISI greater than zero, whether the sentence or the picture is presented first becomes an issue. Clearly, subjects left to their own devices may choose varying strategies, such as converting a sentence to a pictorial representation (or vice versa).

● ●
Expected Running Time = 25 minutes
● ●

Questions

1. What are the dependent and independent variables in this experiment? What are some important controls? Describe the use of randomization in this experiment.

2. Describe your results. For each independent variable, state whether the predicted difference in RTs occurred.

3. Are your data consistent with those of Clark and Chase?

Extension Experiments

1. What is the effect of presenting the picture first, followed by the sentence? See Clark and Chase's (1972) Experiment 2.

2. Clark and Chase (1972) presented their sentences and pictures simultaneously, with the sentence on the left, and instructed their subjects to read the sentence first (Experiment 1). In another experiment, they varied the instructions and the left-to-right order of the sentence and picture. Gough (1966; also see Clark and Chase, p. 502) has reported a similar experiment, but with the sentence appearing three seconds before the picture (presumably enough time to complete encoding it). Does the timing matter? Could the effects of reading time on the verification task be measured by placing it under the subject's control?

3. What is the effect of giving instructions to use a visual-spatial strategy versus a verbal strategy? See above for various studies that tried either to determine subjects' strategies or to actively manipulate them.

References

Carpenter, P. A., & Just, M. A. (1975). Sentence comprehension: A psycholinguistic processing model of verification. *Psychological Review, 82*, 45-73.

Clark, H. H. (1971). More about "Adjectives, Comparatives, and Syllogisms": A reply to Huttenlocher and Higgins. *Psychological Review, 78*, 505-514.

Clark, H. H., & Chase, W. G. (1972). On the process of comparing sentences against pictures. *Cognitive Psychology, 3*, 472-517.

Gardner, H. (1975). *The shattered mind: The person after brain damage.* New York: Knopf.

Gough, P. R. (1966). The verification of sentences: The effects of delay of evidence and sentence length. *Journal of Verbal Learning and Verbal Behavior, 5*, 492-496.

MacLeod, C. M., Hunt, E. B., & Mathews, N. N. (1978). Individual differences in the verification of sentence-picture relationships. *Journal of Verbal Learning & Verbal Behavior, 17*, 493-507.

Mathews, N. N., Hunt, E. B., & MacLeod, C. M. (1980). Strategy choice and strategy training in sentence-picture verification. *Journal of Verbal Learning & Verbal Behavior, 19*, 531-548.

Neubauer, A. C., & Freudenthaler, H. H. (1994). Reaction times in a sentence-picture verification test and intelligence: Individual strategies and effects of extended practice. *Intelligence, 19*, 193-218.

Reichle, E. D., Carpenter, P. A., & Just, M. A. (2000). The neural bases of strategy and skill in sentence-picture verification. *Cognitive Psychology, 40*, 261-295.

Sternberg, S. (1969). The discovery of processing stages: Extensions of Donders' method. *Acta Psychologica, 30*, 276-315.

Thought Questions

1. Which seemed harder, sentences with "is" or those with "isn't"?

2. Which seemed harder, true sentences or false ones?

3. Which seemed harder, sentences with "above" or those with "below"?

2.5 Executive Control, Planning, and the Tower of London

Abstract

The Tower of London is a problem-solving task devised to test executive function in brain-injured patients. Persons with frontal-lobe injuries often have impaired ability on this type of problem-solving, which requires planning a series of moves ahead of time, then executing them. That sort of planful, deliberate cognition is often referred to as executive control, in the sense that it involves a series of decisions that are then executed by lower-level cognitive processes such as perception, attention, and control of action. The Tower of London has now become a research tool for studying normal executive functioning, as well as that impaired by frontal brain injury.

An area of increasing interest within cognitive psychology and the cognitive neurosciences is *executive control*. Executive control refers to a number of aspects concerning the control of thought and of action. These include the processes that coordinate habits and skills, monitor and correct performance, make choices among tasks, and plan future actions (Logan, 2003). These can be contrasted usefully with automatic processes that proceed without much deliberate, conscious control (see Chapter 2.8, *Automatic vs. Controlled Processing*).

Logan (2003) has recently argued that the study of executive control is "the next step in the cumulative investigation of cognition" (p.45). He notes that various, basic cognitive processes, such as perception, attention, memory, and categorization, are now reasonably well understood (though clearly not without plenty of remaining controversies). But theories of memory and the like tend to treat these cognitive processes as freestanding modules that are turned on and used as needed. It is, then, the executive control that does this turning on or off. The difficulty is to specify how *executive control* works, without resorting to a *homunculus*, or "little man" in our head, who controls, chooses, adjusts, and so on. Of course, assuming a homunculus who does these things is a completely hollow explanation, since one then has to explain how the homunculus does his job.

Baddelay (1986) proposed the widely-accepted model of working memory which has working memory consisting of a "central executive" and two slave systems for visual and auditory rehearsal. Much of his research program has been an attempt to specify the workings of the central executive in such a way that he can "pension off" the homunculus (Baddelay, 1995, p. 760).

The importance of executive control goes beyond traditional cognitive psychology to include neuropathology, cognitive neuroscience, and developmental psychology, among other fields.

Studies of psychopathology and brain injury find that basic cognitive processes are often intact in schizophrenics or persons with brain injuries, who nevertheless show severe problems in thinking. Impairments in executive control have been invoked to explain such cases (Logan, Schachar, & Tannock, 2000). Shallice (1982) reviews early literature on the nature of impairments following frontal damage. An early and notorious case that seems to fit this category is that of Phineas Gage, a railroad man who, in 1848, had an inch-think iron bar blown through his head, causing considerable frontal damage, but (amazingly!) not killing him. Despite retaining apparently normal intelligence, vocabulary, and motor ability, after he recovered from the immediate effects, "Gage was no longer Gage," in the words of a friend. He became highly impulsive, irresponsible, quarrelsome, and difficult—the opposite of his personality prior to his injury. For a detailed account, see Damasio, Grabowski, Frank, Galaburda, & Damasio (1994).

In a more recent study of a brain-injured patient—referred to as "J. Z."—Meyers, Berman, Scheibel, and Hayman (1992) also report a distinct personality change with no apparent change in intelligence or general functioning. Described as "honest, stable, and reliable" (p. 122) prior to surgery to remove a tumor in his left frontal lobe, "J. Z." became essentially psychopathic in his behavior after the left frontal area was damaged.

Cognitive-neuroscience studies of basic processes suggest that basic processes are in relatively posterior areas of the brain (basic visual processes being in the occipital cortex, for example). Frontal-lobe structures seem to be more involved in executive control of those posterior structures (Miller & Cohen, 2001). Indeed, in the cases of Phineas Gage and "J. Z.," the main damage was to such frontal regions. (Figure 2.5.1 shows various areas of the brain.)

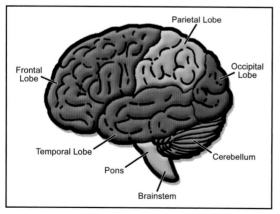

FIGURE 2.5.1 – *Areas of the brain*

How is executive control studied? Tasks studied have included error detection and correction,

inhibition of responses, dual-task performance (in which subjects must try to do two things at once), and task-switching (in which subjects must switch between different tasks). (See Logan, 2003, for references. For dual-task performance, see Wickens and Hollands, 2000.) In addition to these, a task of considerable interest to cognitive psychologists and cognitive neuroscientists is one concerned with planning for action—the Tower of London Task (TOL)—first described by Shallice (1982). It has become a standard test of frontal involvement in the Supervisory Attentional System (a term used by Shallice for something very much like executive control).

Shallice reported impairment in TOL performance for patients with left anterior lesions of the frontal lobe, relative to patients with right anterior lesions, those with left or right posterior lesions, and healthy control subjects. In the experiment accompanying this chapter, you will complete a version of the TOL that is very similar to that of Shallice (1982). Figure 2.5.2 shows the basic TOL task with two-, four-, and five-move goal states.

The pattern on the left is the starting position of a set of three balls fitted onto three pegs of different lengths. One peg can hold three balls, one can hold two, and the last can hold only one. The task is to move one ball at a time to reproduce the various goal states on the right, making the minimum number of moves possible. The solution to the two-move problem is to move the blue ball to the third peg, then move the red ball to the second peg. Note that many of the TOL problems involve *subgoal specification*. That is, some initial moves are required in order to permit the moves you need to make to achieve the final goal. For the four-move problem shown in Figure 2.5.2, for example, you must move the blue ball to the right-hand peg, then move the red and green balls to the middle peg. Only then can you move the blue ball to its goal position on the first peg.

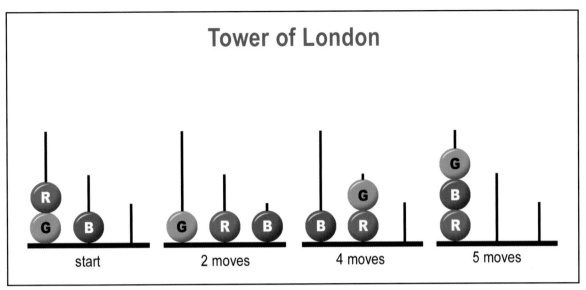

Tower of London

start   2 moves   4 moves   5 moves

FIGURE **2.5.2** – *The initial and goal positions of a two-move, a four-move, and a five-move Tower of London problem. The goal is to move the balls from the starting position to the goal position one at a time, in the minimum number of moves. After Shallice (1982, Figure 2).*

A related problem-solving task is the Tower of Hanoi, shown in Figure 2.5.3. Here, the problem is to move the stack of disks to another peg by moving them one at a time and never putting a smaller disk on top of a larger one.

This task also requires subgoal specification. It is less important for the study of planning and problem-solving than the Tower of London in part because there is only a single problem to solve—albeit a difficult one.

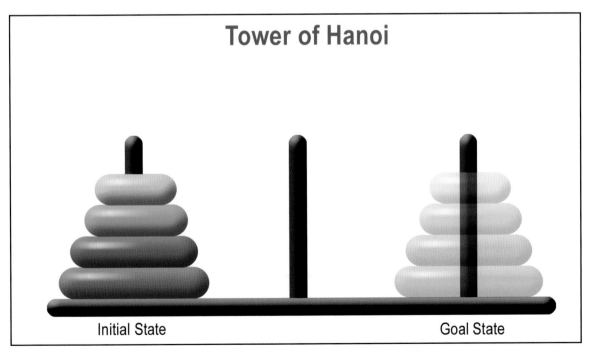

Tower of Hanoi

Initial State   Goal State

FIGURE **2.5.3** – *The initial and goal states of the Tower of Hanoi problem. The player can move only one disk at a time and is not allowed to put a larger disk on top of a smaller one. It can be shown that the minimum number of moves is $2^D – 1$, where D is the number of disks.*

Studies of Executive Function Using the Tower of London

A wide variety of approaches to the study of executive function have made use of the TOL. A few of those are considered here. Because the literature on the TOL has a very definite starting point in Shallice's 1982 paper, you can extend this review fairly easily by searching under "Tower of London" as a subject search in PsycInfo and in PubMed (a medical literature search engine at the National Library of Medicine, a branch of the National Institutes of Health, which you can access at *www.nlm.nih.gov*—select Library Services, then Databases, then PubMed).

Clinical Studies

The TOL was devised as a test of frontal-lobe functions (Shallice, 1982), and much of the literature is devoted to studies with clinical populations. Many confirm the relationship between frontal-lobe injury and TOL performance (e.g., Carlin, Bonerba, Phipps, Alexander, Shapiro, & Grafman, 2000), but a few do not (Cockburn (1995).

Sonuga-Barke, Dalen, Daley, and Remington (2002) report that executive function is not related to Attention Deficit Hyperactivity Disorder, at least in pre-schoolers, though it does appear that children with poor arithmetic skills (but not those with poor reading skills) do significantly poorer on the TOL (Sikora, Haley, Edwards, & Butler, 2002).

Imaging Studies

Both Positron Emission Tomography (PET) and functional Magnetic Resonance Imaging (fMRI) methods of forming images of areas of brain activation have been used to study the brain regions that underlie TOL performance (e.g., Dagher, Owen, Boecker, & Brooks, 1999; Rowe, Owen, Johnsrude, & Passingham, 2001; van den Heuval et al., 2003). These have confirmed the role of dorsal prefrontal brain regions in the TOL, but also implicate other brain regions, such as premotor cortex (which is involved in the execution of the moves). Using fMRI, Newman, Carpenter, Varma, and Just (in press) showed a very clear increase in the activation of the prefrontal cortex and superior

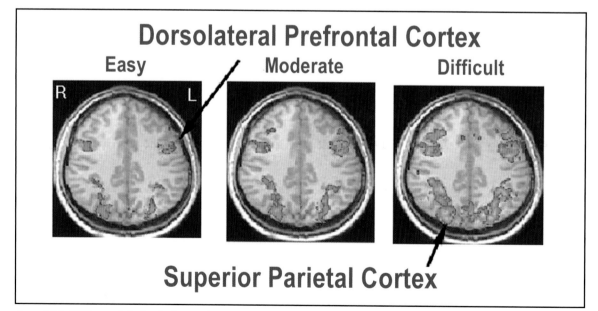

FIGURE *2.5.4 –"fMRI scans indicating the increase in activation of dorsolateral prefrontal cortex and superior parietal cortex as the difficulty of the TOL problem increases from easy (1-2 moves) to moderate (3-4 moves) to difficult (5-6 moves)."* [Newman, Carpenter, Varma, and Just, in press]

parietal cortex as they increased the difficulty of the TOL problems from 1 to 6 moves (see Figure 2.5.4).

Other Approaches

The TOL has been shown to be sensitive to developmental trends, with improvements in performance across grade levels (P. Anderson, V. Anderson, & LaJoie, 1996; Krikorian, Bartok, & Gay, 1994). Developmental psychologists note that basic cognitive processes develop relatively early in life, but that executive control takes longer to develop. In old age, on the other hand, executive control seems to decline before the basic processes (Williams, Ponesse, Schachar, Logan, & Tannock, 1999).

Methodological Considerations

The version of the TOL that is implemented for this chapter is based on the instructions and method of scoring devised by Schnirman, Welsh, and Retzlaff (1998). They noted that several studies have questioned the reliability or consistency of the TOL. Humes, Welsh, Retzlaff, and Cookson (1997), for example, found a value of Chronbach's α of only 0.25, while the consistency of the Tower of Hanoi was $\alpha = 0.90$. (Chronbach's α is a measure of consistency that can range from 0 to 1, with 1 representing perfect consistency. This use of α should not be confused with the usage in statistics of α as a symbol for the confidence level.) Kafer and Hunter (1997) reported similar results, arguing that difficulties in validating the TOL as a measure of planning/problem-solving lies largely in the poor psychometric properties of the standard test. Schnirman et al. attempted to improve on the test and develop an instrument with good reliability and internal consistency.

Their study consisted of three phases. In the first, they devised a large set of potential TOL problems, with various starting positions. Their problems ranged from 3 to 6 moves required for a solution. They then tested 50 college students on the whole set. The three-move problems turned out to be so easy that there was little variability in performance from subject to subject, so those were eliminated. Their final problem set consisted of the 10 items in each of the 4-, 5-, and 6-move sets that had the highest inter-item correlations. They called this the Tower of London-Revised (TOL-R).

In their second phase, they tested a new group of 50 college students to obtain an independent measure of reliability (represented by r). Odd/even, split-half reliability was calculated by taking the score based only on the odd-numbered items and the score based only on the even-numbered items for each subject and then measuring the correlation, which was $r = 0.74$. Chronbach's α, which measures reliability conceptually by considering every way the set of items could be divided, was 0.74—clearly superior to the original 12-problem TOL, for which α was only 0.25.

The third phase of the Schnirman et al. (1998) study tested the same group of 34 subjects twice each on the 30-item TOL-R, with a 5- to 7-week period between the two tests. Test-retest reliability is another way of assessing the reliability of a test; it consists of the correlation between the two scores at the first administration and the scores at the second. Test-retest reliability of the TOL-R was $r = 0.70$, which is usually regarded as an acceptable level of reliability.

The version of the TOL that you will complete consists of the TOL-R, but with some changes in the scoring. Schnirman et al. (1998) scored their test simply as the number of items correct out of the total of 30. In addition to an overall score, we record two other dependent variables, as described by Krikorian et al. (1994). *Latency* or *planning time* is the time between the introduction of the problem and the first move. *Execution time* is the time from the first move to completion of the final move. Note that the subject may begin making their moves before having completed their planning of the moves.

(Karat, 1982, has shown exactly this result with the Tower of Hanoi.) We also record the *total time*, which is simply the sum of the planning time and the execution time.

For this version, we also added a letter (R, G, or B) to each of the "balls" to avoid the problem of an occasional color-blind subject. *Protonopia*, or red-green color blindness, is the most common, affecting about 1% of males and 0.02% of females (Goldstein, 1999).

● ●

Expected Running Time = 35 minutes

● ●

Questions

1. What are the independent and dependent variables? What are some important controls?

2. What were your results? You can discuss these in terms of the score (number correct), mean planning time, mean execution time, and mean total time, each as a function of the task complexity (i.e., number of moves).

3. Williams et al. (1999) reported a study of executive function that examined a *stop-signal task*. In that task, their subjects performed a two-choice RT task. On some trials, however, an auditory stop signal was presented shortly after the stimulus; on those trials, the subjects were to try to inhibit their response. Their independent variable was age—from childhood through old age. What developmental trends did they report?

Extension Experiments

1. Welsh, Satterlee-Cartmell, and Stine (1999) reported a significant correlation—$r = 0.40$—between performance on the TOL-Revised (Schnirman, Welsh, & Retzlaff, 1998) and Stroop interference. While they used a different scoring system from the one used here and did not specify with any precision the nature of their "interference score," it would be interesting to correlate performance on this TOL task with a measure of interference in the Stroop task (see Chapter 1.5, *Attentional Interference and the Stroop Effect*). An interference score could be calculated for the Stroop test by subtracting the mean RT (for the single-trial versions) or mean *reading time* (for the multiple-item version) for the neutral condition (naming the colors in which "X's" are presented), from the mean for the *incongruent* condition (naming the colors when the letters form the names of conflicting colors).

   (Welsh et al., 1999, actually used a measure of *resistance* to Stroop interference as a measure of ability to inhibit interference and found a positive correlation. The interference score as described above thus should yield a negative correlation.)

   Welsh et al. also reported correlations between the TOL-R and both visual and spatial working memory. They describe those tests, which would be easy to perform with little equipment. In addition, you easily could measure working memory "capacity" using a digit-span test. For a digit-span test, set up lists of random digits from 4 to 11 digits long. To test subjects, read them the list of digits and ask the subjects to repeat them back immediately. The score is the maximum number a subject can correctly repeat, which is usually in the range of 5 to 9 digits (Miller, 1956).

2. Van der Linden, Frese, and Meijman (2003) showed that two hours of work on cognitively demanding tasks led to a lengthening of planning time on the TOL, but did not affect a simple memory task. This should be easy to replicate. If you can find some willing subjects, a manipulation of time of day might be interesting, as well. Do people who self-report that they are "morning people" do better in the morning? Do you get the opposite effect with "afternoon people"?

References

Anderson, J. R. (2000). *Cognitive psychology and its implications.* New York: Worth.

Anderson, P., Anderson, V., & LaJoie, G. (1996). The Tower of London test: Validation and standardization for pediatric populations. *The Clinical Neurologist, 10,* 54-65.

Baddeley, A. (1986). *Working memory.* Oxford, UK: Oxford University.

Baddeley, A. (1995). Working memory. In Gazzaniga, M. (Ed.), *The cognitive neurosciences* (pp. 755-764). Cambridge, MA: MIT Press.

Carlin, D., Bonerba, J., Phipps, M., Alexander, G., Shapiro, M., & Grafman, J. (2000). Planning impairments in frontal lobe dementia and frontal lobe lesion patients. *Neuropsychologia, 38,* 655-665.

Cockburn, J. (1995). Performance on the Tower of London test after severe head injury. *Journal of the International Neuropsychological Society, 1,* 537-544.

Dagher, A., Owen, A., Boecker, H., & Brooks, D. (1999). Mapping the network for planning: A correlational PET activation study with the Tower of London task. *Brain, 122,* 1973-1987.

Damasio, H., Grabowski, T., Frank, R., Galaburda, A., & Damasio, A. (1994). The return of Phineas Gage: Clues about the brain from the skull of a famous patient. *Science, 264,* 1102-1105.

Goldstein, E. B. (1999). *Sensation and perception.* New York: Brooks-Cole.

Humes, G., Welsh, M., Retzlaff, P., & Cookson, N. (1997). Towers of Hanoi and London: Reliability and validity of two executive function tasks. *Assessment, 4,* 249-257.

Jersild, A. T. (1927). Mental set and shift. *Archives of Psychology, 14,* 81.

Johnson-Laird, P. (1995). Mental models, deductive reasoning, and the brain. In M. Gazzaniga (Ed.), *The cognitive neurosciences* (pp. 999-1008). Cambridge, MA: MIT Press.

Kafer, K., & Hunter, M. (1997). On testing the face validity of planning/problem-solving tasks in a normal population. *Journal of the International Neuropsychological Society, 3,* 108-119.

Karat, J. (1982). A model of problem-solving with incomplete constraint knowledge. *Cognitive Psychology, 14,* 538-559.

Krikorian, R., Bartok, J., & Gay, N. (1994). Tower of London procedure: A standard method and developmental data. *Journal of Clinical and Experimental Neuropsychology, 16,* 840-850.

Logan, G. (2003). Executive control of thought and action: In search of the wild homunculus. *Current Direction in Psychological Science, 12,* 45-48.

References *(continued)*

Logan, G., Schachar, R., & Tannock, R. (2000). Executive control problems in childhood psychopathology: Stop-signal studies of attention deficit disorder. In. S. Monsell & J. Driver (Eds.), *Attention and performance XVIII: Control of mental processes* (pp. 653-677). Cambridge, MA: MIT Press.

Meyers, C. A., Berman, S. A., Scheibel, R. S., & Hayman, A. (1992). Case report: Acquired antisocial personality disorder associated with left orbital frontal lobe damage. *Journal of Psychiatry and Neuroscience, 17*, 121-125.

Miller, E. K., & Cohen, D. (2001). An integrative theory of prefrontal cortex. *Annual Review of Neuroscience, 24*, 167-202.

Miller, G. (1956). The magical number seven, plus or minus two: Some limits on our capacity for processing information. *Psychological Review, 63*, 81-97.

Newman, S. D., Carpenter, P. A., Varma, S., & Just, M. A. (in press). Frontal and parietal participation in problem solving in the Tower of London: fMRI and computational modeling of planning and higher-level perception. *Neuropsychologica.*

Rowe, J., Owen, A., Johnsrude, I., & Passingham, R. (2001). Imaging the mental components of a planning task. *Neuropsychologia, 39*, 315-327.

Schnirman, G., Welsh, M., & Retzlaff, P. (1998). Development of the Tower of London-Revised. *Assessment, 5*, 355-360.

Shallice, T. (1982). Specific impairments of planning. *Philosophical Transactions of the Royal Society of London B, 298*, 199-209.

Sikora, M., Haley, P., Edwards, J., & Butler, R. (2002). Tower of London test performance in children with poor arithmetic skills. *Developmental Neuropsychology, 21*, 243-254.

Sonuga-Barke, E., Dalen, L., Daley, D., & Remington, B. (2002). Are planning, working memory, and inhibition associated with individual differences in preschool ADHD symptoms? *Developmental Neuropsychology, 21*, 255-272.

van den Heuval, O., Groenewegen, H., Barkhof, F., Lazeron, R., van Dyck, R., & Veltman, D. (2003). Frontostriatal system in planning complexity: A parametric functional magnetic resonance version of the Tower of London task. *Neuroimage, 18*, 367-374.

van der Linden, D., Frese, M., and Meijman, T. (2003). Mental fatigue and the control of cognitive processes: Effects of perseveration and planning. *Acta Psychologica, 113*, 45-65.

Welsh, M. C., Satterlee-Cartmell, T., & Stine, M. (1999). Towers of Hanoi and London: Contribution of working memory and inhibition to performance. *Brain and Cognition, 41*, 231-242.

Wickens, C., & Hollands, J. (2000). *Engineering psychology and human performance.* Upper Saddle River, NJ: Prentice Hall.

Williams, B., Ponesse, J. S., Schachar, R., Logan, G., & Tannock, R. (1999). Development of inhibitory control across the lifespan. *Developmental Psychology, 35*, 205-213.

2.6 Organization in Memory as an Aid to Recall

Abstract

The experiment accompanying this chapter concerns the effects of organization on learning and recall; it replicates a study by Bower, Clark, Lesgold, and Winzenz (1969). Subjects study four lists of words for one minute each, then have five minutes for free recall. The study and recall are then repeated. The lists (totaling 104 words) are either hierarchically organized by categories or randomly ordered. The typical result is a striking difference in recall between the organized and random conditions. Recall is better for the second presentation for both groups. This chapter is intended to provide a starting point for discussions of memory, to demonstrate the importance of organization, and to illustrate a simple *factorial* design.

*T*he effect of organization on memory has long been studied. Materials that are arranged in a meaningful manner are thought by most of us to be easier to remember. However, Bower, Clark, Lesgold, and Winzenz (1969) noted that many previous experiments had shown only a fairly weak effect when comparing memory for organized and random word lists. They felt that a well-designed experiment should show organization to be a powerful variable for recall. You will replicate that experiment.

Why should organization matter? One effect of organization on memory is that it provides better *retrieval cues*. (Refer to Chapter 2.7, *Recognition, Recall, and Encoding Specificity* to learn more about the importance of retrieval cues.) Recalling one word sometimes can provide a retrieval cue for another, but only if they are related in memory. But there is more than just a *retrieval* effect involved. *Storage*, or encoding, is also affected by

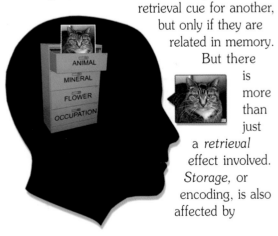

organization, because organized material suggests strongly how and where the material should be stored. One limitation to learning isolated facts is that we don't know "where" in memory to store them (and, subsequently, upon retrieval, might have a hard time figuring out where to look for them). When materials are organized, on the other hand, we can more easily and quickly decide where they fit best in memory. Thus, encoding, as well as retrieval, is improved.

Methodological Considerations

This experiment replicates Experiment 1 of Bower et al. (1969) with some modification. Subjects study four lists of 26 words each for one minute per list. At the end of the four minutes of study time, subjects are given five minutes for free recall (i.e., recall in any order) during which they are to write down as many of the words as they can remember. After the recall period, an alphabetized list of all 104 words is presented so that the subjects can verify which words were correct. They enter both the number recalled correctly and the number of *intrusions*, or false recalls. The whole procedure is then repeated a second time.

Subjects are assigned to one of two conditions, counterbalanced on subject number. Subjects in

Methodological Considerations *(continued)*

one condition (*organized* lists) see four lists of words arranged in a hierarchical fashion, with a heading at the top, subheadings below that, and three or four words in each subcategory below that. Subjects in the other condition (*unorganized* lists) see the same 104 words in the same physical arrangement, but with the words rearranged randomly across lists (including the headings and subheadings). Subjects are instructed to recall all words, including the headings.

This experiment illustrates a *mixed factorial* design. Independent variables ("IVs) usually are classified as *within-subjects* or *between-subjects* IVs. Between-subjects IVs are those where assignment of subjects to groups is independent. That is, each subject serves in only one level of the IV (one group), and assignment of one subject to the level of the IV does not affect assignment of others. Within-subjects IVs (also called *repeated-measures* IVs) involve testing each subject at each level of the IV.

Expected Running Time = 35 minutes

Questions

1. What are the dependent and independent variables in this experiment? What are some important controls?

2. What are the results of the experiment?

3. Examine the recall sheets for the group in the *unorganized* condition. Did subjects sometimes recall a word and then recall other, related words? If this happened, how does this fit with the notion of spreading activation in memory? (See Chapter 2.1, *Lexical Decisions*.)

4. One of the organized lists was taken from the Bower et al. (1969) article. Which one was it?

5. Bower et al. (1969) also report a similar experiment that employed a recognition test instead of a recall test. What was the result?

Extension Experiments

1. The experiment you performed used conceptual (categorical) hierarchies. Would organization affect the learning of associative hierarchies in the same way? See Bower et al. (1969).

2. Would the same effect be seen if a recognition test were employed? See Bower et al. (1969).

References

Bower, G. H., Clark, M., Lesgold, A., & Winzenz, D. (1969). Hierarchical retrieval schemes in recall of categorized word lists. *Journal of Verbal Learning and Verbal Behavior, 8*, 323-343.

Tulving, E., & Pearlstone, Z. (1966). Availability versus accessibility of information in memory for words. *Journal of Verbal Learning and Verbal Behavior, 5*, 381-391.

2.7 Recall, Recognition, and Encoding Specificity

● ●

Abstract

Recall and recognition tests of memory for learned word lists are demonstrated. While recognition is better than recall in most situations, the experiment accompanying this chapter demonstrates that, under certain circumstances, we can recall words that we cannot recognize. This replicates the Tulving and Thomson (1973) experiment designed to test "episodic" and "tagging" theories of memory for word lists. The roles of context and retrieval cues in memory are illustrated.

● ●

Which is easier, recall or recognition? Most people's intuitive belief is that recognition is easier, and psychologists long ago confirmed this belief with laboratory studies of recall and recognition. Anyone who has studied a foreign language knows that you can learn to understand the language much earlier than you can speak it. Most of us have had the experience of not being able to recall someone's name, but recognizing it instantly when we see or hear it. And most students prefer multiple-choice exams to essay exams because they feel more confident that they will recognize the right answer among several choices than that they will recall the information. These examples illustrate that recognition is usually easier than recall.

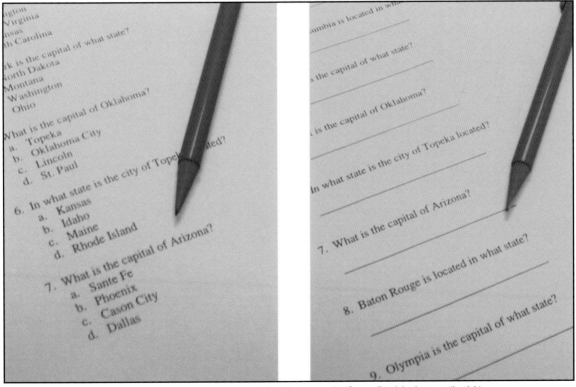

FIGURE 2.7.1 – *An example of a recognition task is shown on the left, while an example of a recall task is shown on the right*

But why is recognition easier? Any time a regularity in the data is as strong as the recognition-superiority effect, it cries out for an answer. We hardly can claim to understand memory if we do not have a satisfactory account of so strong an effect.

Tulving and Thomson (1973) performed an experiment designed to test several competing theories (or models) of the recognition-superiority effect. Here, we will consider only two of the competing theories, but note that other theories share a common problem with what Tulving and Thomson called the *generation-recognition* model. This model holds that the main process of memory retrieval is recognition, and that recall really consists of two steps—first, generation of likely alternatives, followed by a *recognition* of one of those alternatives. This model has been proposed by a number of persons, including Kintsch (1971). Note that this model accounts for the recognition-superiority effect because recall has recognition embedded in it—in other words, *recall = generation + recognition*. Therefore, recall will not occur if you fail to generate the right candidate item *or* if you fail to recognize it. According to this account, recall could be equal to recognition (if you generate all of the correct items). Recognition is usually superior to recall because we fail to generate some of the right candidates, in addition to failing to recognize some. But note that this model makes a strong claim: Recall can *never* be superior to recognition, because recall *requires* recognition—i.e., if you cannot recognize an item, then you cannot recall it, even if you generate the item.

Tulving and Thomson (1973) offered a different theory of why recognition is usually easier than recall that can account for recognition failure as well. Their theory is based on the principle of *encoding specificity*. This principle states that (a) we can retrieve only what has been stored and (b) how it can be retrieved depends upon how it was stored. To-be-remembered items are stored in a context, such as in relation to other

words in a list. The reason recognition is usually easier than recall is because the to-be-remembered item is present on a recognition test, thereby providing a retrieval cue. Thus, recognition is essentially *cued* recall. Tulving and Thomson proposed that it should be possible to construct a recognition test with poor retrieval cues and, likewise, a recall test with good retrieval cues. They theorized that if there were more retrieval cues present in the recall task than in the recognition task, you could actually reverse the usual recognition-superiority effect. The experiment accompanying this chapter replicates a version of their research showing the recognition failure of recallable words.

Controversy on Recognition Failure of Recallable Words

Tulving and Wiseman (1975) proposed a mathematical model of the relationship between the probability of recognizing and then recalling individual items in experiments such as the one discussed above. This Tulving-Wiseman law has generated a considerable literature, both supporting and challenging the law. To review this rather lively literature, enter "Tulving-Wiseman," "recognition failure," or "recognition failure of recallable words" as a search term in PsycINFO. (You will then need to select that term at the bottom of a list of headings as a keyword.)

Kintsch (1978) has argued that his generation-recognition model can handle the finding of recognition failure of recallable words if "the possibility is admitted that Ss [subjects] employ a considerably less stringent criterion for the editing of implicitly retrieved responses in recall than in a recognition task" (p. 470).

Despite the theoretical confusion, the general topic of recognition failure of recallable items continues to have some interest. Noice and Noice (2002) examined very long-term recall and recognition of parts memorized by actors up to 28 years previously, and they report instances of recognition failure of recallable passages.

Methodological Considerations

This experiment uses *paired-associate* learning, in which subjects are presented with lists of pairs of words. They are instructed that, at recall, they will be given the left-hand ("stimulus") words in a new, random order, and they will be asked to write down the right-hand words ("response") words. Note that this is *cued* recall. In most paired-associate learning experiments, the pairs of words are chosen randomly, so that there is no association between the words. For their lists, Tulving and Thomson instead used pairs of words that were associated, so that the stimulus words can serve as retrieval cues for the response words.

In recognition tests, the to-be-remembered items typically occur in a random order in the midst of other, unassociated "distracter" words (or "foils") that were not studied. Recall is usually tested by presenting the to-be-remembered items for some period of time for the subject to study, and then, perhaps after a delay, giving the subject a blank sheet of paper on which to write down all the items they can recall. For Tulving and Thomson's recognition test, however, the distracters were all strong associates of the target words, and their recall tests used cued recall.

The word lists used for this experiment employ the target words from Tulving and Thomson's (1973, p. 361) List A. The recognition test consists of the target words from the study list, plus distracters which were generated by having approximately 100 students in an Introductory Psychology class write down "the first word that came to mind" for each target word. The three most frequently occurring associates for each word, along with the target words, make up the recognition test. The cue words used in the paired-associate learning and recall were weak associates of the targets, defined as words that only a single person gave as an associate.

For example, Tulving and Thomson's list contained the words COLD and BUG. For COLD, the three strong associates were ICE, HOT, and WINTER, and those are used as distracters in the recognition test. Only one person gave HAND as an associate, and that was used for the paired-associate learning and recall. The three strong associates for BUG were INSECT, FLY, and BEE. Only one person gave WINDSHIELD as an associate. Of course, while WINDSHIELD was a rare associate for BUG, anyone seeing the pair "WINDSHIELD-BUG" could easily recall BUG given the cue WINDSHIELD.

As a check, another group of Introductory Psychology students were given the list of cue words and asked to write down "the first word that came to mind" for each. For several items, strong asymmetries of association were found. One of the rare cue words was DIAPER, which only one person gave as an associate to BABY. However, given DIAPER, almost everyone gave BABY as an associate. Using DIAPER on a recall test, therefore, might lead to a false high "recall" rate, simply because of the strong association between DIAPER and BABY (but not between BABY and DIAPER!). We replaced DIAPER with LITTLE. Similarly, given CHAIR, only one person wrote down ROCKING, but given ROCKING, almost everyone wrote down CHAIR. We replaced ROCKING with HIGH, another weak associate that did show a strong asymmetry in association.

For the sake of time, the version of the experiment for which you are a subject uses some of the simplifications suggested by Watkins and Tulving (1975).

• • • • • • • • • • • • • • • • • • •
Expected Running Time = 15 minutes
• • • • • • • • • • • • • • • • • • •

Questions

1. What are the dependent and independent variables in this experiment? What are some important controls?

2. What are the results? Is recall consistently better than recognition under these conditions?

3. Watkins and Tulving (1975) reported that, in experiments like this one, subjects often fail to recognize words that they can remember. They claimed that this evidence rules out a "tagging theory" of recognition and recall and is in favor of an "episodic theory." What are those theories, and why do their data support episodic over tagging theory? (Note: See the first two paragraphs of the summary on page 5 of Watkins and Tulving, 1975.)

Extension Experiments

1. The distracter words used in the recognition test of this experiment were all related semantically to the test items. Would you obtain different results if you used distracters that were not related in meaning to the test items? See Watkins and Tulving (1975, Experiment 5).

2. Does the order of the tests (recognition and then recall) matter for the outcome of this experiment?

3. Can subjects sometimes recognize words that they previously could not? Wallace (1978) argued that failure to recognize words you can recall is actually a special case of a more general class of context effects, which includes recognition failure of words that later can be recognized.

References

Kintsch, W. (1971). Models for free recall and recognition. In D. A. Norman (Ed.), *Models of human memory*. New York: Academic Press.

Kintsch, W. (1978). More on recognition failure of recallable words: Implications for generation-recognition models. *Psychological Review, 85,* 470-473.

Noice, T., & Noice, H. (2002). Very long-term recall and recognition of well-learned material. *Applied Cognitive Psychology, 16,* 259-272.

Tulving, E., & Thomson, D. M. (1973). Encoding specificity and retrieval processes in episodic memory. *Psychological Review, 80,* 352-373.

Tulving, E., & Wiseman, S. (1975). Relation between recognition and recognition failure of recallable words. *Bulletin of the Psychonomic Society, 6,* 79-82.

Wallace, W. P. (1978). Recognition failure of recallable words and recognizable words. *Journal of Experimental Psychology: Human Learning and Memory, 4,* 441-452.

Watkins, M. J., & Tulving, E. (1975). Episodic memory: When recognition fails. *Journal of Experimental Psychology: General, 104,* 5-29. (See also the critique and reply following this paper.)

Winograd, E., & Rivers-Bulkely, N. T. (1977). Effects of changing context on remembering faces. *Journal of Experimental Psychology: Human Learning and Memory, 3,* 397-405.

2.8 Automatic versus Controlled Processing

● ●

Abstract

Many tasks of everyday life are so well-practiced that they become automatic. An example would be putting your foot on the brake as you approach a stop-sign while driving. Other tasks, however, require more intentional, conscious control. For example, the first time you ever drove a car, you probably had to think quite deliberately about what to do when you approached a stop sign. These types of tasks are called controlled. In addition to differing in the amount of attention they require, automatic processes are highly inflexible, while controlled processes are relatively easy to change. In the experiment accompanying this chapter, the acquisition of automatic processing is illustrated through the use of a category-search task with either consistent or varied mapping (either the same or different categories). Consistent mapping promotes automatic processing through extended practice.

● ●

Automaticity is a research area that has been of considerable interest to psychologists. Indeed, William James, in his *Principles of Psychology* (1890) noted that "habit diminishes the conscious attention with which our acts are performed" (p.114). Modern research has greatly improved our understanding of automaticity. Schneider and Shiffrin (1977; also Shiffrin and Schneider, 1977) reported extensive research on the conditions under which automatic attentional search processes develop. The experiment accompanying this chapter illustrates one of the types of experiments they performed.

Laberge and Samuels (1974) helped formalize the notion of automaticity, developing a theory of how reading becomes automatic. The automatic nature of reading—at least for skilled readers—is discussed further in Chapter 1.5, *Attentional Interference and The Stroop Effect*. As researchers became aware of the rather powerful effects of automaticity, they began to apply the idea to domains beyond attentional search and reading. Chapter 3.5, *Automaticity and Stereotyping*, illustrates one such application. Social psychologists have found that priming by male- or female-stereotyped

words (such as "cigar" or "cosmetics") influenced the speed of classification of first names as male or female (Blair and Banaji, 1996) under conditions that suggest that the stereotyping occurs automatically.

This chapter is concerned with automatic and controlled cognitive processing. Controlled processing occurs when we do cognitive acts that are not well practiced. This type of processing requires a lot of attention, but can be changed fairly easily. An example from everyday life would be following a recipe. You have to read each ingredient carefully and pay attention to what you are doing. But you also can switch easily to another recipe and follow it, instead. Automatic processing, on the other hand, occurs only with large amounts of practice, and it is difficult to change. An example is writing the previous year when writing dates during the month of January. This type of action is automatic and difficult to change. In fact, the altering of writing the date requires controlled processing. In the experiment accompanying this chapter, the development of an automatic process from one that is initially controlled is illustrated.

A task that has been widely studied by experimental psychologists is the search of short-term memory. In this type of experiment, a subject is shown a set of letters (the memory set) and then shown a single letter (the probe). The subject's task is to decide whether that probe is a member of the memory set, and the subject indicates the decision by pressing an appropriate key. In the usual version of this experiment (Sternberg, 1966; also, see Chapter 2.2, *Scanning Short Term Memory*, in the *PsychMate Student Guide*), the letters in the memory set are changed after every probe, or after every few probes. Subjects take longer to respond as the memory set size increases—that is, reaction time (RT) is an increasing function of the number of items to which the probe must be compared. This kind of search has all the hallmarks of controlled processing. It requires effort, the probe seems to be compared to the members of the memory set one at a time, and it is easy to switch from one memory set to another.

Now suppose that you were given a great many trials with the same memory set on each trial. This is the basic experimental paradigm used by Schneider and Shiffrin (1977), whose subjects had as many as 24 hours of practice. With this degree of practice, subjects become very good at doing the memory search—so good, in fact, that RTs are no longer for large memory sets than for small ones, suggesting that the subjects now are able to search the entire memory set at once (in parallel). This well-practiced search is now automatic. It requires little effort or attentional capacity. Also, this search is difficult to change— if a new memory set is given, it must be searched in a controlled manner. Similarly, the automatic search is hard to suppress—if a member of that memory set is now used as a distracter or negative probe with a new memory set, it often will be responded to incorrectly.

Schneider and Shiffrin (1977) presented evidence that the development of automaticity occurs with large amounts of practice on a task, but they also noted that it must be a particular type of practice. That type of practice uses what they termed *consistent mapping* of stimulus to response. This simply means that a specific stimulus always calls for the same response. This is in contrast to *varied mapping*, in which a particular stimulus sometimes requires one response and sometimes another. To use the analogy to driving again, a stop-sign provides consistent mapping, because it always means "Stop." But consider a yield sign. Depending on whether there is other traffic coming, it may mean either "Stop" or "Go." Thus, the yield sign provides varied mapping, and drivers do not develop automatic responses to yield signs.

Issues in Automaticity

Identifying Automatic & Controlled Processes

An issue raised early in research on automaticity concerned the identifying features of automatic processes that distinguish them from controlled processes. Posner and Snyder (1975) offered three criteria for automaticity. Automatic processes, they held, occur without intention, do not involve conscious awareness (indeed, they contrasted automatic and conscious processing), and are efficient, in that they do not interfere with other mental activities. A fourth feature of automatic processes often added to their list is lack of controllability. As research on automaticity has advanced, however, it has become clear that this simple formulation will not do. Logan and Cowan (1984) have noted that most actions used as examples of automaticity, such as reading, driving, walking, and typing, are in fact absolutely dependent upon intent. While braking at a stop-sign may be automatic, it occurs only when we have the intention of driving. Reading words is automatic for skilled readers, and this process is sometimes described as *autonomous*, implying that it is initiated without intent, or even against intent (as in the Stroop effect—see Chapter 1.5, *Attentional Interference and The Stroop Effect*). But it is hardly unconscious or outside of awareness. Indeed, it is the (automatically induced) awareness of the word that seems to produce Stroop interference.

Bargh (1992, 1994) notes that activation of stereotypes is unintentional, efficient, and outside of awareness, but much research suggests that it is nevertheless under control—with proper motivation, persons can ignore stereotyping and act on the basis of individual, rather than group, characteristics (see Chapter 3.5, *Automaticity and Stereotyping*). Shiffrin (1997) treats at length the claim that automatic processes proceed outside awareness, concluding that there is no good case to be made for relating the distinction between controlled and automatic processes to that between conscious and unconscious processes. In this regard, Carlson (1997) notes that if automaticity involves some restructuring of a task, such as the switch from an algorithm to memory retrieval in Logan's instance theory (discussed below), then subjects will not report awareness of some mental processes during an automatic task because they simply are not using them.

Indeed, Bargh (1992) argues that the four characteristics of automaticity may be independent dimensions of cognitive processes and that it may be a signal error to assume that all four are needed for automaticity. He notes, in examining a variety of phenomena said to be automatic, the one shared characteristic was autonomy, meaning that, once a process is started, it can proceed without conscious guidance. Carlson (1997), in considering autonomous processes, notes that this does not mean necessarily that the process cannot be controlled consciously ("ballistic" processes), only that it need not be.

Automaticity is also context-dependent. Bargh (1992) notes that a person would, while driving,

automatically brake at a stop-sign. But, if walking, the same person would not feel compelled to put her foot on an imaginary brake.

An important aspect of many real-world tasks is that they involve many components. Driving involves component tasks such as monitoring speed and location in the lane, monitoring for pedestrians and other vehicles, and responding to each of these. In this complex task, some components become automatic, such as braking at a stop-sign. But as Schneider and Shiffrin (1977) noted, this type of automaticity modifies an ongoing controlled process by attracting attention to aspects of the environment. Indeed, Shiffrin and Schneider (1977) noted that most mental tasks of any interest are likely to be so complex that they cannot be characterized as wholly automatic or controlled, but rather are made up of components of each type.

What Changes to Permit Automatic Performance?

An early view of automaticity relies on the notion of attentional resources (Kahneman, 1973). The basic idea is that we have a certain amount of attention available to us at any moment, and we can spread that attention among multiple tasks, provided that each is easy enough—that is, requires little in the way of resources. On this view, automaticity arises when a task is so well-practiced that it no longer requires more than minimal attention, freeing up attentional resources for other tasks. For example, when you were first learning to drive, you almost certainly could not hold a conversation while driving—the act of driving required so much attention that none was left for monitoring a conversation. But, as some of the components of driving become automatic, enough attention is available to permit a conversation. Of course, under poor driving conditions, such as a snowstorm or rush-hour traffic, driving will again demand so much attention that a conversation cannot take place. Unfortunately, resource theories of attention and, by extension, resource theories of automaticity, fell on hard times. Logan (1997) has reviewed the failures of the resource notion, which are more complex than can be addressed here.

A very different theoretical approach to automaticity which has been developed in various forms by several researchers relies on the notion that automaticity reflects ease of memory. Novices trying to solve a problem must carefully think through an algorithm for generating an answer. Experts, because they have solved the same problem many times, can skip the algorithm and directly recall the answer. One example of this approach is Logan's (1988) *instance theory*. (Logan, 1988, also outlines a number of other theories of automaticity.) According to Logan, "Automaticity is memory retrieval: Performance is automatic when it is based on single-step direct-access retrieval of past solutions from memory" (p. 493).

In Logan's theory, a task initially requires that we solve an algorithm. However, as we gain experience, we may have solved an algorithm repeatedly, so that we can now remember the solution, rather than solving the algorithm again. An example would be learning to add. Children first learn to add by the algorithm of counting. Given four red circles and four blue circles, they can count all the circles to solve "4 + 4 = 8." But after the child has solved that particular problem several times, she may simply remem-

ber that "4 + 4 = 8," rather than solving it. An instance you may relate to more easily is multiplication. Consider the task of multiplying 17 times 13. You would probably need to solve the algorithm something like "3 times 7 is 21. Write down 1 and carry the 2," etc. But if asked to solve 3 times 2, you do not solve the algorithm at all—you simply remember the answer. Applying this to automatically stopping at a stop-sign, recall the first time you ever drove a car. You probably had to really think about what to do when you saw a stop-sign—you still had to solve an algorithm. But after enough instances, you simply remember what to do.

Logan's theory assumes that every time we solve an algorithm for a particular problem, we store another instance of the solution. As more such instances are stored in memory, it becomes more likely that you will simply remember the solution, rather than have to work it out. Automaticity is acquired through consistent practice. Logan's theory accounts for that finding this way. "Practice is important because it increases the amount retrieved and the speed of retrieval; consistency is important because it ensures that the retrieved instance will be useful" (p. 492). Note that with a varied-mapping task, whatever algorithm is solved will produce different answers on different occasions, so one cannot rely on recall of specific instances to guide behavior. According to Logan's theory, then, the poor performance of a novice is due to lack of knowledge.

While no final solution has been reached in regard to competing theories of how automaticity arises, the competing theories give an excellent example of science-in-progress. An important issue for automaticity, to some degree transcending specific theoretical accounts, is how automaticity arises. Schneider and Shiffrin (1977) addressed this issue in a lengthy series of experiments, concluding that it is both the amount and the nature of practice that leads to automaticity.

Methodological Considerations

In this experiment, subjects make speeded responses to indicate whether one of two words presented is a member of a category named earlier (such as "furniture"). There are eight categories, with six exemplars of each. Each category is searched for equally often, in random order. See Fisk and Schneider (1983) for a discussion of category-search tasks.

In this experiment, subjects are given a category (such as "vehicles" or "geographical features") and must decide whether or not probe words are members of that category. The principal design consideration in this experiment concerns how the words and categories are presented. Two of the categories are presented in the consistent-mapping (CM) condition. The exemplars of these two categories never appear as distracter items when other categories are tested. Thus, when one of those exemplars appears, the correct response is always to indicate that they were in the category being searched for. The remaining categories are presented in the varied-mapping (VM) condition. Exemplars of these categories may appear as positive probes for their own category or as negative probes (distracters) for the other VM categories.

How can we tell that a task is becoming automatic? With much practice, both CM and VM targets should be responded to more quickly, but there should be a greater reduction in RT for the CM targets as they become automatized. But high levels of automaticity require far longer to achieve than would be practical in a teaching laboratory. For that reason, in the experiment, automaticity is tested by giving you a more difficult version of the task in the last block. In the fourth block only, the memory set size will increase from one to two, i.e., two categories will be named on each trial. This should have the effect of exaggerating the difference in RT between CM and VM conditions. It is worth emphasizing, in this context, that automaticity is a matter of *degree*. That is, there is a continuum from controlled to automatic processing (MacLeod & Dunbar, 1988). In this experiment, there will be a partial development of automaticity—time constraints do not permit the thousands of trials needed for a well-developed automatic process.

Expected Running Time = 55 minutes

Questions

1. What are the dependent and independent variables in this experiment? What are some important controls?

2. What were the results of the experiment? What aspect of the data would indicate that the CM category search is becoming automatic? Note that a great many trials are needed for fully developed automaticity, and time may not have permitted enough in this experiment. There should still be some clear differences between your ability to search the CM category and the VM categories, though.

3. This experiment used a category-search task. Another important task that has been used for research on automaticity is a version of the Sternberg (1966) letter-search task (see Chapter 2.2, *Scanning Short-Term Memory*). Describe the version of that task as developed by Schneider and Shiffrin (1977).

Extension Experiments

1. Run subjects for extended periods of practice (e.g., 2 hours of category search) and see if performance changes with really extended practice in the consistent-mapping and varied-mapping conditions. Examine what happens when you reverse the previously learned set (i.e., words which were trained originally as targets become distracters). See Schneider & Shiffrin (1977), Experiment 2.

2. How might consistency be important in more complex real-world tasks (e.g., processing order forms; see Myers & Fisk, 1987) or games (e.g., chess moves; see Fisk & Lloyd, 1988)? Design an experiment to examine learning of consistent and inconsistent rule sets.

References

Bargh, J. A. (1992). The ecology of automaticity: Toward establishing the conditions needed to produce automatic processing effects. *American Journal of Psychology, 105*, 181-199.

Bargh, J. A. (1994). The four horsemen of automaticity: Awareness, intention, efficiency, and control in social cognition. In R. S. Wyer & T. K. Srull (Eds.), *Handbook of social cognition: Vol. 1. Basic processes* (pp. 1-40). Hillsdale, NJ: Lawrence Erlbaum Associates.

Carlson, R. A. (1997). *Experienced Cognition.* Mahwah, NJ: Lawrence Erlbaum Associates.

Fisk, A. D., & Lloyd, S. J. (1988). The role of stimulus-to-rule consistency in learning rapid application of spatial rules. *Human Factors, 30*, 35-49.

Fisk, A. D., & Schneider, W. (1983). Category and word search: Generalizing search principles to complex processing. *Journal of Experimental Psychology: Learning, Memory, and Cognition, 9*, 177-195.

James, W. (1890). *The principles of psychology* (Vol. 1). New York: Henry Holt.

Kahneman, D. (1973). *Attention and effort.* Englewood Cliffs, NJ: Prentice-Hall.

LaBerge, D., & Samuels, S. J. (1974). Toward a theory of automatic information processing in reading. *Cognitive Psychology, 6*, 293-323.

Logan, G. D. (1988). Toward an instance theory of automaticity. *Psychological Review, 95*, 492-527.

Logan, G. D. (1997). The automaticity of academic life: Unconscious applications of an implicit theory. In R. S. Wyer (Ed.), *The automaticity of everyday life* (pp. 157-180). Mahwah, NJ: Lawrence Erlbaum Associates.

Logan, G. D., & Cowan, W. B. (1984). On the ability to inhibit thought and action: A theory of an act of control. *Psychological Review, 9*, 295-327.

MacLeod, C. M., & Dunbar, K. (1988). Training and Stroop-like interference: Evidence for a continuum of automaticity. *Journal of Experimental Psychology: Learning, Memory, and Cognition, 14*, 126-135.

Myers, G. L., & Fisk, A. D. (1987). Application of automatic and controlled processing theory to industrial training: The value of consistent competent training. *Human Factors, 29*, 255-268.

Posner, M. I., & Snyder, C. R. R. (1975). Attention and cognitive control. In R. L. Solso (Ed.), *Information processing and cognition: The Loyola symposium* (pp. 55-85). Hillsdale, NJ: Lawrence Erlbaum Associates.

Schneider, W. (1985). Training high-performance skills: Fallacies and guidelines. *Human Factors, 27,* 285-300.

Schneider, W., Dumais, S. T., & Shiffrin, R. M. (1984). Automatic processing and attention. In R. Parasuraman, R. Davies, & R. J. Beatty (Eds.), *Varieties of attention* (pp. 1-27). New York: Academic Press.

Schneider, W. & Fisk, A. D. (1984). Automatic category search and its transfer. *Journal of Experimental Psychology: Learning, Memory, and Cognition, 10,* 1-15.

Schneider, W. & Shiffrin, R. M. (1977). Controlled and automatic human information processing: I. Detection, search, and attention. *Psychological Review, 84,* 1-66.

Shiffrin, R. M. (1997). Attention, automatism, and consciousness. In J. Cohen & J. W. Schooler (Eds.), *Scientific approaches to consciousness. Carnegie Mellon Symposia on cognition* (pp. 49-64). Mahwah, NJ: Erlbaum.

Shiffrin, R. M. & Schneider, W. (1977). Controlled and automatic human information processing: II. Perceptual learning, automatic attending, and a general theory. *Psychological Review, 84,* 127-189.

Sternberg, S. (1966). High-speed scanning in human memory. *Science, 153,* 652-654.

2.9 Mental Comparisons

• •

Abstract

The exercise accompanying this chapter concerns the process of comparing two objects when the objects themselves are not present, but rather must be remembered; it is designed to illustrate the symbolic distance, congruity, and end effects. In the experiment, animals are compared for size. The symbolic distance effect is reflected in faster RTs for two animals that are very different in size than for two that are similar. The congruity effect occurs when judgments of "Which is smaller?" are made faster for two small animals than for two large ones, while judgments of "Which is larger?" show the opposite pattern. The end effect occurs when judgments are faster if both animals are close to one end of the continuum of sizes and slower if both are of intermediate size. Various theories of the nature of the comparison process are reviewed.

• •

Comparative judgments, or mental comparisons, are a common form of cognitive process in everyday life. These are judgments of largest, heaviest, greenest, or whatever dimension is of interest. Whenever you say that one person is taller than another, or that one object is above another, you are making a comparative judgment. The study of these types of judgments has been of interest to psychologists for some time. In a typical experiment, subjects are asked to compare two animals in size, judging either which is larger or which is smaller of two animals. In many such studies, the subjects are seeing either the animal names or pictures of them. Thus, the comparison is based on *memory* (a mental comparison) rather than being a direct perceptual judgment (see Chapter 2.4, *Sentence-Picture Comparison* for an example of a study with perceptual comparison). In addition to studying comparisons per se, experiments like this can also help us learn something about how concepts (such as *animal* or *dog*) are stored in memory.

The experiment accompanying this chapter replicates a study by Čech and Shoben (1985) that illustrates the three standard findings in this area which any theory of mental comparisons must address. One common outcome of comparison experiments (mental or perceptual) is that the greater the difference in size of the two animals, the faster a subject can answer the question (Moyer, 1973). This has been termed the *symbolic distance effect* (Moyer & Bayer, 1976). Also of interest to the study of comparisons is the finding that it takes less time to answer "Which is smaller?" than "Which is larger?" if both objects to be compared are small. If both objects are large, it takes longer to answer "Which is smaller?" Known as the *congruity effect*, this was first noted by Audley and Wallis (1964; Wallis & Audley, 1964) for persons judging the brightness or pitch of perceptual stimuli (though they called this the *crossover effect*). A third empirical finding in mental comparisons (it does not appear to have a perceptual counterpart) is that it takes less time to compare two stimuli that are both at the *ends* of the range of stimuli (e.g., the largest and smallest animals) than for those in the middle of the range. This finding is known as the *end effect* (Leth-Steenson & Marley, 2000).

Two general classes of explanations have been offered for the symbolic distance effect. One is based on imagery (Paivio, 1975). This explanation assumes that we have an analog representation of the objects stored in memory. When the subject sees SQUIRREL and ELEPHANT, he or she calls up an image of each and compares them for size. According to this explanation, the image is analogous to the actual object in important ways, such as relative size.

A second class of explanation assumes that we store in memory a set of propositions about the objects. In this context, you can think of a proposition as a basic statement, such as "Elephants are large" or "Squirrels are small." One type of information we have stored about elephants is that they are large; similarly, we have stored the information that squirrels are small. We can compare these stored facts in order to answer the question and, thus, don't need images. (Clearly there would be many other propositions stored with each animal beyond just

size, but that doesn't change the basic point.) Banks (1977) and Holyoak (1978) present the basic arguments in regard to imagery versus propositional accounts of relational judgments.

Categorization and the Comparison Process

A number of studies have established the importance of categorical knowledge[15] and processes in making relational judgments. Čech[16] and Shoben (2001) review the evidence that categorization plays a strong role in the symbolic distance, congruity, and end effects.[17] Čech and Shoben offer examples of how categorization affects processing of relational information.

The symbolic distance effect can be attenuated or even eliminated if the two objects to be compared are from different categories. Sailor and Shoben (1993) had subjects make judgments about buildings and animals, where all of the small objects were animals and all of the large objects were buildings. For pairs such as BARN-DEER or SKYSCRAPER-BEAR, no symbolic distance effect occurs, presumably because subjects could make the judgments based on their knowledge of the relative sizes of buildings and animals, rather than their knowledge of barns and deer. They made an important comparison to another experiment using the categories *animals* and *weapons*, where all the large objects were weapons and the small ones were animals. Although there was a correlation between categories and sizes, just as in the first experiment, it is an artificial association. In the real world, weapons may be larger or smaller than animals. The usual symbolic distance effect occurred, strengthening the claim that real-world

---

[15] See also chapter 2.3, *Typicality in Categorization.*

[16] Pronounced "check."

[17] Čech and Shoben (2001) use the term "bowed serial position effect" for what others call the "end effect." We prefer "end effect" because "serial position effect" is so strongly associated with the study of memory (referring to the usually superior recall for items at the beginning and end of a list).

knowledge of relative sizes was what eliminated the symbolic distance effect with the *animals* and *buildings* categories.

The congruity effect is also altered by categorization. Čech and Shoben (1985) showed that subjects were faster at choosing the smaller of two small pairs, such as RABBIT-BEAVER, when larger animals such as HORSE and ELEPHANT were also present. However, when RABBIT and BEAVER were the two largest items on the list, subjects were faster at choosing which of the two was *larger*. In the context of a list ranging in size from FLEA to ELEPHANT, RABBIT and BEAVER are

small animals. But in a list going from FLEA to BEAVER, RABBIT and BEAVER are large animals. Čech and Shoben (1985) suggested that there is a distinct advantage in judging which is smaller if the items to be compared are both small. If both are classified as large, then additional processing is required to match the instruction to determine which is smaller. There is also a large advantage in classification if the two animals are classified differently. If asked to judge which is smaller for the pair FLEA-HORSE, the subject can simply note that fleas are small and horses are large and then base the judgment on that information. When beaver is the largest animal, reclassifying the largest animals on the list (such as beaver) as large increases the number of cross-classifications, improving efficiency.

Čech and Shoben (2001) also argue for a role of categorization in the end effect. While most researchers have attributed the end effect to the relative difficulty of discriminating where an item falls in a list, Čech and Shoben suggest instead that it may depend on the relative ease with which subjects can classify the animals as large

or small. Animals that are intermediate in size, such as BEAVER, are not as readily classified as large or small. FLEA and ELEPHANT, on the other hand, are easily classified as large or small. Consistent with this claim, Shoben and Wilson (1998) showed that the speed of classification of animals as small was fastest for the very smallest animals. Speed of classifying animals as large was fastest for very large animals.

Based on a series of experiments that manipulated the ease with which categories could be formed, Čech and Shoben (2001) argue that "people attempt to group items so as to facilitate processing consistent with the efficiency principle" (p.810). In other words, categorization created on demand can structure the objects in ways that make classification more efficient.

Other Approaches to Mental Comparisons

While Čech and Shoben (2001) point out the importance of categorization in mental comparisons, other approaches have also been offered. These are not reviewed in depth here, but the interested student will find a rich review of the theories and data in the articles referenced below.

Petrusic (1992) has extended the congruity effect to perceptual judgments such as visual proximity (nearer or farther) and verticality/horizontality. Petrusic argues, on the basis of several experiments, that a propositional view of congruity effects cannot account for such perceptual congruity effects. Petrusic compares several theories of the congruity effect, favoring an *evidence accrual* model, in which evidence about the nature of the comparison is built up over time.

Leth-Steenson and Marley (2000) present a formal connectionist model of the symbolic distance, congruity, and end effects based on variants of the basic comparison task. They extensively review the literature on all three effects. They extend their theorizing to also account for lexical markedness effects (see

Chapter 2.4, *Sentence-Picture Comparison*, for a brief description of "marked" forms).

The argument over the basic mechanisms of relational judgments and how the symbolic distance, congruity, and end effects arise is ongoing, and no final answer seems likely for some time. In regard to this issue, a comment by Adams (1980) some years ago still seems apt: "Some may find theoretical indecisiveness like this uncomfortable, but it does not bother scientists very much because the world is clouded with uncertainty in their eyes and they are tolerant of it. At any moment, given the facts available, a scientist will pass tentative judgments on the mechanisms that are required to explain the facts, and then will get on with the job of research to refine the judgments and reduce the uncertainty" (p. 283).

Methodological Considerations

Counterbalancing and Randomization

To minimize any possible order effects, this experiment uses a complete randomization and counterbalancing of the order of the stimuli. On each trial, two animal names are presented, one above and one below a fixation mark. In the first block of trials, subjects are instructed to answer "Which is larger?" by indicating either the top (above fixation) or bottom name. In the second block, they are asked to indicate which is smaller. The order of the blocks is counterbalanced across subjects.

Within each block, each animal is paired with each other animal twice.[18] On one pairing, the larger animal is listed above the fixation, while on the other pairing, the larger one is below the fixation. With 12 animals in the list, there are 66 possible pairings. Each is presented twice in each of the two blocks, resulting in 264 trials (66 x 2 presentations x 2 blocks) of this experiment.

Formats for Studying the Comparison Process

While our discussion has centered largely on comparisons of size, researchers have examined the comparison process in a wide variety of settings. Cattell (1902, cited in Petrusic, 1992) was perhaps the first to examine the comparison process, showing that RTs to select the brighter of two stimuli were faster the larger the difference in illumination. A very incomplete list of comparison processes reported in the experimental literature includes 2-digit numbers (Dehaene, Dupoux, & Mehler, 1990), alphabetical order (Hamilton & Sanford, 1978), which of two points along a line was closer to (or further from) a central fixation (Petrusic, 1992), relative verticality/horizontality (Petrusic, 1992), and arbitrarily ordered stimuli (subjects memorized the relative heights of six fictional people by name (Leth-Steenson & Marley, 2000).

• •

Expected Running Time = 30 minutes

• •

---

[18] Six "small" animals (flea, snail, mouse, chipmunk, rabbit, and beaver, in ascending order) and six "large" animals (sheep, deer, lion, horse, rhino, elephant) are used as stimulus words. These lists are taken from Čech and Shoben (1985), with the exception that we substituted "deer" for "crocodile," because some subjects were confused as to whether a crocodile or a lion is larger. According to the *Encyclopedia Britannica*, the most wide-ranging of the crocodile species routinely reaches 20 feet in length. Lions average about 10 feet, including the tail.

Questions

1. What are the dependent and independent variables for this experiment? What are some important controls?

2. Is there a symbolic distance effect? What pattern in the data indicates this?

3. Is there a congruity effect? What pattern in the data indicates this?

4. In there an end effect? What pattern in the data indicates this?

5. Do you feel that you are using imagery to make the judgment, or are you using propositional information about the animals?

6. Čech and Shoben (1985) report two experiments on symbolic magnitude comparisons that had subjects make relational judgments about the same animals as in the experiment for this exercise, but, instead of using *all* the animals, they used either only the small animals (Experiment 1) or only the large ones (Experiment 2). What did they find?

Extension Experiments

1. Suppose that the animals to be compared were only the small animals used in this experiment. In this case, RABBIT and BEAVER are the largest animals. Would a congruity effect occur, such that "larger" judgments about this pair were made faster than "smaller" judgments? See Čech and Shoben (1985).

2. In the experiment for this exercise only a limited number of animal names were used. Would the results change if members of different categories were compared for size (e.g., SNAIL-LAMP)? See Paivio (1975) for this and several other interesting manipulations of this basic experiment. Sailor and Shoben (1993) also describe variants of this.

References

Adams, J. A. (1980). *Learning and memory: An introduction.* Homewood, IL: Dorsey Press.

Audley, R. J., & Wallis, C. P. (1964). Response instructions and speed of relative judgments: I. Some experiments on brightness discrimination. *British Journal of Psychology, 55,* 59-73.

Banks, W. P. (1977). Encoding and processing of symbolic information in comparative judgments. In G. H. Bower (Ed.), *The psychology of learning and motivation* (Vol. 11, pp. 101-159). New York: Academic Press.

Čech, C., & Shoben, E. J. (1985). Context effects in symbolic magnitude comparisons. *Journal of Experimental Psychology: Learning, Memory, and Cognition, 11,* 299-315.

Čech, C., & Shoben, E. J. (2001). Categorization processes in mental comparisons. *Journal of Experimental Psychology: Learning, Memory, and Cognition, 27,* 800-816.

Dehaene, S., Dupoux, E., & Mehler, J. (1990). Is numerical comparison digital? Analogical and symbolic effects in two-digit number comparison. *Journal of Experimental Psychology: Human Perception and Performance, 16,* 626-641.

References *(continued)*

Hamilton, J. M., & Sanford, A. J. (1978). The symbolic distance effect for alphabetic order judgements: A subjective report and reaction time analysis. *Quarterly Journal of Experimental Psychology , 30*, 33-41.

Holyoak, K. J. (1978). Comparative judgments with numerical reference points. *Cognitive Psychology, 10*, 203-243.

Leth-Steenson, C., & Marley, A. A. J. (2000). A model of response time effects in symbolic comparison. *Psychological Review, 107*, 62-100.

Moyer, R. S. (1973). Comparing objects in memory: Evidence suggesting an internal psychophysics. *Perception and Psychophysics, 13*, 180-184.

Moyer, R. S., & Bayer, R. H. (1976). Mental comparison and the symbolic distance effect. *Cognitive Psychology, 8*, 228-246.

Paivio, A. (1975). Perceptual comparisons through the mind's eye. *Memory and Cognition, 3*, 635-647.

Petrusic, W. M. (1992). Semantic congruity effects and theories of the comparison process. *Journal of Experimental Psychology: Human Perception and Performance, 18*, 962-986.

Sailor, K. M., & Shoben, E. J. (1993). Effects of category membership on comparative judgment. *Journal of Experimental Psychology: Learning, Memory, and Cognition, 19*, 1321-1327.

Wallis, C. P., & Audley, R. J. (1964). Response instructions and speed of relative judgments: II. Pitch discrimination. *British Journal of Psychology, 55*, 121-132.

2.10 Additive Factors Methodology

• •

Abstract

Additive factors methodology is a method for verifying theoretical stages in human informa-tion processing. In the case of the search of short-term memory, this permits separating the stages of encoding, comparing, and responding, even though the dependent measure—the time it takes the subject to respond—is always the sum of the times for the three stages. Additive factors method-ology assumes that processing occurs in a series of processing stages carried out in sequence, with each stage being completed before the next begins. This technique relies on an examination of the interaction of the effects of two different experimental manipulations. If those manipulations affect different stages of processing, they should have additive effects on the time needed to complete the task. If, on the other hand, two manipulations affect the same stage, their effects should interact. Examination of the joint manipulation of two variables can thus be used to determine the validity of the stages proposed by information-processing models of cognition. This methodology is illustrated in relation to the search of short-term memory to determine whether a target letter is part of the memory set the subject has just seen.

• •

Cognitive psychologists are often interested in describing the stages of processing involved in mental activities. For example, when you search for a book on a shelf, you must encode the visual patterns of what you see into some sort of internal representation, then compare those patterns to the mental image of the book you are seeking. Finally, you must actually reach for and retrieve the book when you find it. These activities comprise a series of stages. Sternberg (1969) was concerned with how we can determine the nature of the stages of a mental process, such as a simple compari-son. The exercise accompanying this chapter is a demonstration of the method Sternberg devised to study stages of mental processing, which he called *additive factors methodology.*

The additive factors methodology is concerned with showing that certain mental processes take place in a series of stages. Sternberg's immedi-ate interest was his model of search of short-term memory (STM), but the same logic applies to any model of a process that involves a series of discrete stages. Recall from Chapter 2.2, *Scanning Short-Term Memory,* that the

Sternberg (1966) memory search experiment was concerned with two issues. One was whether the search through items in short-term memory is serial (one at a time) or parallel (all at once). The other issue was whether the serial search is self-terminating (stopping when a match was found) or exhaustive (continuing to the end, even if a match was found). On the basis of experiments like this, Sternberg (1969) proposed a model of the search of short-term memory that treated the process as a series of discrete stages of processing, with each stage being completed before the next begins. The first stage is *stimulus encoding*, or putting a representation of the stimulus into memory for purposes of comparison to the members of the memory set. The next stage is that of the *comparisons* themselves (actually a series of substages—one for each comparison required). Next comes a *binary decision* stage, where a binary ("yes"/"no") decision is made. This is followed by a *response organization* stage, where the appropriate button-press is organized. The actual mechanical *response* is then carried out. Total reaction time (RT) is the sum of the processing time for each stage, plus the time to carry out the response.

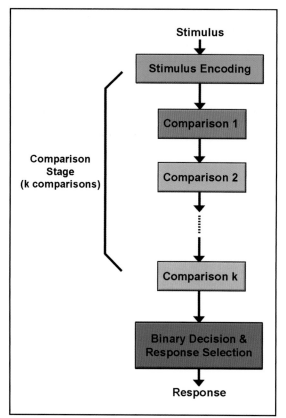

FIGURE 2.10.1 – *Sternberg's model of the stages of mental comparison, where k is the number of comparisons required to decide whether the probe matches a member of the memory set.*

How do you verify the existence of these separate stages? The attempt to decompose RT into the durations of a series of stages has a long history in psychology. Donders (1868/1969), a Dutch physiologist, proposed the *subtractive method*. The basic idea of this approach is to

measure RT on two tasks that differ only in the presence or absence of a single stage. The difference between the RTs for these two tasks would then be a measure of the duration of that stage. For example, Donders compared the mean RTs for a simple RT task (a single response is made when the stimulus is detected) and a choice RT task (one of several stimuli occurs and the appropriate response is chosen and executed). The difference between these two tasks is that the first requires only a stimulus detection stage and a response execution stage, while the second adds a stimulus identification stage and a response selection stage. This difference in RT was taken as measuring the duration of these two "extra" stages. (It lumps them together, of course, and does not measure how long each of them takes alone.) This approach to measuring the duration of stages of processing remained popular for some time (e.g., Jastrow, 1892). A problem arose for this method, however. Suppose that inserting a new stage also affected how long the other stages took? If this were the case, you would not have a pure measure of the time of the inserted stage. For example, Woodworth (1938) cites a study by Ach suggesting that "in preparing for a simple reaction, motor readiness was at a higher pitch than in preparing for a disjunctive [choice] reaction" (p. 309).

The validity of what Sternberg has termed "pure insertion" was difficult to demonstrate. Külpe (1895), reviewing studies of reaction time, argued that "this assumption is not justified" (p. 380), and this eventually led Woodworth (1938, p. 309-310), in his *Experimental Psychology*, to advocate discarding the method altogether. In the second edition of this book, Woodworth and Schlosberg (1954) relegate mention of this method to an "historical sketch." Reaction time remained important as "a means of studying the *total reaction* as dependent on the stimulus, the task, and the conditions in which the task is performed" (Woodworth, 1938, p. 310), but not as a measure of the duration of stages of mental processing. Pachella (1974) offers a detailed and excellent critique.

Sternberg (1969a, 1969b, 1975, 2001) proposed the *additive factors* methodology as a way to overcome this difficulty and to verify his stage model of search of STM. This method discards what Sternberg calls the *assumption of pure insertion* for a "weaker and more plausible *assumption of selective influence*" (1969, p. 436). Rather than trying to insert or remove a processing stage without affecting other stages, Sternberg sought to find ways to influence the duration of one stage without influencing other stages. This new method is not concerned with measuring the duration of each stage, but rather with verifying a particular stage model by providing evidence that the stages exist and are independent of one another.

Here's the logic: Recall the memory search task. The subject is given a small set of letters to remember, then the subject is probed by being shown a letter. The subject must respond differently (i.e., press a different button) depending on whether the letter is or is not a member of the memory set. Total RT, according to Sternberg's model, is the sum of encoding, comparison, decision, and response organization stages, plus the time to make the overt response. Suppose we identify factors that influence the various stages. If the stages are truly independent, then manipulating the factors in an experiment should result *only* in a "main effect" of one or the other factor (or both), but there should be no interaction.

Let's take a simple example. We know already that memory set size affects RT. It is reasonable to assume that this is because more comparisons must be made during the comparison stage. A

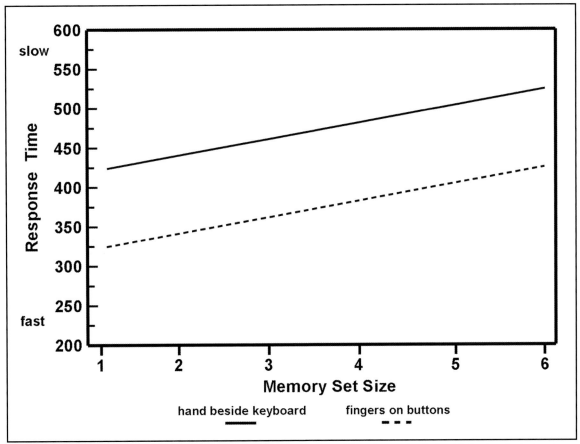

FIGURE **2.10.2** – *An example of an additive effect. Increasing the memory set increases RT, as does moving the hand further from the keyboard, but the two factors do not interact with each other.*

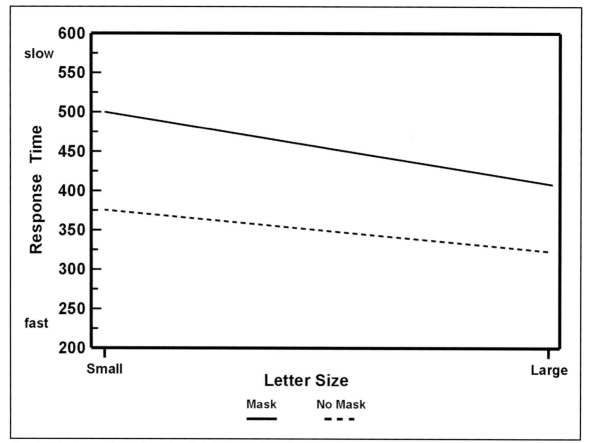

FIGURE **2.10.3** – *An example of an interactive effect. RT is slower for smaller letters, and for masked letters, but the effect of a mask is greater for small letters than for large letters.*

factor that would influence the overt response would be how far you had to move to reach the response keys. If you have your finger on the button you should be faster than if you start each trial with your hand beside the keyboard. If we did an experiment in which we manipulated memory set size *and* response distance, we would expect to get a result like the idealized one in Figure 2.10.2. There is a clear effect of memory set size—RT increases as you must make more comparisons. There is an equally clear effect of response distance—the further you have to move, the longer it takes. But there is no interaction—the lines are parallel. These factors are *additive*. They each add their own constant amount to RT, but the *combination* has no effect. We have strong evidence, therefore, that the comparison stage and the overt response are independent, separate stages, each of which adds some amount to overall RT.

Here is another example illustrating an interaction. Suppose I manipulate stimulus discriminability in two ways. One is by using small versus large letters and the other is by the presence or absence of a "mask" that partly obscures the stimulus. It seems reasonable that both of these factors would influence the encoding stage, and so should interact. Idealized results of such an experiment are presented in Figure 2.10.3. Note that small letters, being harder to see, result in slower RTs, and that the mask also increases RT because it, too, makes it harder to see. But what happens when we combine a small letter and a mask? That ought to result in even worse performance, as the graph indicates. The interaction occurs because both factors affect the same stage.

To summarize, *two experimental manipulations that affect the same stage will interact, while* two manipulations that affect different stages will be additive. With this logic in mind, Sternberg sought to find factors that would affect various stages in an additive fashion. If successful, he would have strong evidence for his model of a series of discrete stages of processing in the search of STM. The experiment accompanying this chapter replicates one of Sternberg's experiments, testing for additivity in factors affecting the stimulus encoding stage and the comparison stage. The two experimental manipulations are memory set size (which should affect the comparison stage) and whether or not the stimulus is degraded by a pattern mask (which should affect the encoding stage).

Wickens and Hollands 2000) review experiments testing additivity and interaction of a number of variables with tasks like the Sternberg search task. The 20 studies cited, involving nine different manipulations, generally confirm the existence of four stages—stimulus encoding, recognition, response selection, and response execution.

Applications of the Additive Factors Methodology

The effect of sleep deprivation on information processing has been explored using the additive factors methodology. Sanders and Reitsma (1982) had subjects perform a task in which they indicated whether two stimuli were the same or different. The stimuli to be compared were either close or far apart. The amount of sleep deprivation showed a clear interaction with the time to identify the first stimulus and the time to make a response after seeing the second stimulus, but had an additive effect on the time needed to shift fixation from the first to the second stimulus. Sanders, Wijnen, and van Arkel (1982) varied clarity of the stimulus and stimulus-response compatibility and also showed an interaction between amount of sleep deprivation and clarity of the stimulus, but the effects on stimulus-response compatibility were additive. Again, stimulus identification seems strongly affected by sleep deprivation.

Another area of application of the additive factors methodology has been to identify which stages in information processing are affected by various environmental or physiological changes. In these applications, an independent variable is manipulated between subjects, rather than by exposing the same subjects to the different levels of the independent variable, as in the studies cited above. Strayer, Wickens, and Braune (1987) studied the effects of aging on a memory-search task by comparing performance of older and younger subjects. While additive factors methodology (in conjunction with electroencephalograms and examination of speed-accuracy tradeoff) showed that aging affected the speed of the stages of perceptual encoding and response execution, it showed a smaller effect on the memory-search stage. They conclude that "the difference in performance [of older and younger subjects] lies predominantly in the perceptual-motor systems. Thus, input-output processes seem to be the locus of the large decrements in response performance with age" (p. 109).

Smith and Langolf (1981) studied the effect of mercury exposure on the Sternberg memory-search task. Performance differences between persons exposed to mercury in industry and those not exposed showed an effect on the comparison stage, but not on the encoding and response execution stages. This led them to conclude that the effect of mercury was on the central nervous system (brain and spinal cord), rather than on the peripheral nervous system (the sensory and/or motor nerves). Lindeis, Nathoo, and Fowler (1996) examined the effects of hypoxia (low blood oxygen) on performance of a mental rotation task (essentially the same as Version 2 of the *PsychMate* experiment in Chapter 1.3, *Rotation of Mental Images*). On the basis of an additive effect of hypoxia and degree of rotation, they concluded that hypoxia affects early stages of visual processing, rather than having a more general effect on information processing stages in general.

Other Issues Regarding the Additive Factors Logic

Sternberg's additive factors method assumes processing is done in discrete stages (e.g., the perceptual stage outputs nothing to the comparison stage until perceptual processing is complete). McClelland (1979) has provided an elaborate analysis of additive and interactive effects. McClelland examined cascaded processes where input is cascaded through several stages quickly before one stage is complete (e.g., the perceptual stage outputs partial information to the comparison stage while the perceptual stage is still clarifying the stimulus). For cascaded processes, interactions can occur even for variables that affect different stages. This complicates interpretation and is the subject of current research. Eriksen and Schultz (1979) argued for what they called a "continuous flow" model, which also has later stages of information processing operating on the partial output from previous stages. Sanders (1990) has suggested that some types of continuous processing still can be handled by the additive factors methodology.

The issue of how, experimentally, to detect and verify stages of processing is an ongoing problem for psychology. Sternberg's (1969) additive factors methodology made a major contribution to this problem. For a review of more recent contributions, see Schweickert and Giorgini (1999). They review and extend methods that go beyond mean reaction times and, instead, are based on distributions of reaction times.

Methodological Considerations

The general method used is the same as in the first memory search experiment, but with the addition of a second factor of stimulus discriminability. This is manipulated by adding a pattern mask to the stimulus letter that makes it harder to recognize. In this experiment, the stimulus is "masked" by presenting the stimulus letter alternating every 20 ms with a mask consisting of a grid of dots. The choice of a pattern is crucial. Some patterns will mask a letter almost beyond recognition, while others have surprisingly little effect.

Expected Running Time = 20 minutes

Questions

1. What are the dependent and independent variables in this experiment? What are some important controls?

2. What are your findings? Are the lines parallel, or is there an interaction? What specific stages are affected by each independent variable?

3. Sternberg (1969) actually found an interaction between stimulus clarity and memory set size for the *first* session of testing of his subjects. This interaction disappeared in the second session. What did he suggest accounted for this finding?

4. Sternberg (1969, p. 438) suggested that a factor affecting the binary decision stage is response type—whether the response indicated a positive probe or a negative probe. You already examined the combined effects of probe type and memory set size when you did the experiment on *Scanning Short-Term Memory* (see Chapter 2.2). What do those data say about the separability of the serial comparison and binary decision stages?

Extension Experiments

1. In the discussion above, we mentioned manipulating memory set size (affecting the comparison stage) and the distance to move to the response keys (affecting the response execution stage). This could be done using the experiment from Chapter 2.2, *Scanning Short-Term Memory*, but performing the experiment once with the fingers poised just above the response keys and once with the fingers positioned several inches away when each trial is begun—perhaps by having the fingers resting on the *7* and *8* keys of the numeric keypad, instead of the *1* and *2* keys.

2. What other factors could you manipulate to try to determine whether other pairs of stages could be shown to be independent? Sternberg (1969, p. 438) mentioned several. For a more recent discussion of a number of studies using additive factors methodology, see Wickens and Hollands (2000).

References

Donders, F. C. (1868/1969). On the speed of mental processes. In W. G. Koster (Ed. & Trans.), *Attention and human performance II*. *Acta Psychologica, 30*, 412-431.

Eriksen, C. W., & Schultz, D. W. (1979). Information processing in visual search: A continuous-flow conception and experimental results. *Perception and Psychophysics, 25*, 249-263.

Jastrow, J. (1892). Classification time. *American Journal of Psychology, 4*, 411-415.

Külpe, O. (1895). *Outlines of psychology*. New York: Macmillan.

Lindeis, A. E., Nathoo, A., & Fowler, B. (1996). An AFM investigation of the effects of acute hypoxia on mental rotation. *Ergonomics, 39*, 278-284.

McClelland, J. L. (1979). On the time relations of mental processes: An examination of systems of processes in cascade. *Psychological Review, 86*, 287-330.

Pachella, R. (1974). The interpretation of reaction time measures in information processing research. In B. H. Kantowitz (Ed.), *Human information processing* (pp.41-82). Hillsdale, NJ: Erlbaum.

Sanders, A. F. (1990). Issues and trends in the debate on discrete vs. continuous processing of information. *Acta Psychologica, 74*, 123-167.

Sanders, A. F., & Reitsma, W. D. (1982). The effect of sleep loss on processing in the functional visual field. *Acta Psychologica, 51*, 149-162.

Sanders, A. F., Wijnen, J. L. C., & van Arkel, A. E. (1982). An additive factor analysis of the effects of sleep loss on reaction processes. *Acta Psychologica, 51*, 41-59.

Schweickert, R., & Giorgini, M. (1999). Response time distributions: Some simple effects of factors selectively influencing mental processes. *Psychonomic Bulletin and Review, 6*, 269-288.

Smith, P. J., & Langolf, G. D. (1981). The use of Sternberg's memory-scanning paradigm in assessing effects of chemical exposure. *Human Factors, 23*, 701-708.

Sternberg, S. (1966). High-speed scanning in human memory. *Science, 153*, 652-654.

Sternberg, S. (1969a). Memory scanning: Mental processes revealed by reaction-time experiments. *American Scientist, 57*, 421-457.

References *(continued)*

Sternberg, S. (1969b). The discovery of processing stages: Extension of Donder's method. *Acta Psychologica, 30*, 276-315.

Sternberg, S. (1975). Memory scanning: New findings and current controversies. *Quarterly Journal of Experimental Psychology, 27*, 1-32.

Sternberg, S. (2001). Separate modifiability, mental modules, and the use of pure and composite measures to reveal them. *Acta Psychologica, 106*, 147-246.

Strayer, D. L., Wickens, C. D., & Braune, R. (1987). Adult age differences in the speed and capacity of information processing: 2. An electrophysiological approach. *Psychology and Aging, 2*, 99-110.

Wickens, C. D., & Hollands, J. G. (2000). *Engineering psychology and human performance* (3rd ed.). Upper Saddle River, NJ: Prentice Hall.

Woodworth, R. S. (1938). *Experimental psychology.* New York: Henry Holt.

Woodworth, R. S., & Schlosberg, H. (1954). *Experimental psychology* (Rev. ed.). New York: Holt, Rhinehart and Winston.

2.11 The Generation Effect

Abstract

The *generation effect* refers to a common finding that words generated by a subject's own efforts are remembered better than those that are presented by the experimenter. Slamecka and Graf (1978) described the general phenomenon, and the experiment accompanying this chapter replicates one of theirs. Some subjects see pairs of words related by some rule (e.g., rhymes or words in the same category). Other subjects see one word and a letter, and they must generate the second word according to the rule. Both groups are then tested for recognition.

"*Most* of us have probably encountered the informally expressed sentiment that there is an especial advantage to learning by doing, or that some kind of active or effortful involvement of the person in the learning process is more beneficial than merely passive reception of the same information" (Slamecka & Graf, 1978, p. 592). The *generation effect* is a term given to a very robust finding in memory research: Subjects remember words that they have generated themselves far better than words that were merely presented for study. In a series of experiments, Slamecka and Graf (1978) provided a "delineation" of the phenomenon. Here is their basic experiment: In the "read" condition, subjects were given lists of pairs of related words (e.g., LONG/SHORT) and were required to read each pair out loud. In the "generate" condition, the subject was given the left-hand word and the first letter of the right-hand word (e.g., LONG/S) along with a rule, such as "generate an antonym." The subject had to think of a word that would fit (here, sHORT) and say that word out loud. They were then tested for how well they remembered the right-hand member of each pair. In many experiments under variations of this procedure, subjects' memory for words they had generated was better than for the same words when supplied by the experimenter in the "read" condition.

Mulligan (2002b), citing reviews by Greene (1992) and Mulligan (2001), noted the range of conditions under which the generation effect has been demonstrated: "The generation effect has been observed with a variety of materials (e.g., single and compound words, sentences, abbreviations, numbers), in which a variety of generation tasks (e.g., generation from antonyms, semantic associated, rhymes, anagrams, word fragments, second-language translations, definitions) have been used, and on a variety of memory tests (e.g., free recall, cued recall, recognition, comprehension)" (p. 850).

Jacoby (1978) found the effect with a problem-solving task like a crossword puzzle. Subjects were given a crossword-puzzle clue and a partial word. Again, subjects who had to solve the

puzzle themselves performed better on a subsequent memory task than subjects who were given the solutions. The effect is not limited to memory for words, however, as shown by Gardiner and Rowley (1984). Their subjects were given multiplication problems that either required that they work out the solution themselves (generate) or had the correct solutions supplied (read). Again, the generation effect was clear: Memory was better for problems the subjects solved themselves than for problems where the answer was supplied. However, the generation effect does not always occur. Interestingly, the effect does not seem to occur when the re-sponse terms (right-hand terms) are nonwords. McElroy and Slamecka (1982) had subjects read or generate pronounceable non-words by either a rhyming rule (e.g., PRAB/F is a cue to generate "FRAB") or a letter-transposition rule (e.g., take the first three letters of the stimulus term and add them to the first letter in backward order; PREET/T is a cue to generate "TERP"). In neither case did they find any advantage of "generate" over "read" conditions. Lutz, Briggs, and Cain (2003) also suggest that the generation effect does not occur with new or unfamiliar material.

This sort of regularity in data compels attention. What is the basis for the effect? If you are already familiar with the "levels-of-processing" approach in memory (see Chapter 3.4, *Levels of Processing and the Self-Reference Effect*), that might occur to you as a candidate (but see Slamecka & Katsaiti, 1987, p.606). This approach says that how long you remember something is a function of how you processed it; i.e., materials that receive deeper processing for meaning are remembered better. The generation effect could thus be interpreted as being due to the deeper processing required of words that are generated as opposed to words that are merely read. This approach, and several variants of it (see McElroy & Slamecka, 1982), assume that semantic memory is the locus of the effect, since it did not occur when they had subjects generate non-words. (Semantic memory refers to memory for word meanings, as well as knowledge of the world.) Another class of explanations assumes

that the difference is due to inherent differences in the two tasks—generating and reading. For example, Jacoby (1978) suggested that arousal might be heightened during generation as compared to during reading (but see Donaldson & Bass, 1980).

While we cannot review all of the theoretical approaches to the generation effect, we must note a couple of others. McNamara and Healy (2000) offered a "procedural" explanation for the generation effect, arguing that generation is superior because it makes it easier for subjects to reinstate, at the time of retrieval, the cognitive operations they had used at the time of encod-ing. In essence, they argue that previous theo-retical accounts were typically couched in terms of the nature of the items to be remembered, rather than the process of encoding. Mulligan (2002a) and MacLeod and Daniels (2000) tie the generation effect to the distinction between direct and indirect (or explicit and implicit) tests of memory. The student who wants to pursue this topic should search PsycINFO for the keyword "Generation Effect."

The generation effect remains a topic of consid-erable research, largely because it is clear that we do not yet have an accepted explanation. When one is found, it is likely to advance considerably our understanding of the nature of memory.

Methodological Considerations

"False" generations. Subjects in the "gener-ate" condition may sometimes generate some word other than the one used for the "read" condition. Slamecka and Katsaiti (1987) reported only about 1% generation of the "wrong" words, using generation of antonyms and synonyms, with the first letter of the target word given. Slamecka and Graf (1978) reported a similar figure for rhymes, but considerably higher for related words or words from a given category. In the *PsychMate* version of this experiment, subjects are tested using the word they gener-ated. Fortunately, relatively few subjects gener-ate the "wrong" words.

A confound. In the experiment accompanying this chapter (which replicates Slamecka and Graf's, 1978, Experiment 1), there is a confound. In the "generate" condition, subjects have to type in their response. As a result, the time spent on processing each pair of words is longer in the "generate" condition than in the "read" condition. Fortunately, we can be reasonably certain that this confound is not a problem. In Slamecka and Graf's original version, they had subjects read or generate the words out loud, which provides a better control of the time needed to process each pair, and they still found a robust generation effect.

Between-subjects versus within-subject designs. In the literature on the generation effect there is a considerable discussion of the issue of *pure* versus *mixed* lists—see Slamecka and Katsaiti (1987). Experiments on pure lists employ a between-subjects design, in which each subject is assigned to either the "read" or the "generate" condition. Experiments on mixed lists employ a within-subject (repeated-measures) design, in which each subject reads some items and generates others. In a series of experiments, Slamecka and Katsaiti showed that the generation effect occurred only for mixed lists. Slamecka and Katsaiti argued against a number of possible theoretical accounts of the generation effect on the basis of this finding. However, the experiment replicated here (Slamecka and Graf's, 1978, Experiment 1) routinely produces a large generation effect with pure lists. Moreover, Slamecka and Graf's Experiment 2 was exactly the same as their Experiment 1, except that it employed mixed lists. A comparison of their Figures 1 and 3, showing probability of recall as a function of the rule type and "generate" versus "read" instructions, showed nearly identical results for pure and mixed lists. We are unable to resolve this paradox. See Mulligan and Duke (2002) for a further discussion of this issue.

⬤ ⬤ ⬤ ⬤ ⬤ ⬤ ⬤ ⬤ ⬤ ⬤ ⬤ ⬤ ⬤ ⬤ ⬤ ⬤
Expected Running Time = 20 minutes
⬤ ⬤ ⬤ ⬤ ⬤ ⬤ ⬤ ⬤ ⬤ ⬤ ⬤ ⬤ ⬤ ⬤ ⬤ ⬤

Questions

1. What is the dependent variable in this experiment? What are the independent variables? Specify whether these are within-subject or between-subjects variables. What are some important controls?

2. Did a generation effect occur? If so, does it occur for all rules? Specifically, are there any differences depending on the rule used?

3. Compare your results to those of Slamecka and Graf's (1978) Experiment 1. Is the mean percent recall about the same?

Extension Experiments

1. Most studies of the generation effect use short retention intervals. Indeed, most use immediate tests of memory. Would it make any difference if there were a relatively long period before the retrieval test? Lutz, Briggs, and Cain (2003, p. 183) note a dearth of studies of this issue.

2. An interesting extension experiment would be to perform Slamecka and Katsaiti's Experiment 3, which compared pure and mixed lists.

3. A comparison that Slamecka and Katsaiti discuss is that of recognition versus recall tests. Do these two types of tests lead to different results? If so, why?

4. Jacoby (1978) found a generation effect with a "problem-solving" task similar to a crossword puzzle, and Gardiner and Rowley (1984) found it with simple multiplication problems. What other sorts of situations might yield a generation effect?

References

Donaldson, W., & Bass, M. (1980). Relational information and memory for problem solutions. *Journal of Verbal Learning and Verbal Behavior, 19*, 26-35.

Gardiner, J. M., & Rowley, J. M. C. (1984). A generation effect with numbers rather than words. *Memory and Cognition, 12*, 443-445.

Green, R. L. (1992). *Human memory: Paradigms and paradoxes.* Hillsdale, NJ: Erlbaum.

Jacoby, L. L. (1978). On interpreting the effects of repetition: Solving a problem versus remembering a solution. *Journal of Verbal Learning and Verbal Behavior, 17*, 649-667.

Lutz, J., Briggs, A., & Cain, K. (2003). An examination of the value of the generation effect for learning new material. *Journal of General Psychology, 130*, 171-188.

MacLeod, C. M., & Daniels, K. A. (2000). Direct versus indirect tests of memory: Directed forgetting meets the generation effect. *Psychonomic Bulletin and Review, 7*, 354-359.

McElroy, L. A., & Slamecka, N. J. (1982). Memorial consequences of generating nonwords: Implications for semantic-memory interpretations of the generation effect. *Journal of Verbal Learning and Verbal Behavior, 21*, 249-259.

McNamara, D. S., & Healy, A. F. (2000). A procedural explanation of the generation effect for simple and difficult multiplication problems and answers. *Journal of Memory and Language, 43*, 652-679.

Mulligan, N. W. (2001). Generation and hypermnesia. *Journal of Experimental Psychology: Learning, Memory, and Cognition, 27*, 436-450.

Mulligan, N. W. (2002a). The effects of generation on conceptual implicit memory. *Journal of Memory and Language, 73*, 327-342.

Mulligan, N. W. (2002b). The generation effect: Dissociating enhanced item memory and disrupted order memory. *Memory and Cognition, 30*, 850-861.

Mulligan, N. W., & Duke, M. D. (2002). Positive and negative generation effects, hypermnesia, and total recall time. *Memory and Cognition, 30*, 1044-1053.

Slamecka, N. J., & Graf, P. (1978). The generation effect: Delineation of a phenomenon. *Journal of Experimental Psychology: Human Learning and Memory, 6*, 592-604.

Slamecka, N. J., & Katsaiti, L. (1987). The generation effect as an artifact of selective displaced rehearsal. *Journal of Memory and Language, 26*, 589-607.

SOCIAL PSYCHOLOGY

SOCIAL PSYCHOLOGY

3

Introduction

Humans, like many other organisms, are social creatures. Any psychology that claims to give a general account of how we function must deal not just with how we function in isolation, but also with how we function within a social context. How we make judgments about others; how we act toward others; what we remember about others; and why we judge, act, or remember are all part of social psychology.

We all must make social judgments: Is this person honest? Friendly? Hard-working? But what controls those judgments? A major area of social psychology is concerned with these questions of social judgment. We all must interact with others, also. How does our behavior influence theirs? Should I cooperate with this person, or not? Which will be of the most benefit to me? To them? To society? Another major issue for social psychology is social behavior—our actual behavior in social settings. Of course, that behavior is partly determined by other persons' behaviors, so the situation is quite complex. Despite that complexity, social psychologists have made progress in understanding humans in their social context.

Some of the approaches of social psychology are illustrated in the exercises of this section. Many of these issues also have importance beyond the realm of psychology itself. Economics, business, political science, and sociology are all disciplines concerned with the actions of individuals in social contexts, and the study of social psychology can give interesting insights into those disciplines as well.

The connection of social psychology to cognitive psychology is now well established. This has proven to be a very fruitful enterprise, with the concepts and findings of cognitive psychology helping to improve our understanding of our perception and memory of ourselves and others.

3.1 The Prisoner's Dilemma

● ●

Abstract

"The prisoner's dilemma" is the name given to a type of competitive game in which a player tries to win points by choosing to defect or cooperate with his or her opponent. The number of points each player scores depends upon the choices they both make. If they both cooperate, they both score more points than if they both defect. However, if one player defects and the other cooperates, the one who defects earns more points than the one who attempted to cooperate. This game has interested social scientists because it is akin to many real-life situations, such as the nuclear arms race, union-management negotiations, and even two friends deciding what movie to attend!

● ●

An early pioneer in the mathematics of game theory, A. W. Tucker, gave the name "prisoner's dilemma" to a certain class of games of strategy. Here is how the prisoner's dilemma was described by Luce and Raiffa (1957) in their book, *Games and Decisions*:

> Two suspects are taken into custody and separated. The district attorney is certain they are guilty of a specific crime, but he does not have adequate evidence to convict them at trial. He points out to each prisoner that each has two alternatives: to confess to the crime the police are sure they have done, or not to confess. If they both do not confess, then the district attorney states he will book them on some very minor trumped-up charge such as petty larceny and illegal possession of a weapon, and they will both receive a minor punishment; if they both confess they will be prosecuted, but he will recommend less than the most severe sentence; however, if one confesses and the other does not, then the confessor will receive lenient treatment for turning state's evidence whereas the latter will get "the book" slapped at him. (p. 95)

As you can see, there is a basic conflict in this situation between each individual's goals and their common rewards (or punishments). Unable to talk directly to your partner in crime, should you hold out or confess? If you know that your partner will also hold out, then clearly you should, too. But if you distrust your partner, or if you want to minimize your own sentence, you should probably confess.

The prisoner's dilemma game (PDG) is a way to formalize this situation, and the exercise you will do with the PDG has you play it in varying ways to illustrate the possible outcomes. Of course, the situation described above would be of interest only to criminals and prosecutors, and this exercise would not be of much interest. But the PDG turns out to be a very good model for a great many situations of interest to social psychologists, sociologists, economists, political scientists, biologists, and mathematicians. An excellent introduction to the complexities of the PDG can be found in Rapoport and Chammah (1970).

Now we will develop a more formal analysis of the prisoner's dilemma game (see Advanced Question 1 for a further development). When you play the computer version of the PDG, your opponent will be the computer, which will play each of several strategies. You will be shown a "payoff matrix" like the one in Figure 3.1.1, which shows the number of points you will win under various conditions. The actual numbers are arbitrary, but you can assume that larger numbers represent larger rewards (or smaller punishments). One choice is to **cooperate**; the

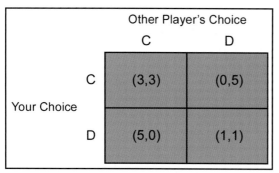

FIGURE 3.1.1 – A payoff matrix for the prisoner's dilemma game

other choice is to **defect** (i.e., fail to cooperate). In the original prisoner's dilemma cited above, where the "opponent" is your partner in crime, "cooperating" would mean refusing to confess, while "defecting" would be to confess. For this version, you will earn "points," rather than shorter sentences, but the basic situation is otherwise the same. The numbers in parentheses in the payoff matrix in Figure 3.1.1 represent the points each player earns for a given pair of choices. The first number represents your points, and the second number represents your opponent's points. Note that you are to try to win as many points as possible.

With this payoff matrix, you have two choices in each round—cooperate or defect. What should you do? Suppose that your opponent cooperates. Your best choice then is to defect (earning 5 points) rather than to cooperate (which earns only 3 points). On the other hand, if your opponent defects, cooperating would earn you zero points, so you would be better off if you defected, also (earning 1 point). As you can see, your point earnings will depend on whether or not you can determine your opponent's strategy (and also on what that strategy is). If only one round of the game is played, and you cannot predict your opponent's choice, there is a best strategy—you should defect. This is easily demonstrated. If you cooperate, you win either 3 points or 0 points, for an average of 1.5 points. If you defect, you win either 5 points or 1 point, for an average of 3 points. But this is true only if you play a single round.

A more realistic version of the prisoner's dilemma game is the one you will play, where there are a number of rounds in each game (this is called an *iterated* PDG). In this case, the best outcome for you would be if your opponent always cooperated and you always defected. But it is not very realistic to expect any opponent to behave that foolishly. Nobody likes to lose all the time!

The best mutual outcome is for you and your opponent to cooperate with each other. That is, cooperation will lead to the most points won by you and your opponent together (though your individual earnings may not be as high as they would be if you sometimes defected). True, mutual cooperation thus involves each person making a small sacrifice for the overall good. For this reason, the situation embodied in the PDG is sometimes called the "tragedy of the commons" (Hardin, 1968)—if some resource is held in common (such as grazing land), and each person attempts to maximize his or her own use (by grazing more cattle), then soon there will be no resources left for anyone.

Other examples of "real-world" situations that are comparable to the PDG follow. Try to consider, as you read them, how they fit the payoff matrix above. A classic example of a situation that parallels the prisoner's dilemma is the "price war" in retail sales. If two retail stores competing for the same customers "cooperate" by keeping prices high, both benefit. If one

lowers prices in order to attract customers away from the other store, his or her profits climb—there is a benefit to "defecting." But what if both stores lower their prices (i.e., defect)? Then both lose—neither has a competitive advantage, and both now make lower profits.

A recent example of the tragedy of the commons is Internet usage, because most people pay a flat fee for Internet usage, rather than paying proportionally to the "bandwidth" or capacity of Internet resources they use. The result is that some individuals do a lot of "surfing," using a proportionally large amount of the (limited) capacity. When enough people do so at the same time, it results in a slowing of transmission of information from site to site, and everyone suffers. When such congestion occurs (called an Internet "storm"), people then may quit trying to use the Internet for the moment, leading to a sudden reduction in usage, and the storm passes. Huberman and Lukose (1997) have analyzed these storms, showing that they can be modeled successfully after the tragedy of the commons, as well as the notions of cooperation and defection from the PDG. Their analysis leads to some suggestions for relieving Internet congestion—the most straightforward of which is to charge people according to bandwidth usage, thereby avoiding the tragedy of the commons (at least as long as there is enough bandwidth usually to accommodate all Internet users).

Consider the "arms race" that existed in the mid- to late 20th century between the United States and the former Soviet Union. If both sides decided to arm themselves, the cost to each would be very high. If both sides agreed not to arm themselves, they both would benefit economically. But if one side decided not to arm itself, and the other side did arm itself, the outcome would be a disaster for the side that failed to arm itself. Of course, there are many other factors affecting such decisions, such as verifiability if the two sides decided to cooperate. But, in many ways, this situation is parallel to

the prisoner's dilemma described above—the costs or benefits to each side depend on what *both* sides do.

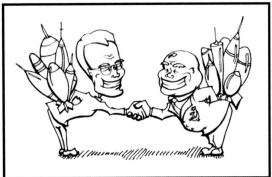

© 2003 Kristal Kamholz

Another (less deadly) form of the PDG is played if you and a friend discuss where to go for dinner. Suppose you want Chinese food, while your friend has a yen for pizza. You do not like pizza and your friend does not like Chinese food. If you both insist on having your way, you may end up not going out at all, and you both would lose. If, on the other hand, one of you insists on your choice and the other goes along, then one of you gets what you want, but the other person either goes hungry or has a meal that he or she does not enjoy. Finally, if you both cooperate, you may decide on another restaurant that you *both* like. In this case, neither of you gets what you want most, but both of you get meals you like.

Bargaining between a union and the management of a company is also like an iterated PDG, in that the bargaining for a new contract involves a series of agreements over various terms of the contract. In bargaining on each term of the contract, the two sides can cooperate by settling on a mutually satisfactory compromise, or either side can insist that its bargaining position cannot be compromised. Cooperation by both sides leads to the maximum mutual benefit. Either side can increase its own "winnings" by defecting and insisting on its own terms, but there is always a risk in this case. If management always defects, the workers will likely go out on strike, while if the union always defects, it may drive the company into bankruptcy.

Axelrod (1984) describes "cooperation without friendship" that occurred between British and German soldiers in the trench warfare of WWI. Despite considerable effort by the high commands on both sides, there developed some fairly elaborate devices for avoiding killing each other, based on the fact that aggressive action led to retaliation. This "live-and-let-live" system of mutual cooperation is illustrated by a soldier's description:

> It would be child's play to shell the road behind the enemy's trenches, crowded as it must be with ration wagons and water carts, into a bloodstained wilderness...but on the whole there is silence. After all, if you prevent your enemy from drawing his rations, his remedy is simple: he will prevent you from drawing yours. (Hay, 1916, pp. 224-225, cited in Axelrod, 1984).

A simple, personal case of the prisoner's dilemma game occurs whenever you buy material you could illegally copy (e.g., text books, journals, video/audio tapes, computer software). For example, with computer software, if you cooperate by purchasing the software and the manufacturer cooperates by keeping prices low, many people can afford to have programs they could not possibly afford to develop themselves. However, if too many people use pirated copies, either prices go up for the people who cooperate or the company goes out of business. The net effect is that everyone loses.

An interesting advance in studying the PDG comes from research by Rilling et al. (2002) who examined the brain activity of subjects playing the PDG for an actual monetary reward. Brain activity was monitored using functional magnetic resonance imaging (fMRI). Two findings emerged. First, patterns of neural activation depended on whether the subject was competing against another human or against a computer. The second, and more fascinating, discovery was

that mutual cooperation led to a pattern of activation that previously had been identified as part of the "reward circuitry" of the brain. Social cooperation is intrinsically rewarding to the brain. The authors note, of course, that this study does not establish whether this intrinsic reward system is genetically programmed or whether it is acquired through socialization in childhood and adolescence.

Game Theory

The PDG is one of many "games" studied in a branch of mathematics called *game theory*. The goal of game theory is to analyze games like the PDG to determine whether there are principled solutions—i.e., is there a "correct" strategy? There is one term from game theory that you may have heard used (or, frequently, misused). That term is *zero-sum game*. A zero-sum game is one in which the amount won is equal to the amount lost. In order for you to win, someone else must lose. An example would be if you and another person were tossing coins. Each person tosses a coin, in turn, and the other must call "heads" or "tails." If you toss a coin and your opponent correctly calls it, he or she wins the coin. Otherwise, you keep it. Note that if you each start with 20 coins of equal value and play a while, there will still be 40 coins—the money is the same, only the distribution changes. Similarly, if five people each bring $100 to a poker game and play for some time, for each person who takes away more than $100, others must have lost the same amount. The sum of the winnings is equal to the sum of the losses—a zero-sum game.

It turns out that most zero-sum games can be analyzed completely—the best play (that which will, on average, maximize winnings or minimize losses in each round) can be specified by mathematical game theory. But the PDG, like many other games, is a *non*-zero-sum game. If both people cooperate in a PDG, they both win. For you to win does not require that someone else loses. These games are enormously more complex, and most defy complete mathematical analysis. For a fascinating biography of John von Neumann, one of the founders of game theory, and a particularly good discussion of the PDG and a number of other non-zero-sum games, we recommend *Prisoner's Dilemma*, by William Poundstone. A beginning treatment of game theory may be found in *The Encyclopedia Britannica*. Davis (1970, chapter 5) also provides a good, non-technical introduction to the game-theory analysis of the PDG. Almost any book on the mathematics of game theory will contain a more technical discussion. Rapoport and Chammah (1970) provide a very good general account of mathematical analysis of the PDG.

Game theory has recently begun to play an important role in economic theorizing. The 1994 Nobel Memorial Prize in Economic Science was awarded to three of the major developers of game theory. And the auctions held by the Federal Communications Commission to sell wavelengths used for wireless personal communications like cell phones was not only designed with game theory principles in mind, but *every* major participant in the auction hired academic game theorists to advise them (Passell, 1994). Budescu, Erev, and Zwick (1999), in a festschrift[19] honoring Amnon Rapoport, document some of the interaction of economics with cognitive and social psychology.

Methodological Considerations

When you begin this experiment, you will get complete instructions for playing the PDG against the computer. A payoff matrix is presented which tells you how many points you and your "opponent" (the computer) will earn for each combination of choices. You will then make your choice, and your opponent will also make a choice according to one of four strategies. Then the points you each earned will be reported. There will be four games of ten rounds each, and your goal is to earn as many points as possible. Please note that you are to try to maximize your winnings, which does not mean necessarily that you want your opponent to win fewer points.

In each game, your opponent will adopt one of four strategies. Those strategies will not be known to you in advance. You should try to determine the strategy your opponent is using in order to maximize your points.

● ● ● ● ● ● ● ● ● ● ● ● ● ● ● ● ● ● ●
Expected Running Time = 18 minutes
● ● ● ● ● ● ● ● ● ● ● ● ● ● ● ● ● ● ●

Questions

1. One purpose of this exercise was to compare the success of the different strategies employed by the computer. For that comparison, what are the independent and dependent variables?

2. Which of the computer's strategies works best against the various strategies employed by the students? Against which of the computer's strategies do students win the most points?

3. Can you tell what strategies the computer employed? Describe what you thought they were. Describe the strategies you tried to employ.

---

[19] A *festschrift* is a collection of articles or essays presented as a tribute or memorial of a scholar. It is from the German (fest=festival, schrift=writing); it is now treated as an English word.

Questions (continued)

4. What might be the effect on this game of being able to meet with your opponent and discuss what you should both do? Of course, in "real-world" situations such as bargaining between governments, such discussion is possible—but later reneging on agreements is possible as well. Insko et al. (1987) present a report of a group version of the PDG with varying possibilities for contact between the groups or between representatives of the groups.

5. What sort of strategy might you adopt to try to "signal" your willingness to cooperate if you cannot communicate with your opponent and your opponent is initially uncooperative? Is the strategy called Tit-for-Tat able to do this?

6. What is the effect of not being "nice"? Compare the computer's points for Tit-for-Tat and Suspicious Tit-for-Tat.

Extension Experiments

1. What is the role of *group* decision-making in the PDG? What is the role of *contact* between the groups? Insko et al. (1987) tested issues such as these.

2. What are the most effective strategies? Axelrod (1984) discusses several. One way to explore this issue is to play strategies of your own against the strategies detailed at the end of this chapter.

3. Luce and Raiffa (1957) were the first to point out that, if the number of rounds of a repeated PDG is fixed, the "best" strategy is to defect always (assuming no communication between the players). The logic is as follows. Suppose you play a single-round PDG and that you do not know what choice your opponent will make. If you cooperate, you will win either 3 or 0 points, depending on your opponent's choice. If the probability of your opponent cooperating is 50%, then your expected earnings would be 1.5 points. If you defect, on the other hand, you will win either 1 point or 5 points, for expected earnings of 3 points. So, you are (at least in a probabilistic sense) better off defecting in a single-round PDG.

   Now suppose there are several rounds and that you know how many rounds there will be. The analysis above would still hold for the last round. But, if you know what you are going to do on the last round, the next-to-last is effectively the last one on which you make a choice. That being so, the same logic applies to the next-to-last round, as well, and so on in a backward fashion.

Despite this analysis, the behavior of real humans playing the finitely-repeated PDG usually show much more cooperation than is predicted. Andreoni and Miller (1993) report on several experiments on single-round and finitely-repeated PDGs and also discuss the development of reputations among the players that strongly push some toward cooperation, at least in the early rounds. (Cressman, 1996, also discusses these issues, though from a mathematical perspective.)

Advanced Questions

1. The various payoffs to a player can be described as follows (Axelrod & Dion, 1988):

    R = *R*eward for mutual cooperation

    S = *S*ucker's payoff (you cooperate, your opponent defects)

    T = *T*emptation to defect

    P = *P*unishment for mutual defection

    The PDG is defined by a situation where $T > R > P > S$, and $R > (S + T)/2$.

    → Show that the payoff matrix for the games you played (the same as in the beginning of this chapter) fits the requirements for the PDG.

    → Explain why the PDG has these requirements.

2. Milinski (1987) has described experiments with three-spined stickleback fish that suggest they have evolved a Tit-for-Tat strategy for how a pair of sticklebacks approach a predator. How did he simulate cooperation and defection, and what were the results?

3. Can species evolve the ability to employ certain strategies in real-world situations that are analogous to the PDG? See Axelrod (1984) and Axelrod and Dion (1988), as well as Milinski (1987) for discussions.

4. What strategies are best? The answer depends, in part, on what strategies are being played against. Axelrod (1984) and Axelrod and Dion (1988) report the results of a computer tournament pitting various strategies against each other. More recent work in this area includes both actual games played by humans (Wedekind & Milinski, 1996), as well as mathematical analysis (Cressman, 1996).

5. How did you respond to the Change of Heart strategy? Did you learn to "trust" your opponent? Compare this to the problem facing the United States of how to deal with the former Soviet Union: a long-time enemy is now offering unilateral reductions in troop strengths and nuclear weapons.

6. The PDG as we have considered it so far involves only two people (or two "sides"). But many real-world problems involve competition for resources among many people, each of whom can make an individual decision. Such a situation occurs in problems of overpopulation (decision to have few or many children), pollution (decision of whether or not to pollute), and behavior in panic situations (decision of saving yourself versus helping others). What factors might influence competition and cooperation in this "N-person" PDG? See Komorita, Sweeney, and Kravitz (1980) for a discussion of the N-person PDG, as well as for references to a number of real-world dilemmas that it models (including those listed above).

7. How might your memory (or lack of memory) for the previous moves affect the play? In general, what is the effect of "noise" on the outcome of the PDG? See Axelrod and Dion (1988) for a discussion.

References

Andreoni, J., & Miller, J. H. (1993). Rational cooperation in the finitely-repeated prisoner's dilemma: Experimental evidence. *The Economic Journal, 103*, 570-585.

Axelrod, R. (1984). *The evolution of cooperation.* New York: Basic Books.

Axelrod, R., & Dion, D. (1988). The further evolution of cooperation. *Science, 242*, 1385-1389.

Budescu, D., Ereve, I., & Zwick, R. (Eds.). (1999). *Games and human behavior: Essays in honor of Amnon Rapoport.* Hillsdale, NJ: Erlbaum.

COMAP (1988). *For all practical purposes: Introduction to contemporary mathematics.* New York: W. H. Freeman.

Cressman, R. (1996). Evolutionary stability in the finitely repeated prisoner's dilemma game. *Journal of Economic Theory, 68*, 234-248.

Davis, M. D. (1970). *Game theory: A nontechnical introduction.* New York: Basic Books.

Hardin, G. (1968). The tragedy of the commons. *Science, 162*, 1243-1248.

Hay, I. (1916). *The first hundred thousand.* London: Wm. Blackwood.

Huberman, B. A., & Lukose, R. M. (1997). Social dilemmas and Internet congestion. *Science, 277*, 535-537.

Insko, C. A., Pinkley, R., Hoyle, R., Dalton, B., Hong, G., Slim, R., et al. (1987). Individual versus group discontinuity: The role of intergroup contact. *Journal of Experimental Social Psychology, 23*, 250-267.

Komorita, S. S., Sweeney, J., & Kravitz, D. (1980). Cooperative choice in the N-person dilemma situation. *Journal of Personality and Social Psychology, 38*, 504-516.

Luce, R. D., & Raiffa, H. (1957). *Games and decisions.* New York: Wiley.

Milinski, M. (1987). TIT FOR TAT in sticklebacks and the evolution of cooperation. *Nature, 325*, 433-435.

Passell, P. (1994, October 12). Game theory captures a Nobel. *The New York Times*, p. C1.

Poundstone, W. (1992). *Prisoner's Dilemma.* New York: Doubleday.

Rapoport, A. & Chammah, A. (1970). *Prisoner's Dilemma: A study in conflict and cooperation.* Ann Arbor, MI: University of Michigan Press.

Rilling, J. K., Gutman, D. A., Zeh, T. R., Pagnoni, G., Berns, G. S., & Kilts, C. D. (2002). A neural basis for social cooperation. *Neuron, 35*, 395-405.

Wedekind, C., & Milinski, M. (1996). Human cooperation in the simultaneous and alternating Prisoner's Dilemma: Pavlov versus Generous Tit-for-Tat. *Proceedings of the National Academy of Sciences, USA, 93*, 2686-2689.

Thought Questions

1. Was the description that you wrote of the person generally positive or generally negative?

2. Did you feel that you could identify the strategy your opponent was using?

3. Were your opponent's choices usually predictable?

4. Did you feel that there were times when you could trust your opponent to cooperate?

5. Were you able to devise strategies of your own to counter your opponent's strategies?

6. Could you remember the choices made in previous rounds and use that information to help evaluate your opponent's choices?

Description of Strategies—Prisoner's Dilemma Game

In the PDG exercise, you play against the computer, which is programmed to employ one of four strategies in each game. Those strategies are described below. Please note that the order in which the strategies were presented to you was random, and so probably was *not* the same as the order in which they are discussed below.

Tit-for-Tat[20]

This strategy was suggested by Anatol Rapoport for a "tournament" held by Robert Axelrod that played a number of strategies against each other (Axelrod, 1984; Axelrod and Dion, 1988). This strategy turned out to be the best of those tested and is very simple: cooperate on round one and then, in later rounds, do whatever your opponent did on the last round. If your opponent cooperates, you cooperate on the next round. If your opponent defects, you defect on the next round. Why is this a good strategy? "What the analysis shows is that an effective strategy is not to start defecting: never be the first to defect. But if the other side defects, be provokable. It also pays to be forgiving after you've been provoked, so as to keep the conflict as short as possible. It pays to respond promptly if someone does something you do not like" (Axelrod, quoted in COMAP, 1988, p. 223). Note that if you figured out that the computer was using this strategy, your earnings would be maximized by cooperating on all remaining trials. This strategy has been described by Axelrod (1984) as nice, provokable, and forgiving. Nice means that the strategy calls for you always to cooperate in the first round. Provokable means that a defection by your opponent is responded to by you defecting in the next round. Forgiving means that if the other player returns to cooperating, you do, too.

---

[20] The term "tit for tat" is a variant of "tip for tap." A tap, of course, is a light blow. "Tip" means a glancing blow, and the use of this word survives in baseball—a foul tip is when the ball is barely touched and knocked foul. Thus, "tit for tat" means "blow for blow."

Description of Strategies *(continued)*

Suspicious Tit-for-Tat

This strategy is the same as Tit-for-Tat, except that the computer defects on the first move. All the remaining rounds are played the same—make whatever choice your opponent made on the last round. The intent of this strategy is to see how your behavior is affected when the initial signal from your opponent is one of non-cooperation. Does that make it harder for you to realize the computer's strategy? In the terms used above, this strategy is provokable and forgiving, but not nice.

Hardball

"Hardball" is the name we have given to a strategy of almost total defection. In this game, the computer chose to defect in all rounds except 5 and 10. Note that the computer made its choices without regard to yours—what you did had no effect. The expectation is that this strategy will lead to relatively low points earnings for both the computer and you, because the best response to consistent defection is to reply with defection. This strategy is a modification of what Axelrod (1984) calls All D (for "always defect").

Change of Heart

We named this strategy "Change of Heart" because the computer defected on rounds 1-5, then changed to Tit-for-Tat for all the remaining rounds. The expectation is that you would take a while to learn to "trust" your opponent when the change of heart occurred and your opponent began to cooperate.

3.2 Measures of Personality Traits

● ●

Abstract

In addition to experiments and other studies designed to discover the psychological processes that humans have in common, there are also studies designed to determine how people differ. Examples of such studies of "individual differences" include intelligence tests and personality tests. In the exercise accompanying this chapter, students complete abbreviated versions of several personality tests. While these brief versions generally are not adequate for actually testing the students' responses, they do serve to show the types of items each test uses. The personality traits tested are anomie, self-monitoring, locus of control, social desirability, and self-esteem.

● ●

*I*n most of the experiments in PsychMate, the purpose is to discover what aspects of psychological functioning people have in common. But, in addition to those shared attributes, people also differ in many ways. A second tradition in psychology has been to study these "individual differences" to see what they have to say about psychological functioning. The exercise on personality testing is intended to acquaint you with some examples of this approach. A common research tactic with personality tests, as well as other measures of individual differences, is to see whether scores on the tests correlate with scores on other measures of personality, as well as demographic measures such as income, ethnicity, and education.

Below are brief descriptions of the various scales that you will see illustrated, with definitions of the personality traits being measured and some discussion of other variables with which they are correlated.

Anomie

The anomie (pronounced AN-uh-me, and spelled either *anomie* or *anomy*) scale illustrated in the exercise accompanying this chapter is the same nine-item scale used by McClosky and Schaar (1965), who conducted two large surveys in which people completed this scale, as well as a number of other scales designed to measure various social attitudes. The concept of anomie comes originally from the work of the sociologist Durkheim (1897/1951), who described it as a condition of normlessness, or not having a feeling of sharing social norms. Durkheim saw this condition as arising from the loss of customary restraints in a capitalistic society devoted to greed and wealth. For him, anomie marked the loss of social restraints and moral limits. McClosky and Schaar have taken a somewhat different approach (and a more research-oriented one), asking what personal factors might be related to feelings of anomie. Their scale consists of items such as "With everything so uncertain these days, it is almost as if anything could happen." High scores indicate high levels of anomie, while low scores are associated with low anomie.

McClosky and Schaar report a number of relationships between other variables and anomie. Educational level was negatively related to anomie—persons with higher educational levels were more likely to score low on anomie. A scale of "mysticism," which was designed to reveal the degree to which people believe that supernatural forces affect their destiny, showed a strong positive relationship to anomie—persons with high scores on the mysticism scale were also more likely to have high levels of anomie. "Psychological inflexibility" also was positively related to anomie, as were manifest anxiety and aggression. One rather interesting finding came from scales of agreement with extreme left- and right-wing political positions. Persons scoring high on either of these scales also tended to have high anomie scores. McClosky and Schaar discuss the degree to which anomie reflects social conditions, as well as the degree to which it is determined by psychological factors.

Self-Monitoring

"Individuals differ in the extent to which they monitor (observe and control) their expressive behavior and self-presentation. Out of a concern for appropriateness, the self-monitoring individual is particularly sensitive to the expression and self-presentation of others in social situations and uses these cues as guidelines for monitoring and managing his own self-presentation and expressive behavior. In contrast, the non-self-monitoring person has little concern for the appropriateness of his presentation and expression, pays less attention to the expression of others, and monitors and controls his presentation to a lesser extent" (Snyder, 1974, p. 536). Snyder and Simpson (1984) have further described persons high in self-monitoring as "particularly responsive to situational and interpersonal cues," while persons low in self-monitoring are "individuals whose actions typically reflect underlying attitudes, dispositions, and other personal attributes" (p. 1281). These quotes describe the sort of personality trait that Snyder attempted to measure with his 25-item scale of self-monitoring. The version used in the exercise for this chapter is only 10 items in length, with those items taken from Snyder's original scale.

An example of an item designed to measure self-monitoring is, "I may deceive people by being friendly when I really dislike them." For this scale, high scores reflect high levels of self-monitoring. Snyder conducted several studies to offer evidence of the validity of this scale. One was based on the assumption that actors would have higher-than-usual levels of self-monitoring, since their profession requires that they adopt different roles and portray them convincingly.

This turned out to be the case, with a group of professional actors scoring significantly higher in self-monitoring than a group of Stanford University undergraduates. On the other hand, psychiatric patients are argued to show less variation in their responses across situations, and Snyder found that they score lower in self-monitoring on average than did his Stanford undergraduate controls. In other studies, Snyder found that persons who scored high on self-monitoring were better at expressing emotion when asked to read a passage out loud. More recently, Snyder and Simpson (1984) reported differences between high- and low-self-monitoring individuals in the patterns of their dating behavior, with persons high in self-monitoring more likely to adopt an "uncommitted" approach to dating and persons low in self-monitoring tending toward more committed relationships.

Locus of Control (LOC)

Rotter (1966) devised the original scale of locus of control, with the intent of measuring the degree to which persons perceive reinforcements (rewards) as being due to their own behavior (*internal* locus) or due to forces outside themselves, such as luck or fate (*external* locus). Rotter argued that persons' responses in many learning situations may depend  powerfully upon the degree to which they feel that the outcome is either under their control or controlled by fate or powerful others. In this scale, subjects must choose which of two statements they agree with the most, with one statement reflecting an external locus of control and the other an internal one. An example of a sentence pair in the LOC scale follows:

"What happens to me is my own doing."

vs.

"Sometimes I feel that I do not have enough control over the direction my life is taking."

The actual version of the LOC scale that you will complete in the exercise is an 11-item scale devised by Valecha (1972). The items are a subset of Rotter's original scale.

Social Desirability

One aspect of personality is the degree to which we tend either to seek the approval of others or to avoid disapproval. Crowne and Marlowe (1964) reported studies using a scale of "social desirability" that they devised. The scale consists of 30 statements that subjects are to rate as true or false in regard to themselves. The statements were carefully chosen, however, to have two main attributes: "First, they are 'good,' culturally sanctioned things to say about oneself; and second, they are probably untrue of most people" (p.21). An example is, "I am always courteous, even to people who are disagreeable." Notice that, while most of us would like to think that we are unfailingly courteous, in truth, hardly anyone can claim that they *always* are so. Thus, this scale is designed to determine the degree to which a person is motivated by approval and avoids doing or saying things that may lead to disapproval. Crowne and Marlowe (1964) report a number of studies showing differences between high- and low-need-for-approval subjects. One example involved subjects having to decide which of two briefly presented cards had the most dots on it. The subject performed this experiment along with four other students who were confederates of the experimenters. On a number of trials, the confederates gave the incorrect answer. The issue was whether the actual subject would tend to agree with this choice or not. Persons with a high need for approval as measured by the scale were consistently more likely to agree (at least publicly!) with the confederates' choices.

Self-esteem

Another important individual difference between people is their degree of self-esteem. Do you think well of yourself, or do you feel like a failure? Rosenberg (1965) attempted to measure self-esteem with a simple 10-item scale, which is reproduced as part of the exercise that you will do. An example of an item from this scale is "I certainly feel useless at times." Rosenberg's main concern was self-esteem in adolescence, and he tested a large number of high-school students with his scale to see if self-esteem is related to other variables in their lives.

Among Rosenberg's findings were that only-children tended to have higher self-esteem than children with siblings (though the number of siblings made no difference). The adolescents' perceptions of how interested their parents were in them also was related to self-esteem. Adolescents with low self-esteem were found to be less likely to participate in extra-curricular activities (though the size of the differences here was not large). When Rosenberg tested the adolescents' expectations for success in a career, he found that those high in self-esteem were more likely to expect to be successful. Research in industrial/organizational psychology has found that persons with low self-esteem are less apt to choose jobs that are suited to their needs and abilities (Korman, 1967). Other research indicates that the "vicious cycle" of low self-esteem (in which low self-esteem leads to failure, which reinforces low self-esteem, and so on) can be broken by getting a person to attribute failure to the difficulty of a task, rather than to his or her own inadequacies (Brockner & Guare, 1983).

Recent Research

In this chapter, we endeavor to present the early research on each of these concepts. All of these remain areas of continuing research, especially self-esteem and locus of control. The literature is too vast to be reviewed here, but the interested student is referred to the PsycInfo database, where anomie, self-monitoring, locus of control, self-esteem, and social desirability are all highest-level search terms. Over 10,000 articles have been published on locus of control and on self esteem! While not as vast, the literature on the other topics includes hundreds of articles.

Concerns in Testing

Two major concerns must be addressed in regard to any test, whether it is a personality scale such as those just outlined, a standardized test such as the SAT or an IQ test, or an experimental test of memory. Those concerns are the *validity* and *reliability* of the test.

Validity

Validity refers to whether a test measures what it claims to measure. As an example, suppose you devised an "intelligence" test that consisted of measuring how many sit-ups a person could do. That test would clearly be invalid—it simply doesn't measure intelligence. Often, of course, problems of validity are more subtle. For example, if an intelligence test has many items with vocabulary that you do not know, it would

not be a valid test for you. Your low score would not reflect a lack of intelligence, but simply that you don't have the same vocabulary as the test maker.

Unfortunately, it is difficult to measure validity. We must be content to estimate it in various ways. Three such approaches are described briefly below.

Face validity refers to a sort of common-sense approach. Counting how many sit-ups someone can do and calling it a test of intelligence lacks face validity. On the other hand, an item like "At times I think I'm no good at all" does appear to have face validity as a measure of self-esteem, because it seems clear that someone with high self-esteem probably would not agree with it, while someone with low self-esteem more likely would. While you should be concerned about face validity, it should be obvious that this is a limited approach—what seems obvious "on its face" to you may seem quite implausible to others, and there is no good way to settle the argument.

Predictive validity, another approach to estimating validity, is concerned with how well the results of a test predict how well you will do on other measures that *should* be related. For example, an intelligence test should correlate reasonably well with school performance. Put another way, scores on an intelligence test should predict school performance fairly well if the test is valid, since how well you do in school is determined, in part, by intelligence. In this case, predictive validity is fairly high. In many practical situations, however, predictive validity is quite low. For example, almost any time a test is used to select persons for training (such as using the SAT to select who gets into college), the measured predictive validity is actually low due to what is known as *restriction of range*. Whenever we have restricted access to training to only those with high scores on an entrance exam (such as the SAT), we have restricted the range of abilities of those who can participate in training. When we graduate only those who did well in school (who had high GPAs), we have further restricted the range of abilities. Even if there is an underlying high predictive validity (high SATs mean that one will do well in school and graduate) , the *measured* predictive validity will be low—not because the SAT is invalid, but because of restriction of range.

Concurrent validity refers to whether a test correlates well with other tests designed to measure the same trait. If I devise a new test for a medical problem, for example, its results should agree well with those of other tests already in use. For many psychological traits, however, we have no agreed-upon measure against which to check a new measure. Suppose scores on a new test of intelligence correlate highly with scores on another intelligence test. We can certainly conclude that they measure the same thing, so *if* the old test is measuring intelligence, the new one is, too. But we then have the problem of figuring out whether the old test is valid!

Reliability

Reliability refers to how well a test measures whatever it is measuring. If a test is reliable, it should yield consistent results. As an example, a bathroom scale is designed to measure your weight and is probably fairly reliable. But suppose you had a five-year-old guess peoples' weights. That would almost surely be highly unreliable. Reliability turns out to be easier to measure than validity, and two approaches to measuring it are detailed below.

Test-retest reliability refers to the correlation between scores on the same test given twice. If an intelligence test is reliable, you should get about the same score each time you take it, since intelligence presumably doesn't change much across short periods of time. But there can be problems with this approach. This method of measuring reliability assumes that taking the test will not change future scores on the test. For long intelligence tests or achievement tests, this is likely true, but it could be a problem for a test where you have a chance to practice before taking it again (or where you can look up the answers while taking it again).

Split-half reliability is a way to measure reliability when test-retest reliability will not work. This method consists of calculating the correlation between one half of the test and the other half. In practice, this is often done using odd- and even-numbered items. On the SAT, for example, it is reasonable to assume that your score based on the odd-numbered items will be about the same as your score based on even-numbered items, thus indicating that the test is reliable. Split-half-reliability gets around some of the problems of test-retest reliability, but should be used only when there is a fairly large number of items on the test. (More sophisticated approaches of the same general sort include Kuder and Richardson's KR-20, or Chronbach's Alpha.)

One thing to remember about reliability and validity is that they are *only partly independent*. That is, a test could be reliable, but not valid, and vice versa (though any measure of validity will be reduced if reliability is low). An example would be measuring intelligence by how many sit-ups someone can do. Test-retest reliability would be high (i.e., if you can do only 10 sit-ups today, there is no reason to think you would be able to do many more or fewer two days from now), but the test still would not be a valid measure of intelligence. Although a test can have high reliability without being valid, an unreliable test will have poor validity. Reliability is necessary, but not sufficient, for validity (Ghiselli, Campbell, & Zedeck, 1981). To illustrate why this is so, imagine a test that is completely unreliable, with a correlation of zero between test and retest. Since reliability concerns how well a test measures something, we would conclude that this test measures nothing. But that is just another way of saying it is invalid, since, if it measures nothing, it cannot be measuring what we want it to measure.

Methodological Considerations

In this exercise, you will complete five brief personality tests. Two of the tests (the 9-item anomie scale and the 10-item self-esteem scale) are presented in their complete form. The other three are abbreviated for the sake of time. The 11-item locus-of-control scale uses a subset of Rotter's original 29 items that was devised and tested by Valecha (1972). Twelve of the 33 items from Crowne and Marlowe's social-desirability scale are included, as are nine of the 25 items from Snyder's self-monitoring scale.

When your instructor reports the data, they will be scored in the following way. The "proportion correct" will indicate the proportion of items on which you indicated the trait being measured. For the locus-of-control scale, a high score indicates a highly *external* locus of control, while a low score indicates an *internal* LOC. On the other scales, higher scores indicate higher degrees of the trait being measured.

Because of the rather sensitive nature of some of these scales, your regular subject number will not be used. The computer will assign a random number, and you will be given a chance to write it down if you wish. The regular subject numbers will be encrypted so that the data analysis program can give your instructor a list of the persons completing the assignment, without permitting him or her to associate particular results with individual students (if several students complete the assignment).

. . . .
Expected Running Time = 12 minutes
. . . .

Questions

1. Discuss the reliability of one test. How has that reliability been measured by researchers or by the author(s) of the scale? Do you feel that it was reliable? That is, would you be likely to make the same responses if you took the test again?

2. Discuss the validity of one test. How has validity been estimated in research on the test? Does the test appear to have good face validity? Do you feel that you easily could make yourself "look better" by giving dishonest answers?

3. Think about what each scale measures. Would you predict that scores on any of the scales would be correlated? Which ones, and why? Compare your answer to the obtained correlations.

References

Brockner, J., & Guare, J. (1983). Improving the performance of low self-esteem individuals: An attributional approach. *Academy of Management Journal, 26,* 642-656.

Crowne, D. P., & Marlowe, D. (1964). *The approval motive.* New York: John Wiley.

Durkheim, E. (1951). *Suicide.* (J. A. Spalding & G. Simpson, Trans.). Glencoe, IL: Free Press. (Original work published 1897)

Ghiselli, E., Campbell, D., & Zedeck, S. (1981). *Measurement theory for the behavioral sciences.* New York: W. J. Freeman.

Kelly, K., Cheung, F. M., Singh, R., Becker, M. A., Rodrigues-Carillo, P., Wan, C. K., et al. (1986). Chronic self-destructiveness and locus of control in cross-cultural perspective. *Journal of Social Psychology, 126,* 573-577.

Korman, A. (1967). Self-esteem as a moderator of the relationship between perceived abilities and vocational choice. *Journal of Applied Psychology, 51,* 484-490.

McClosky, H., & Schaar, J. H. (1965). Psychological dimensions of anomy. *American Sociological Review, 30,* 14-40.

Rapoport, A., & Chammah, A. (1970). *Prisoner's dilemma.* Ann Arbor, MI: University of Michigan Press.

Rosenberg, M. (1965). *Society and the adolescent self-image.* Princeton, NJ: Princeton University Press.

Rotter, J. B. (1966). Generalized expectancies for internal versus external control of reinforcement. *Psychological Monographs, 80*(Whole No. 609), 1-28.

Snyder, M. (1974). Self-monitoring of expressive behavior. *Journal of Personality and Social Psychology, 30,* 526-537.

Snyder, M., & Simpson, J. A. (1984). Self-monitoring and dating relationships. *Journal of Personality and Social Psychology, 47,* 1281-1291.

Valecha, G. K. (1972). *Construct validation of internal-external locus of control as measured by an abbreviated 11-item IE scale.* Unpublished doctoral dissertation, The Ohio State University.

3.3 Impression Formation

Abstract

An important aspect of social psychology is how we form impressions of other people, based on limited knowledge about them. Asch (1946) performed an experiment that is basic to this subject, and that experiment is replicated in the exercise accompanying this chapter. Asch had subjects read a brief set of terms describing a hypothetical person, then tested the subjects' impressions of that person by having them rate the person on a number of dimensions. What he found was that some descriptors are very powerful in determining our impressions of other people.

When you meet new people, how do you form impressions of them? That is, what things about them might influence how you perceive them? In this exercise, you will repeat a famous experiment done some years ago by Solomon Asch (1946). In that experiment (there were actually several versions of it), Asch had subjects listen to a series of adjectives (personality traits) describing a person. The subjects were then asked to write a character sketch of what they thought that person was like. In addition to the character sketch, Asch had his subjects complete checklists of opposing traits (such as "sociable-unsociable"), indicating which of the two terms was most likely to be true of the person described.

Asch found striking differences in ratings given by two groups of subjects when the description of

FIGURE 3.3.1 – How might your perception of this person change based on the descriptors of "adequate" versus "effective" or "smart" versus "shrewd"?

the person they were to rate differed in only one trait. Asch called such traits "central," because he viewed them as especially important for impression formation. Some other traits that were tested yielded very little difference in impressions, and Asch called these "peripheral" characteristics.

Psychologists have long been interested in how we come to know other persons, but a major problem for studying this sort of question was how to approach it experimentally. One important aspect of Asch's work was that he was able to study impression formation experimentally and *quantitatively*. That is, he was able to make repeatable measurements about the effect of various descriptors on judgments of personality, and he was able to show that such judgments could be manipulated systematically.

One question that might seem obvious is whether the results of experiments like Asch's really apply to everyday types of judgments. After all, Asch's subjects were asked to write character sketches and choose traits based on a brief description of a *hypothetical* person. Would the same result occur if the description was followed by actually meeting the person described?

Kelley (1950) performed just such an experiment. Students in a class read a brief career profile and character sketch of a visiting lecturer. The lecturer then led a class discussion for 20 minutes. Subjects were then asked to rate the lecturer on a number of scales (some of which were the same as Asch's). The results were strikingly similar to Asch's, thereby confirming that his results were not just the result of the abstract setting in which the ratings had been made. Moreover, student subjects given descriptions that were expected to lead to a favorable impression were also somewhat more likely to interact with the lecturer by joining the class discussion.

Recent Studies of Impression Formation

Impression formation continues to be an important area of study in social psychology and social cognition. Wyer and Srull (1994) provide references to many studies in this area. While Asch's research dealt with impression formation, social psychologists (e.g. Belmore & Hubbard, 1987, as well as Wyer

and Srull, 1994) also have studied other aspects of how we come to know other people, such as person memory (i.e., memory for information about the target person). Several aspects of research on impression formation are presented in the Advanced Questions section below.

An important historical and contemporary review of research in "ordinary personology,"—the everyday ways we make judgments about others—is that of Gilbert (1998). Gleitman et al. (1997) provide an overview of Asch's work and its importance for recent social psychology.

Researchers have applied Asch's basic paradigm and its extension to many interesting areas of impression formation, including the impressions of persons we "meet" via computer communications (Hancock & Dunham, 2001).

Methodological Considerations

After reviewing a list of traits, the subjects are asked to choose which of a pair of adjectives is most likely to be true of the person described. Because the subject must choose one of the two terms, this is called a "forced-choice" rating. Eighteen adjective pairs are rated in this way.

● ● ● ● ● ● ● ● ● ● ● ● ● ● ● ● ● ● ● ●
Expected Running Time = 10 minutes
● ● ● ● ● ● ● ● ● ● ● ● ● ● ● ● ● ● ●

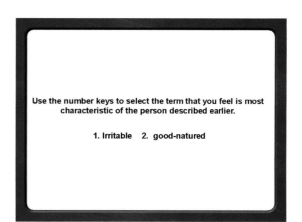

Use the number keys to select the term that you feel is most characteristic of the person described earlier.

1. Irritable 2. good-natured

FIGURE 3.3.2 – *Example of a forced-choice trial from the Impression Formation experiment*

Questions

1. What are the dependent and independent variables? What are some important controls?

2. What are the results? Which of the 18 pairs of adjectives on the checklist show differences between the two groups?

3. Do your results agree with those of Asch (1946)? See p. 263, Table 2, for a report of the percentage of subjects choosing each term.

4. What is the purpose of Asch's Experiment 2? Why is this an important control experiment? What were his results?

Extension Experiments

1. One control experiment that Asch performed (his Experiment 2) was designed to test whether the "warm-cold" distinction affected the overall impression of personality or whether it acted independently of other descriptors. The version of the experiment accompanying this chapter simply omitted the words "warm" and "cold" from the descriptors, but added them to the checklist.

2. What other traits might be "central"? A simple extension of the experiment you have done is to manipulate other pairs of adjectives. Wishner (1960) discusses predicting which traits are central and which are peripheral. Another interesting approach is to use descriptors of *behaviors* (e.g., "Returned a wallet he found to its owner"), rather than personality traits (e.g., honest/dishonest). See Skowronski and Carlston (1987) for examples. Another approach might be to change the other descriptors used. Would the "warm-cold" distinction make the same difference if the other personality traits described were different?

3. Hamilton, Katz, and Leirer (1980) reported an experiment that contrasts memory for trait descriptors depending on whether subjects were asked to form an impression based on those traits (as is Asch's study) or whether subjects were asked to memorize them. They found consistently better recall for subjects asked to form an impression. You might want to consider this finding in light of the levels-of-processing effect (Chapter 3.4).

Advanced Questions

1. One difficulty for interpreting Asch's results was that he classified traits as "central" or "peripheral" depending on the outcome of the checklist ratings. The "warm-cold" trait pair yielded large differences; hence, it was described as central to impression formation. In another experiment, he presented lists of descriptors differing only in describing the person as "polite" versus "blunt." This pair made little difference in the ratings and therefore was described as peripheral. But is there any way to predict—in advance—which traits are central and which are peripheral? Wischner (1960) tackled this problem. How was he able to make such predictions?

2. How do the goals that you bring to bear in social situations influence your perception of other people and your memory for information about them? When you meet someone and form an impression and memories of them, does it matter whether you expect to have to work closely with the person? See Devine, Sedikides, and Fuhrman (1989) for a discussion and some experimental evidence.

3. Suppose that you hear a description of someone you expect to meet later, and you form an impression based on that description. Suppose further that you later are told that part of the description was incorrect. What influence does that have on your impression? Does it matter whether the information you are told to disregard was favorable or unfavorable? Wyer and Budesheim (1987) report several experiments on these issues.

4. Descriptions of a person can vary in many ways. Among these are *morality*-related descriptors (such as honest/dishonest) and *ability*-related descriptors (such as intelligent/stupid). Do we treat these types of descriptors differently in forming impressions of persons? Skowronski and Carlston (1987) suggest that we do, and in some interesting ways.

References

Asch, S. E. (1946). Forming impressions of personality. *Journal of Abnormal and Social Psychology, 41*, 258-290.

Belmore, S. M., & Hubbard, M. L. (1987). The role of advance expectancies in person memory. *Journal of Personality and Social Psychology, 53*, 61-70.

Devine, P. G., Sedikides, C., Fuhrman, R. W. (1989). Goals in social information processing: The case of anticipated interaction. *Journal of Personality and Social Psychology, 56*, 680-690.

Gilbert, Daniel T. (1998). Ordinary personology. In D. T. Gilbert , S. T. Fiske, & G. Lindsey (Eds.), *The handbook of social psychology: Vol. 2.* (4th ed., pp. 89-150). New York: McGraw-Hill.

Gleitman, H., Rozin, P., Sabini, J. (1997). Solomon E. Asch (1907-1996): Obituary. *American Psychologist, 52*, 984-985.

Hamilton, D. L., Katz, L.B., & Leirer, V. O. (1980). Cognitive representation of personality impressions: Organizational processes in first impression formation. *Journal of Personality and Social Psychology, 39*, 1050-1063.

Hancock, J. T., Dunham, P. J. (2001). Impression formation in computer-mediated communication revisited: An analysis of the breadth and intensity of impressions. *Communication Research, 28*, 325-347.

Kelley, H. H. (1950). The warm-cold variable in first impressions of persons. *Journal of Personality, 18*, 431-439.

Skowronski, J. J., & Carlston, D. E. (1987). Social judgment and social memory: The role of cue diagnosticity in negativity, positivity, and extremity biases. *Journal of Personality and Social Psychology, 52*, 689-699.

Wishner, J. (1960). Reanalysis of "Impressions of Personality." *Psychological Review, 67*, 96-112.

Wyer, R. S., Jr., & Budesheim, T. L. (1987). Person memory and judgments: The impact of information that one is told to disregard. *Journal of Personality and Social Psychology, 53*, 14-29.

Wyer, R. S., Jr., & Srull, T. K. (Eds.). (1994). *Handbook of social cognition.* Hillsdale, NJ: Lawrence Erlbaum Associates.

3.4 Levels of Processing and the Self-Reference Effect

Abstract

The levels-of-processing effect refers to the empirical finding that the qualitative nature of processing determines retention in memory of the items processed. The self-reference effect refers to the finding that items processed in reference to the self are remembered better than those processed in non-self-referential ways. The experiment accompanying this chapter replicates a standard level-of-processing experiment in which one of the orienting tasks is a self-reference task.

*T*wo related issues are addressed in this chapter. One is the *levels-of-processing effect*, a well-established, but theoretically troublesome, finding from memory research which states that the way we process information to be remembered affects how well it is later retrieved. The other is the *self-reference effect*: information processed in reference to the self is remembered better than information processed in other ways. The experiment that accompanies this chapter is a standard levels-of-processing study, with a self-reference orienting task added, to replicate Rogers, Kuiper, & Kirker (1977).

Levels of Processing

It was Craik and Lockhart (1972) who first proposed the levels-of-processing approach to the study of human memory. Over the previous decade, most research in memory had focused on elucidating the types or stages of memory through which incoming information was processed, and the relations between those

stages. The "modal model" developed by Atkinson and Shiffrin (1968) was an outcome of that research (see Figure 3.4.1); it proposed that information in short-term memory is transferred to long-term memory by verbal rehearsal. One important aspect of memory *not* treated in models such as Atkinson and Shiffrin's was how the accessibility of information stored in long-term memory was determined. Craik and Lockhart attempted to remedy that problem by proposing that the durability of a memory is determined by the "depth" of processing; in other words, the more semantically involved the processing, the longer the information will remain accessible to retrieval.

Even before Craik and Lockhart's development of a theoretical framework, Hyde and Jenkins (1969) published an experiment concerning the levels-of-processing effect—though not under that name. It is worth describing their study in some detail, since it provides a paradigm for

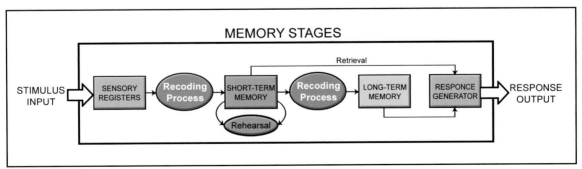

FIGURE 3.4.1 – *The Modal Model proposed by Atkinson and Shiffrin*

much of the other research. Their experiment used an *incidental learning task*, in which subjects first were presented with lists of words and asked to make some sort of judgment about them and then were given a surprise recall task. Because the subjects were not instructed to memorize the lists, any learning that took place was considered to be "incidental."

Hyde and Jenkins used three different *orienting tasks*, which determined how the lists of words were processed by the subjects. One orienting task asked the subjects to estimate the number of letters in each word. Another asked them to state whether the word contained the letter "*e*." A third task was to judge whether the word was pleasant or unpleasant. Finally, there was an *intentional learning* group that was instructed that they would be tested for their memory of the words. Of the 24 words presented, the intentional learning group recalled, on average, 16.1 words. Those who estimated the number of letters recalled an average of 9.9 words. Those asked whether the word contained an "*e*" averaged 9.4 words. And those asked to make a judgment of pleasant vs. unpleasant had an average recall of 16.3 words.

Note two important points. First, *intent to learn did **not** matter*. Subjects who made judgments of pleasant vs. unpleasant—not knowing they would be tested for recall later —recalled as well, in fact, as subjects who were deliberately attempting to memorize the list. Second, *the type of processing **did** matter*. Those subjects who made a judgment (e.g., pleasant vs. un- pleasant) which required a semantic analysis performed much better than those whose judgments were based on structural properties of the words. (Hyde and Jenkins also included three other groups who received the same orienting tasks, but were told explicitly that they would be asked to remember the items. The addition of intentional learning to the orienting tasks made little difference—a point to which we will return.)

Craik and Tulving (1975) published a series of experiments that explored the level-of-process-

ing effect. One experiment was very much like that of Hyde and Jenkins. Subjects were asked to answer "Yes" or "No" to a question asked about a word. The questions and the proportion recognized correctly are shown in Table 3.4.1. Half of the time the question was true of the word ("Yes"), and half the time it was not ("No").

Orienting Task	"Yes"	"No"
Is the word in capital letters?	0.18	0.14
Does the word rhyme with weight?	0.78	0.36
Is the word a type of fish?	0.93	0.63
Would the word fit in the sentence: *"He met a _____ in the street"?*	0.96	0.83

TABLE **3.4.1** – *Results of Craik and Tulving's experiment*

Note the differences. In order to decide whether a word is in capital letters, you need make only an orthographic (i.e., word shape) decision. You could do that quite easily in a language you did not know, provided it had an alphabet similar to English—i.e., you need not process the word *as a word*. To decide whether a word rhymes with weight, you must consider the phonological properties—what the word sounds like. You still do not have to be concerned with the meaning. Indeed, you could do this even with an ortho- graphically regular non-word, such as BLATE. To determine whether the word named a type of fish, you would have to access category informa- tion about the object named, requiring more processing. Finally, to decide whether the word represented an object that one could meet in the street, you would need to consider the properties of the object named. You also might employ imagery to aid in your decision.

As the data reflect, the proportion of words recognized was heavily influenced by the type of processing required. The "deeper" the level of processing, the better the recall. A second finding is that subjects were consistently better when they had answered "Yes" than when they had answered "No."

Two aspects of this experiment are worth noting. The first concerns a possible confound. Craik and

Tulving measured reaction times for answering the question for each word and found that RT correlated positively with level of processing. That is problematic, because it may indicate that recognition is affected—not by the level of processing, *per se*—but by the amount of time spent processing. Craik and Tulving countered that argument by showing that, on individual trials in which RT was slower for the orthographic task than for the semantic task, recognition was still better for the semantic task. They also reported an experiment in which the orthographic task was more difficult, requiring longer processing than the semantic task. Recognition was still better for the semantic task.

A second aspect of Craik and Tulving's experiment concerned the exact conditions of that study. Are their results due to some peculiarity of their methodology? In other experiments, Craik and Tulving showed that the results were the same when a recall test was used instead of a recognition test. They also tested the boundary condition of whether the precise timing of the stimulus presentation was crucial, and also if it really mattered that subjects were unaware whether they would be given a recognition test or a recall test. In a classroom (an advanced psychology course on learning and memory), they did a simplified version of the task, testing all their subjects at once under much less rigorous conditions of timing. The results were nearly identical to their carefully controlled studies. Because this experiment allowed subjects six seconds to study each word (versus only 200 ms in the more formal experiments), it provides further support for the claim that what matters is the *level* of processing, not the amount.

The levels-of-processing *effect* has been well tested and is now a standard classroom demonstration. But *why* does it occur? Two general hypotheses have been advanced. One is that *elaboration* is what matters for memory. According to this account, the more you elaborate on an item, the more retrieval cues you provide, thereby improving the likelihood of later retrieval. Shallow levels of processing require little elaboration, while deeper levels require more. Craik and Tulving found, for example, that asking subjects to indicate whether a word would fit in a sentence led to much better retrieval when the sentence was more complex or when it led to more vivid imagery. At least for "Yes" answers, recall was more than twice as good for a complex sentence such as "The great bird swooped down and carried off the struggling _____" than for the simpler sentence "The _____ is torn."

What of the better retrieval (recall or recognition) for words for which the answer to the question was "Yes"? As Craik and Tulving noted, "It does not seem intuitively reasonable that words associated with *yes* answers require deeper processing before the decision is made. However, if high levels of retention are associated with 'rich' or 'elaborate' encodings of the word (rather than deep encodings), the differences in retention between positive and negative words become understandable. In cases where a positive response is made, the encoding question and the target word can form a coherent, integrated unit" (p. 281). Of course, a "coherent, integrated unit" will provide better retrieval cues.

A second hypothesis concerning the nature of the levels-of-processing effect is *distinctiveness*. According to this account (Eysenck, 1979), the effect of deeper levels of processing is to make the items more distinctive. Because distinctive memories are less easily confused with other memories, they can be retrieved more reliably. Try the following thought experiment. If I read you a list of 20 words, then asked you to recall them in any order, we would typically find a *serial position effect*, with good recall of the first few words and the last few words, but poor recall of the words in the middle of the list. But suppose that, as I read the 10th word, I jumped up in the air and shouted the word. Recall would probably be nearly perfect for that word, because it has been made to stand out from the rest—it has been made more distinctive. Both elaboration and distinctiveness have found experimental support (see Reed, 1996, for a good review). It is also worth noting that the two hypotheses are not necessarily mutually exclusive. Eysenck (1979) has noted that perhaps elaboration makes items more distinctive.

But what of levels-of-processing as a theoretical stance? The *levels-of-processing* **effect** refers to the empirical finding described above—some orienting tasks lead to better retrieval. But is that because of "depth" of processing? Certainly, it is intuitively appealing to conclude that deciding whether the object named could fit in a sentence results in a deeper, semantically richer type of processing than deciding if a word is in capital letters. But the difficulty is that we have no independent means of assessing depth of processing (Nelson, 1977; Craik, 1979). While this problem has led to some serious theoretical difficulties, the robustness of the levels-of-processing effect has made it an area of continuing research.

The Self-Reference Effect

The *self-reference effect* refers to the superiority of a special kind of orienting task. Especially good recall is found in levels-of-processing experiments when subjects are asked to make judgments about whether words describe themselves. There seem to be some unique advantages to the self as a mnemonic aid. A review of the literature on the self-reference effect, with a meta-analysis, is provided by Symons and Johnson (1997). The self-reference effect is part of a relatively new area of social psychology called *social cognition*.

"Social cognition is concerned with how people represent knowledge of people, the situations in which they meet, and the behaviors that they exchange…By far the most important of these objects of social cognition, however, is the person doing the cognizing" (Kihlstrom & Klein, 1994, p. 154). That "person doing the cognizing" is the self. William James (1890/1981; see also Kihlstrom & Klein, 1994) noted that "the universal conscious fact is not 'feelings and thoughts exist' but 'I think' and 'I feel'" (p. 221).

Photo courtesy of Colleen Conn

The "I" doing the thinking or feeling is the self. Not only is the self a basic fact of mental life, but so is our knowledge of self, often called the "self-concept." The self has become an object of intense study in social cognition (Kihlstrom & Klein, 1994; Neisser & Jopling, 1997).

Rogers, Kuiper, and Kirker (1977) began what has become a large literature on one aspect of the self—namely, how the self, or self-concept, is used to guide memory. "Of concern…is the construct of self and how it is implicated in the organization of personal data. Our general position is that the self is an extremely active and powerful agent in the organization of the person's world" (Rogers, Kuiper, & Kirker, p. 677). They reasoned that if the self is used as a reference point to aid the encoding of incoming information, then it might provide a powerful means of organizing and elaborating. The importance of organization for memory is amply demonstrated in the experiment in Chapter 2.6, *Organization in Memory as an Aid to Recall*, and the importance of elaboration was discussed above. The self as a means of organization and elaboration was studied by Rogers, Kuiper, and Kirker in an extension of Craik and Lockhart's (1972) levels-of-processing paradigm.

The basic approach of Rogers, Kuiper, and Kirker (1977) was to add a self-reference task to the orienting tasks used in standard levels-of-processing studies. They presented their subjects with lists of words to be judged under one of several orienting tasks. The shallowest was a *structural* task in which subjects had to decide whether a word was in capital letters. The next was a *phonemic* task—"Does the word rhyme with ____?" They also used a *semantic* task, in which subjects had to judge whether a word meant the same as another word. In addition to these standard orienting tasks, a *self-reference* task was added—subjects had to state whether or not a given word describes them. The words rated in this task were all adjectives that could be used to describe a person.

The results were quite clear (see Figure 3.4.2). First, a strong levels-of-processing effect was found, with the structural task leading to the poorest retrieval on a surprise recall test, the phonemic task resulting in the next best recall, and the semantic task producing better recall than either structural or phonemic tasks. Most

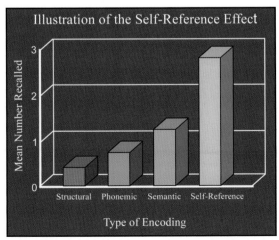

FIGURE **3.4.2** – *Typical results in an experiment looking at the self-reference effect and measuring recall*

important, though, was the finding that recall was best for the self-reference task—recall in this condition was over twice that of the semantic task. Rogers, Kuiper, and Kirker (1977) concluded that the self is, at least in part, a well-organized, highly elaborate structure of self-knowledge, including memory for personal experiences and evaluations of self.

The self-reference effect has been extensively studied. Symons and Johnson (1997) included 129 published studies in their meta-analysis. But the field has not been without controversy. As is often the case, the problem lies not in whether self-referent terms are remembered better than semantically processed terms, but in what conclusions one is justified in drawing from the self-reference effect. Kihlstrom and Klein (1994) review a number of studies that they claim challenge the claim that the self is unique as a memory structure. They conclude that the self-reference task used in many studies simply provides a higher level of elaboration or of organization than the typical semantic task, and that it is quite clear that higher levels of elaboration and/or higher levels of organization result in superior retrieval. For them, then, "the results of these experiments do not mean that the self is not a memory structure. To the contrary, they seem to indicate that the self can be profitably approached as if it were no different from other knowledge structures stored in memory."

While not completely rejecting that claim, Symons and Johnson (1997) present considerable evidence that it is too strong. They base their conclusions on a *meta-analysis*. Meta-analysis refers to a technique for combining the results of many studies that are similar in approach, so that the resulting statistical analysis benefits from the power inherent in the much larger combined sample. This technique, developed in the 1970's (Rosenthal, 1983), expresses the results of each study in terms of the *effect size*. Effect size is the difference between means in two conditions—here, recall in semantic and self-reference tasks—divided by the pooled standard deviations. (Note that this is formally equivalent to Student's *t*.) Expressing differences in terms of effect sizes makes it possible to directly compare the size of differences obtained across studies.

Over the large numbers of studies available to Symons and Johnson, they were able to make a number of interesting comparisons, even when not all studies contributed to each comparison. One finding was that self-reference tasks involving trait terms (such as "tall" or "outgoing") resulted in very strong self-reference effects, while the self-reference effect was nearly absent with self-reference tasks involving nouns (e.g., "student" or "baseball player"). Also, there was no significant difference in the size of the self-reference effect when each person did both the self-reference and semantic tasks (within-subjects design) or when each person did only one or the other (between-subjects design).

More germane is their finding in regard to *other-referenced* tasks. In an other-referenced task, the subject is asked to determine whether a trait-word described some other person, rather than themselves. If the effect of the self in memory is simply to provide a good venue for organization and elaboration, then an other-referenced task that involves an intimate other (such as one's mother) should be as effective as a self-referenced task. Their review, however, showed that

self-reference led to better recall even in comparison to intimate others.

It would require more detail than space permits to review all the predictions and findings of Symons and Johnson's (1997) meta-analysis, but their conclusion is worth noting.

SR [self-reference] works best to facilitate memory when certain kinds of stimuli are used—stimuli that are commonly organized and elaborated on through SR. When these stimuli are used, however, SR appears to be a very efficient, possibly spontaneous mode...Our evidence suggests that SR is a uniquely efficient process; but it is probably unique only in the sense that, because it is a highly practiced task, it results in spontaneous, efficient processing of certain kinds of information that people deal with each day—material that is often used, well organized, and exceptionally well elaborated (p. 392).

Recently, the issue of the self in memory encoding has been explored using positron emission tomography, or PET scans (Craik et al., 1999). They found that self-referential encoding produced different patterns of brain activation than did orienting tasks not involving self-reference. Specifically, self-referential encoding shared the same pattern of activation of the left frontal lobes as the other orienting tasks, but it included activation of the right frontal lobes unique to self-referential encoding.

Methodological Considerations

Stimulus materials were constructed in a manner similar to that described by Rogers, Kuiper, and Kirker (1977). Eight lists of 48 words were constructed. Each consisted of equal numbers of structural, phonemic, semantic, and self-reference items, in a random order. The first four and last four items were fillers, intended to reduce any primacy or recency effects, and recall for those items was not scored. For the main part of the list, an initial list of 40 adjectives that could be self-descriptive traits was generated. Items for the phonemic task were other adjectives that rhyme with the items from the initial list. Items for the semantic task were synonyms of the 40 words on the initial list. Items for the structural task were adjectives (except the word "flies") that neither rhymed nor were synonymous with the items on the initial list. From these items, four lists were constructed. Each had 10 of the potentially self-referential adjectives. An additional 10 items from the initial list were paired either with items from the rhyming list or with non-rhyming words from the initial list. Another 10 items were paired with words from the synonym list or non-synonyms from the initial list. The remaining 10 items from each list were taken from the structural list. Finally, four additional lists were constructed by reversing the items from the original four lists, such that any word responded to by "Yes" on one list would elicit a "No" response on the reversed list. Each subject saw a single list, counterbalanced by subject number. Note that, since the self-reference items did not have an objectively correct answer, counterbalancing of "Yes" and "No" responses was not possible. For the same reason, recall of self-reference items was scored in relation to the answer given during the initial presentation when comparing "Yes" and "No" responses.

Each subject sees a single list of 48 items. On each trial, a cue question is presented, followed by the target item, which remains visible until the subject responds by indicating "Yes" or "No." There is a 2-second interval before the next cue question. Immediately following presentation of the list, the subjects have 3 minutes for free recall.

· · · · · · · · · · · · · · · · · · · ·
Expected Running Time = 10 minutes
· · · · · · · · · · · · · · · · · · · ·

Questions

1. Identify the independent and dependent variables, as well as any important controls. Tell why each control is needed.

2. Did a self-reference effect occur in your data? What indicates that it occurred (or that it did not occur)?

3. Symons and Johnson (1997) consider the possibility that what appears to be a *self*-reference effect may instead be an effect produced by the rating task itself, rather than by the rating specifically of self. What do they conclude?

4. In the discussion above, we have focused on the comparison of semantic and self-reference tasks. What about *other*-referenced tasks? Symons and Johnson treat the data and theoretical implications at some length. Does it matter whether the other person is well-known (such as a celebrity) or is known personally (such as a parent)? If we have well-developed concepts of significant others in our lives, might those function in much the same way as our self-construct?

Extension Experiments

1. An interesting finding that could be replicated easily is one by Rogers, Kuiper, and Rogers (1979) that trait terms such as those used in the self-reference task show a *symbolic distance effect*—if asked to judge which of two traits is more descriptive of them, subjects are faster if the two descriptors are far apart in self-descriptiveness than if they are similar. Interestingly, there is no congruity effect for self-referential traits.

2. Symons and Johnson (1997) do not report any studies that used the task reported by Craik and Tulving as their "deepest" level of processing, namely, "Can you use the word in this sentence? *The great bird swooped down and carried off the struggling ____.*" That condition resulted in much better recall than their semantic task. You could try adding that task. (It might be easiest to substitute that task for the structural task, making sure that half of the items plausibly could be carried off, struggling, by a great bird.)

Extension Experiments *(continued)*

3. See Extension Experiment 3 in Chapter 3.3, *Impression Formation.* The issue is memory for personality trait descriptors (e.g., "intelligent" or "reserved") depending on whether subjects were instructed simply to memorize them or were asked to form a personality impression based on them. This amounts to comparing retrieval following two different orienting tasks.

References

Atkinson, R. C., & Shiffrin, R. M. (1968). Human memory: A proposed system and its control processes. In K. W. Spence & J. T. Spence (Eds.), *The psychology of learning and motivation: Vol. 2* (pp.89-195). Orlando, FL: Academic Press.

Craik, F. I. M. (1979). Human memory. *Annual Review of Psychology, 30,* 63-102.

Craik, F. I. M., & Lockhart, R. S. (1972). Levels of processing: A framework for memory research. *Journal of Verbal Learning and Verbal Behavior, 11,* 671-684.

Craik, F. I. M., Moroz, T. M., Moscovitch, M., Stuss, D. T., Winocur, G., Tulving, E., et al. (1999). In search of the self: A positron emission tomography study. *Psychological Science, 10,* 26-34.

Craik, F. I. M., & Tulving, E. (1975). Depth of processing and the retention of words in episodic memory. *Journal of Experimental Psychology: General, 104,* 268-294.

Eysenck, M. W. (1979). Depth, elaboration, and distinctiveness. In L. S. Cermack & F. I. M. Craik (Eds.), *Levels of processing in human memory.* Hillsdale, NJ: Lawrence Erlbaum Associates

Hyde, T. S., & Jenkins, J. J. (1969). The differential effects of incidental tasks on the organization of recall of a list of highly associated words. *Journal of Experimental Psychology, 82,* 472-481.

Kihlstrom, J. F., & Klein, S. B. (1994). The self as knowledge structure. In R. S. Wyer, Jr. & T. K. Srull (Eds.), *Handbook of social cognition* (pp.153-208). Hillsdale, NJ: Lawrence Erlbaum Associates.

Neisser, U., & Jopling, D. A. (Eds.). (1997). *The conceptual self in context.* Cambridge: Cambridge University Press.

Nelson, T. O. (1977). Repetition and depth of processing. *Journal of Verbal Learning and Verbal Behavior, 16,* 151-171.

Reed, S. K. (1996). *Cognition: Theory and applications* (4th ed.). Pacific Grove, CA: Brooks/Cole.

Rogers, T. B., Kuiper, N. A., & Kirker, W. S. (1977). Self-reference and the encoding of personal information. *Journal of Personality and Social Psychology, 35,* 677-688.

Rogers, T. B., Kuiper, N. A., & Rogers, P. J. (1979). Symbolic difference and congruity effects for paired-comparison judgments of degree of self-reference. *Journal of Research in Personality, 13,* 433-449.

Rosenthal, R. (1983). Meta-analysis: Toward a more cumulative social science. *Applied Social Psychology Annual, 4,* 65-93.

Symons, C. S., & Johnson, B. T. (1997). The self-reference effect in memory: A meta-analysis. *Psychological Bulletin, 121,* 371-394.

3.5 Automaticity and Stereotyping

Abstract

A *stereotype* is an example of a categorical knowledge structure. When we use stereotypes, we make judgments of others based, not on their individual characteristics, but, rather, on their perceived group (category) membership and our memory for the characteristics we believe to be associated with that group. Common stereotypes are based on age (e.g., "Old people have poor memories."), race or ethnicity (e.g., "Asians are over-achievers."), appearance (e.g., "Blondes are ditzy."), religion (e.g., "Baptists are gospel singers."), and sex ("Men can never ask for directions."). Stereotypes, either positive or negative, sometimes have some grain of truth, but often also present an inaccurate depiction of a group. They are almost always inaccurate depictions of some individuals within the group. Most of us recognize that stereotyping is inherently unfair. Surely, it is better to judge people on their individual merits—for example, there are, in fact, many old people with great memories. Yet we continue to stereotype. Below, we consider some of the reasons that stereotyping occurs and the conditions under which it is controllable.

*I*n the experiment accompanying this chapter, you will replicate a study by Blair and Banaji (1996) on stereotyping of sex roles, which examines one of the central claims from the social-cognitive approach—namely, that stereotyping is an automatic process.

Theories and Metaphors of Stereotyping

Social cognition has emerged in recent years as a successful framework for understanding how people make sense of their social worlds. One of the earliest demonstrations of this approach was Bartlett's (1932) experiments on the ability of British undergraduates to recall a Native-American folk tale. He showed that they sometimes misremembered, and, when they did, the misremembering often reflected pre-existing beliefs. This confirmed the constructive nature of remembering, but it also showed that the more general claim also holds—that our evaluations and impressions of others, as well as our memories, are shaped by our previous knowledge and cultural assumptions about the world.

Fiske and Taylor (1984) characterized social perceivers as "cognitive misers." This account of social-cognitive functioning assumes that we rely on categorical knowledge structures in many cases because it is easier than the alternative, which is to form individual judgments about people. Gilbert and Hixon (1991) went even further, suggesting that people are "mental sluggards," preferring easy categorical judgments. They noted that "the stereotype is the sluggard's best friend" (p. 509).

Other metaphors have been offered. Fiske and Taylor (1991) characterized the social thinker as a "motivated tactician," trying to cope with limitations on information-processing in trying to make sense of the world. Macrae, Milne, and Bodenhausen (1994) referred to the social perceiver as an "efficiency expert" who relies on categorical thinking when the cognitive load is high—categorical thinking is simply more efficient. Oakes and Turner (1990) see the social perceiver as a "meaning seeker" who uses categorical thinking while trying to make sense of a complex social world.

Whatever the specific metaphor, it is clear that we often use categorical knowledge of groups to guide our perception and evaluation of others.

Stereotyping and Automaticity

One noteworthy theoretical advance in cognitive psychology that has had enormous impact on social cognition is the development of the concept of *automaticity*, which is treated more fully in Chapter 2.8, *Automatic versus Controlled Processing*. (Additionally, Chapter 1.5, *Attentional Interference and The Stroop Effect* illustrates the automaticity of reading in skilled readers.) The basic idea is that certain mental or motor routines can be automatic, in the sense that—given the right stimulus situation—the routine will be carried out. A classic example is that of an experienced driver stopping at a stop sign. If you have been driving for a number of years, you know that this seems to happen without thinking about it—almost as though your foot put itself on the brake. This illustrates the nature of an automatic process—it requires no effort, it is very difficult to control, and it occurs with little or no conscious, deliberate, decision-making. (Controlled processes have the opposite characteristics.)

Earlier research on stereotyping, while not using the modern vocabulary of automaticity, nevertheless suggested that aspects of person perception, such as stereotyping, occur largely unwittingly. Allport (1954) was among the first

to argue that categorical knowledge, or—to use Bartlett's (1932) term—"schematic" knowledge, often determines how we evaluate and respond to others. "Every event has certain marks that serve as a cue to bring the category of prejudgment into action… A person with dark brown skin will activate whatever concept of Negro is dominant in our mind" (Allport, 1954, p. 21).

One issue facing automaticity theories of stereotyping is that automaticity appears to be a matter of degree. Bargh (1994) argued that few routines meet all of the criteria for automaticity. Others have made similar points, including Logan (1989) who noted that "automatic reactions can be modulated by attention and intention; they can be inhibited and suppressed; and they can be coherent and planful" (p. 70).

Blair and Banaji (1996) usefully distinguish between an automatic *activation* of stereotypes given situational cues (such as a person's age, race, size, sex, etc.) and the *application* of the stereotype to judgments about a person, which, they suggest, are more easily controlled.

While stereotype activation appears to be a (largely) automatic process, thus accounting for the difficulty of controlling stereotyping, there is research that suggests circumstances under which we can successfully avoid stereotyping. Maskowitz et al. (1999) showed that people could avoid race- and sex-based stereotyping when they had a chronic, automatic goal of fairness. In other words, we can automate a habit of not stereotyping! Blair and Banaji (1996), in a follow-up to the experiment that accompanies this chapter, showed that subjects who were asked to assume a counter-stereotypic intention (and who had enough time to activate such intentions) actually could reverse their stereotypical responses. Blair and Banaji (1996, p. 1143) cite a number of studies showing that stereotyping can be reduced under some circumstances.

We will not attempt here to review the literature on automaticity and stereotyping in any detail—it is too large a task and would require a book of its own. But notions of automaticity fit nicely with ideas of stereotyping and cognitive economy. Macrae and Bodenhause (2001) review the literature about "the puzzling issue of exactly when perceivers use generic knowledge structures, such as stereotypes, to guide their dealing with others" (p. 241). Blair and Banaji (1996) also review the literature on automaticity and stereotyping, as do Macrae, et al. (1997). Bargh and Ferguson (2000) present an excellent overview of automaticity research. They also develop at length the implications of a cognitive determinism—the proposition that "for *every* psychological effect (e.g., behavior, emotion,

judgment, memory, perception) there exists a set of causes, of antecedent conditions, that uniquely lead to that effect" (p. 925).

There are a number of demonstrations of the essentially automatic nature of the evaluation of social objects, including words, faces, pictures, and odors (see Bargh and Ferguson, 2000, p. 931, for a review). Blair and Banaji's (1996) study is but one of these. However, it is one of the most straight-forward and thus was chosen to demonstrate this important aspect of social cognition. Banaji and Hardin (1996) report very similar studies.

Methodological Considerations

The accompanying experiment builds on a tradition of *priming* studies, such as those of Meyer and Schwaneveldt (1971)—see Chapter 2.1, *Lexical Decisions*. A more immediate predecessor is Neely (1991).

The basic paradigm used by Blair and Banaji (1996) for demonstrating automaticity of stereotyping involves presenting a word that stereotypically is associated with a social category (in this case, sex), and which is intended to *prime*, or activate, the stereotype. That prime is followed by a stimulus to which the subject must respond, often called the *imperative stimulus*. In this case, the imperative stimulus is a name, which the subject must classify as quickly as possible as either a male or female name. If the reaction time (RT) to the imperative stimulus changes with the nature of the prime, then a *priming effect* has been shown. That priming effect does not, in itself, demonstrate automatic stereotyping. But Blair and Banaji argue (following Neely, 1977) that the *stimulus onset asynchrony* (SOA),[21] or delay between the prime and the imperative stimulus, of only 350 ms precludes the use of a deliberate, effortful, controlled process. In other words, there is not enough time for a controlled process to take place; therefore, any effect of the prime on RT to the imperative stimulus must be due to an automatic process.

Note that the names used in this experiment are chosen to be clearly male or female names (e.g., John or Mary). Names that are ambiguous in their sex (e.g., Leslie, Pat) were omitted. Note that there is a constraint on this experiment in that it would presumably work only with people for whom the primes are, in fact, stereotypical, and for whom the names are familiar as male or female names. Thus, persons whose native language is not English may not show the effect as clearly—obviously depending on their degree of familiarity with the language and culture. This is one reason that the names are restricted largely to "traditional" English names, and do not include names that might not be as widely familiar.

---

[21] Another term for SOA is the *interstimulus interval*, or ISI. The choice of terms is arbitrary.

Methodological Considerations *(continued)*

The primes and names used in this experiment were those originally used by Blair and Banaji (1996) in their Experiment 1 (see their p. 1162). Because they found no stereotyping effect for trait words, we omitted those, and used only their nontrait words as primes. (All neutral primes were nontrait words).

The valence (positive vs. negative) of the primes was established by Blair and Banaji by having 12 undergraduates rate the words on a 7-point scale from "least likeable" to "most likeable." The prime words actually used in the study were those clearly rated as positive or negative.

Blair and Banaji also chose the primes so that they were approximately equal in length and frequency, based on the Kučera and Francis (1967) norms.

· ·
Expected Running Time = 20 minutes
· ·

Questions

1. What are the dependent and independent variables in this experiment? What are some important controls?

2. In Blair and Banaji's (1996) research, primes were classified as masculine (e.g., cigar, mechanic), feminine (e.g., cosmetics, nurse), or neutral (e.g., tree, lice). Prime words were also classified as trait (e.g., "caring" as a feminine trait, "logical" as a male trait) versus nontrait (e.g., "ballet" as feminine, "bald" as masculine). In addition, the primes were classified by valence (positive, negative). Examples of feminine and masculine positive primes were flowers and sports, respectively. Examples of feminine and masculine negative primes were housework and hunting, respectively. They included both male and female subjects. What was their result? Did RT to the sex of the names depend on the prime gender? Did the sex of the subjects matter? Did valence and type (trait, nontrait) of prime matter?

3. Can stereotyping be reversed, and, if so, how? See Blair and Banaji's (1996) Experiments 3 and 4.

Extension Experiments

1. The word lists used by Blair and Banaji for the experiment replicated here were the same as those used for their Experiments 3 and 4, except for changes in the way the primes and target names were paired. Those experiments also differed in the SOA and the introduction of a counter-stereotyping strategy. They reported that they could induce subjects to reverse the usual stereotyping.

References

Banaji, M., & Hardin, C. (1996). Automatic stereotyping. *Psychological Science, 7,* 136-141.

Bargh, J. A. (1994). The four horsemen of automaticity: Awareness, intention, efficiency, and control in social cognition. In R. S. Wyer & T. K. Srull (Eds.), *Handbook of social cognition: Vol. 1. Basic processes* (pp. 1-40). Hillsdale, NJ: Lawrence Erlbaum Associates.

Bargh, J. (1997). The automaticity of everyday life. In R. Wyer (Ed.), *Advances in Social Cognition: Vol. X. The automaticity of everyday life* (pp. 1-61). Mahwah, NJ: Erlbaum.

Bargh, J., & Ferguson, M. (2000). Beyond behaviorism: On the automaticity of higher mental processes. *Psychological Bulletin, 126,* 925-945.

Bartlett, F. C. (1932). *Remembering: A study in experimental and social psychology.* Cambridge, UK: Cambridge University Press.

Blair, I., & Banaji, M. (1996). Automatic and controlled processes in stereotype priming. *Journal of Personality and Social Psychology, 70,* 1142-1163.

Fiske, S. T., & Taylor S. E. (1984). *Social cognition* (1st ed.). Reading, MA: Addison-Wesley.

Fiske, S. T., & Taylor S. E. (1991). *Social cognition* (2nd ed.). New York: McGraw-Hill.

Gilbert, D. T., & Hixon, J. G. (1991). The trouble of thinking: Activation and application of stereotypic beliefs. *Journal of Personality and Social Psychology, 60,* 509-517.

Kučera, H., & Francis, W. (1967). *Computational analysis of present-day American English.* Providence, RI: Brown University Press.

Logan, G. (1989). Automaticity and cognitive control. In J. S. Uleman & J. Bargh (Eds.), *Unintended thought* (pp. 52-74). New York: Guilford.

Macrae, C. N., & Bodenhausen, G. V. (2001). Social cognition: Categorical person perception. *British Journal of Psychology, 92,* 239-255.

Macrae, C. N., Bodenhausen, G. V., Milne, A. B., Thorn, T. M. J., & Castelli, L. (1997). On the activation of social stereotypes: The moderating role of processing objectives. *Journal of Experimental Social Psychology, 33,* 471-489.

References *(continued)*

Macrae, C. N., Milne, A. B., & Bodenhausen, G. V. (1994). Stereotypes as energy-saving devices: A peek inside the cognitive toolbox. *Journal of Personality and Social Psychology, 66,* 37-47.

Meyer, D. E., & Schvaneveldt, R. W. (1971). Facilitation in recognizing pairs of words: Evidence of a dependence upon retrieval operations. *Journal of Experimental Psychology, 90,* 227-234.

Moskowitz, G., Wasel, W., Goldwitzer, P. W., & Schaal, B. (1999). Preconscious control of stereotype activation through chronic egalitarian goals. *Journal of Personality and Social Psychology, 77,* 167-184.

Neely, J. (1977). Semantic priming and retrieval from lexical memory: Roles of inhibitionless spreading activation and limited-capacity attention. *Journal of Experimental Psychology: General, 106,* 226-254.

Neely, J. (1991). Semantic priming effects in visual word recognition: A selective review of current findings and theories. In D. Besner & G. Humphreys (Eds.), *Basic research in reading: Visual word recognition* (pp. 264-336). Hillsdale, NJ: Erlbaum.

Oakes, P. J., & Turner, J. C. (1990). Is limited information processing the cause of social stereotyping? In W. Stroebe & M. Hewstone (Eds.), *European review of social psychology* (Vol. 1, pp. 111-135). Chichester, UK: Wiley.

3.6 Survey Research

Abstract

While much of PsychMate is concerned with experimental research, many researchers in psychology also rely on questionnaires of various kinds to explore both individual differences (for example, scales to measure personality traits) and social-psychological problems such as attitudes towards various social issues. Of course, surveys and questionnaires also are used by sociologists and public-opinion pollsters for studying similar issues. In this chapter, we present some basic information about surveys and questionnaires, including their construction and analysis, and issues of sampling. This brief presentation makes no claim to treat the topic of survey research in more than an introductory manner, and the student is advised to consult one (or several) of the many textbooks on survey research for more details. The reference list at the end of this chapter includes several books that may be helpful.

This chapter is organized very differently from the other PsychMate chapters. The whole chapter is really concerned with **methodological considerations**.

We begin with some suggestions for surveys that you might want to carry out. Next, we address a number of issues of item construction, sampling, and data analysis. Finally, there are two actual surveys that are replicated in the accompanying software. Your instructor has the data from the original surveys.

Suggestions for Surveys

A problem confronting the student who is interested in carrying out a survey as a class assignment or project is to identify a topic for the survey, an appropriate population from which to sample, and a means of sampling. Herewith are two suggestions. In the section below on *sampling*, we give a detailed discussion of how you might sample from (a) students on your campus and (b) citizens in your community.

Replicating a Published Poll

One good approach is to find a public opinion poll of some kind and then administer that same

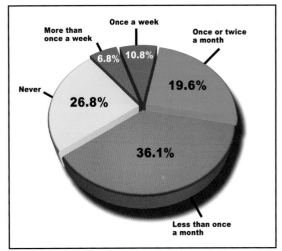

FIGURE 3.6.1 – *Use of a pie chart to graphically present the results of a poll item. This pie chart might represent the results of asking undergraduates how often they call home during the term.*

poll (or some questions from it) to a new sample taken from your community or from students at your college. An excellent source for poll results are the journals *Public Opinion* and *Public Opinion Quarterly*, both of which are published by the American Association for Public Opinion Research (***www.aapor.org***). A great resource for recent polls on a wide variety of issues is available at ***www.pollingreport.com***. Many of the articles there are devoted to discussing the

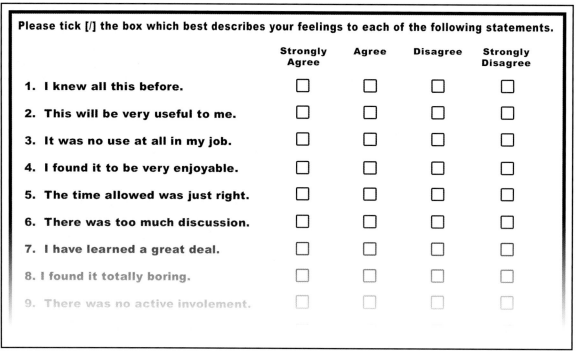

FIGURE 3.6.2 – An example of a Likert scale with four choices.

results of all kinds of polls. Another source is the *General Social Survey* (information is available at **www.norc.uchicago.edu/projects/ gensoc.asp**). If you can find a poll that was based on a national sample of college students, you could do an interesting comparison of your campus to the national figures.

Several recent polls that have questioned under-graduates concerning their knowledge of world events, geography, history, and so on usually have found a rather low level of knowledge. It might be interesting to replicate such a poll, especially if you think your school would do very well. Of course, one limitation of such polls is that they don't usually *compare* the undergradu-ates to another sample (say, of college-educated adults). This limitation means that you really can draw few conclusions. Are students really less well-prepared than they used to be? You should consider, if you undertake this kind of poll, how you can sample from a relevant control group. While the faculty at your school are hardly

representative of the whole adult population, they are handy. And a comparison of students to faculty might prove interesting, whether the survey is based on knowledge, attitude, or belief.

Making Your Own Poll

If you choose to write your own poll, instead of replicating an existing one, you may find that the most convenient populations from which to sample are students at your college or university and citizens of the city where you live. Possible topic areas include subjects of current interest to students or the community, such as crime on campus, the quality of dorm life and cafeteria food, attitudes toward city government, prefer-ences in an upcoming local election, opinions about local public schools, and many others. Try to choose a topic about which people are likely to have an interest. This not only makes it easier to get people to respond, but it also means that the responses will be less haphazard than if you ask for opinions on something about which your respondents know little and care nothing.

The field of survey research is too vast to permit us to give you more than general background information. We recommend that you also consult standard references. *The Survey Kit*, with Arlene Fink (2002) as series editor, is one of the best references available. It consists of a set of brief books covering various areas of survey research, such as sampling, analysis of survey data, telephone surveying, and item design. The second edition includes information on web-based surveys. Earl Babbie's (2001) *The Practice of Social Research*, now in its 10th edition, is another standard text, though it goes beyond just survey research. Krosnick (1999) provides a useful review of a number of issues in survey research.

Ethical Considerations

Before discussing the construction of surveys and issues of sampling, we need to address some ethical problems that easily can arise, especially when sampling from students on your campus.

Informed consent to participate is a necessary part of *any* research using human subjects. Surveys do not have a major problem in this regard, since it is difficult to force people to take a poll against their will. The mere fact that they agree to participate establishes informed consent, since they know precisely what question they are answering—no deception is possible. But problems can arise. **Do not use fraternity or sorority pledge classes as respondents.** If you are in a fraternity or sorority, this might seem like an easy way to get some subjects. However, such persons likely will not feel that they can refuse a request from a fraternity brother or sorority sister to participate. If that is the case (and note that you probably will have no way to tell), then informed consent has *not* been obtained. (In addition to the ethical problem, this group would hardly constitute a representative sample of college students.) Opinion polls are sometimes (but not always) exempt from review by your university's Institutional Review Board (IRB). Consult the IRB before beginning to collect data.

Confidentiality is another potential problem. Respondents have an absolute right to assume that their individual responses will *not* be made public or used against them. Be sure that the survey data are recorded in such a manner that individual respondents cannot be identified later. This is best accomplished by simply not recording the respondents' names. If you do keep a temporary list of names, destroy it as soon as it is no longer needed. Remember that **you** have the responsibility to maintain confidentiality. This is not an abstract principle: **Do not discuss a respondent's individual answers with *anyone*** in a manner that will identify the respondent. That includes your friends, other students with whom you are working on the survey, and the instructor. (Of course, you might have a respondent ask you about various items at a later time. In that case, they are revealing their responses, and you have no ethical problem.)

Revealing how a fellow student responded may seem innocuous, and in many cases it is hard to see how any harm could come. But keep in mind that violating confidentiality may make it harder for you to get additional respondents or may make future surveys by other classes impossible.

Construction of Questionnaires

The construction of good surveys or questionnaires is not an easy task. Our own biases and hidden assumptions can shape the items in ways that seriously affect the responses. We hope that the following discussion can aid you in avoiding some pitfalls. Unfortunately, there are no rules that guarantee success. There is one rule that can at least help you avoid some mistakes: *Always pretest the survey items.* The most careful researcher may sometimes write a bad item. By having a number of people critique the items before they are used, you may at least manage to eliminate ones that are clearly inadequate.

General Considerations

One of the immediate difficulties faced in writing a survey or questionnaire concerns the problem of defining and measuring the concepts in which you are interested. To illustrate: Suppose that you want to survey students at your college or university concerning their attitudes toward religion. You could just ask them to rate their attitude as positive or negative. But, clearly, this leaves a lot to be desired, since attitudes about religion could vary in the *degree* to which they are positive or negative. You could instead ask subjects to give a rating of their attitude along a scale with several points, such as strongly positive, positive, neutral, negative, and strongly negative. But even this may not do so well, since it fails to define "religion." Some persons may feel negatively toward "organized" religion but still feel that religious belief plays a very positive role in their lives. "Religion" may mean vastly different things to different people, so that they are, in effect, answering different questions! In addition, a single item testing this attitude may not serve as well as a series of items designed to reflect different aspects of religion: How often do you attend church? Are you a member of a church? Do you believe that religion is a force for good in the world? (Of course, the use of multiple items attempting to assess the same basic construct then leads to the difficulty of whether or how to combine those items into an overall score of "attitude toward religion." A score based on the average of a set of related items is called a *scale score*.)

The point here is not that *religion* is hard to define and attitudes toward it hard to measure, but that most social constructs, and the terms used to describe them, are ambiguous. But too often we believe that we "know" what a term (like *religion*) means. This belief may not pose a problem if the respondents to the survey share that meaning, but we cannot assume that they do.

The issue of what we assume words to mean is part of the point of the survey called "What is

sex?" that accompanies this chapter. If you ask a person in a poll if they have engaged in sex in the last month, what do they think you mean? The answer is not as straightforward as you might expect.

Content of Items

Survey items usually address one of three content areas: facts, beliefs, and feelings or attitudes. Items dealing with facts are perhaps the easiest to write: Do you contribute to the United Way? Do you use the public library? Do you use Brand X? This class of items usually can be made clear and unambiguous, but may still lead to problems if asking about past behavior. Limitations of memory and availability of the information must be taken into account. A pretest should identify any items that respondents might misinterpret.

Items dealing with beliefs would include such things as: Does the United Way spend your contribution on the most important community needs? Does the public library have the types of books you enjoy reading? Does Brand X get your clothes cleaner than your previous brand? Availability of information is again important. If a pretest indicates that most respondents do not know anything about the content area, then you may want to revise or omit the item, since people will often respond even when they have no knowledge, leading to very "noisy" data.

Feelings and attitudes also can be assessed with surveys, using items such as: How do you feel about the United Way? Do you approve of the way the President is handling his job? Do you enjoy doing laundry? Survey items designed to elicit information about feelings and attitudes often may be more difficult to construct than those simply asking for information because they are more likely to be ambiguous and to depend on context. The same person who admires the President's handling of domestic issues may be disturbed by his foreign policy, for example. In that case, the subject's answer to a question about approval of the President's handling of his

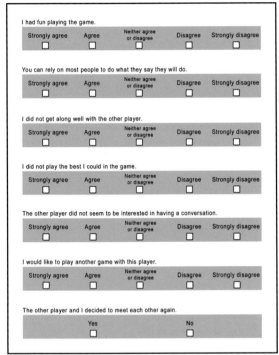

FIGURE 3.6.3 – Example of a survey employing a 5-choice Likert scale.

job may depend on which context (foreign or domestic) is most readily recalled or most recently in the news.

Types of Items

A number of types of items are available for use on surveys. These can take the form of questions ("Do you know anyone who has used illegal drugs?") or statements ("I believe that the death penalty is a deterrent to crime.") with which the respondent must indicate a degree of agreement. You should not feel that you are restricted to only a single type of item—a combination often is used. Suit the item to the information you are trying to gain. No single type is best for all purposes.

In addition to choosing the forms of the items, you also must choose the form of the answers. Answers can be indicated in an *open-ended* or *closed-ended* fashion. In the former, no limit is put on the choice of answers, while in the latter the respondent must choose from the available responses. Open-ended questions have the advantage of not forcing the responses into a

preconceived "mold," but have the serious disadvantage of often being difficult to analyze, especially if the respondent gives long answers. Closed-ended questions have the advantage of ease of scoring, but you must be sure that the alternatives offered cover all relevant categories. The following particularly bad example was actually used on a survey. Respondents were asked to indicate their religion, with alternatives of "Protestant," "Catholic," "Hindu," "Moslem," or "None." Not only are many religions (Judaism, Buddhism, etc.) omitted entirely, but no "Other" category is offered. Are Buddhism and atheism really the same thing? To make matters even worse, many Christians do not regard themselves as either Catholic or Protestant. These include members of the Greek and Russian Orthodox churches, Mormons, and many evangelicals. Krosnick (1999) reviews the literature on the issues concerning open- and closed-ended questions.

Responses to questions and statements are often measured along a scale. One example is the Likert scale, which consists of a series of graded responses indicating degree of agreement with a statement, such as strongly agree, agree, neutral, disagree, strongly disagree (see Figure 3.6.3). Scales usually have from 5 to 9 response categories with which to indicate strength of agreement. Of course, the scale also could be labeled to indicate degree of approval/disapproval, belief/disbelief, or some other dimension. The number of response categories to permit should be neither too large nor too small. With fewer than five categories a problem will arise because respondents tend to avoid the most extreme response categories. At the other extreme, nine categories is about as many as respondents can reliably discriminate. Krosnick (1999) discusses this issue in more detail.

Pretesting

If at all possible, you should perform a pretest of your survey. Pretesting usually involves several interviewers each conducting a small number of surveys, then meeting to discuss their impressions. If a question frequently required further explanation or if many people declined to answer it, you should probably make a change in the item.

Pitfalls

No list of problems that can arise in writing survey items can be exhaustive, but a few can be pointed out.

Clarity. Items should be readily understood. Do not assume that the respondent will know the latest jargon about governmental (or other) matters. An item like "Do you support increased funding for SIDS research?" may well lead to a blank stare instead of an answer, unless the respondent is familiar with the Sudden Infant Death Syndrome (SIDS). Respondents may feel obliged to provide an answer or may not want to appear ignorant, so they give a meaningless answer to what is (to them, and therefore is, in fact) a meaningless question. Again, pretesting may reveal the problem. We are all so close to some areas of our own knowledge that things we take utterly for granted, such as acronyms like SIDS, may be pure gobbledygook to most people.

Items are sometimes unclear because they really ask two questions at once. Suppose respondents are asked to rate their agreement with the following statement: "Military spending is too high, and the money could better be used to clean up the environment." If they say they agree, just what are they agreeing to? One could surely favor reducing military spending without necessarily wanting the government to spend the money on something else! It would be better to first ask about military spending and then to ask those who favor reducing it the additional question of how the savings should be used.

Length. Most respondents will expect to be able to read or hear and understand an item quickly. Long items may not be understood thoroughly, leading to responses that are not truly indicative of the respondent's views. There is often a

tradeoff between length and clarity, and the researcher must weigh that balance. Pretesting can help identify items that are either unclear or too long.

Negative items. Avoid these; they may be misunderstood or misread. Asking respondents to rate their agreement with "The death penalty is a deterrent to crime" will cause fewer misunderstandings than the same rating of agreement with "The death penalty is not a deterrent to crime." If the respondent overlooks the "not" in the statement, he or she may well give the opposite answer from what was intended.

"Biased" items. There are many kinds of bias that can creep into questions, and they cannot all be detailed here. The main point, though, is to avoid wording questions in ways that might make certain types of answers unacceptable. Imagine a question like this: "Do you agree with Adolph Hitler's view that communism will ultimately fail?" Even an ardent anti-communist might not want to appear to be associating himself with Hitler. A positive bias can occur as well in an item such as "The President has warned that we face a growing trade deficit and recommends increased tariffs. Do you agree that increased tariffs are the best solution?" A respondent who has no real opinion of his or her own may reply "Yes" simply based on the President's endorsement.

"Personal" questions. Try to provide alternatives that make it easy for the respondent to reply. For example, it is best not to simply ask people to report their income. Many will feel this is highly intrusive. Asking them instead to indicate into which range of income they fall will often work much better. "Do you earn (a) less than $20,000 per year? (b) more than $20,000 but less than $40,000," etc., is less likely to make the respondent ill-at-ease. Additionally, you should avoid starting a survey with personal questions. Save them for later, when the respondent has relaxed a little and gotten accustomed to the types of questions you are asking.

Ordering of Questions

The ordering of the questions within a survey also may affect the outcome. Imagine, for example, a survey that has a series of questions about the respondent's perception of drug use in the community, followed by a question like "What is the greatest problem facing America today?" You should not be surprised if they rate drug use as one of the worst problems, since you just spent a few minutes bringing it to their attention. The same question asked of the same person in a more neutral context might well elicit a different answer.

Sampling

Populations and Samples

The principle purpose of most surveys is *not* to find out what the *specific* respondents interviewed feel about an issue, but rather to use their answers to try to estimate how the whole community, state, or nation feels. In other words, we use our *sample* to try to estimate something about the whole *population*. A population consists of everyone of the type being studied.

That might mean all adults, all likely voters, all students at your college or university, all citizens of the United States, or all of whatever group you are interested in. If you want to know how the citizens of your city feel about some recent political event, you could, of course, simply ask them all. You could then say with precision that (at least on a certain date), say, 74.2% opposed a bond issue for new schools, while 11.6% favored it, with the rest having not made up their minds. Here, the population is all voters in the town, but clearly you cannot reasonably expect to interview every single one of them, unless you live in a very small town! A major issue for survey research, then, is how to restrict yourself to a small enough number of interviews that you can get the job done, but still have the results reflect the whole population. To do this, you must select a sample of voters in the community. If you are careful in your selection, you can then make reasonable (though not perfect) predictions, based on your sample, about what percent of the whole population have a certain opinion.

Sample Selection

In selecting a sample from a population, the single most important issue is whether the sample is *representative* of the population. If it is not, then the whole survey is simply a waste of time. A number of approaches can be taken for sampling, but the most common is some variety of *random* sampling. The basic idea behind random sampling is to select members of the population in such a manner that each member has the same probability of being in the sample. If this is done, then the proportions of different groups in the sample should be about the same as their proportions in the population. Several problems arise, however. In a large population, it may be nearly impossible in practice to randomly select individual people. In addition, random samples can vary in their characteristics from those of the population. While this does not happen often, it can happen. Several modifications of "simple" random sampling have been developed, and a few are outlined here. Follow-

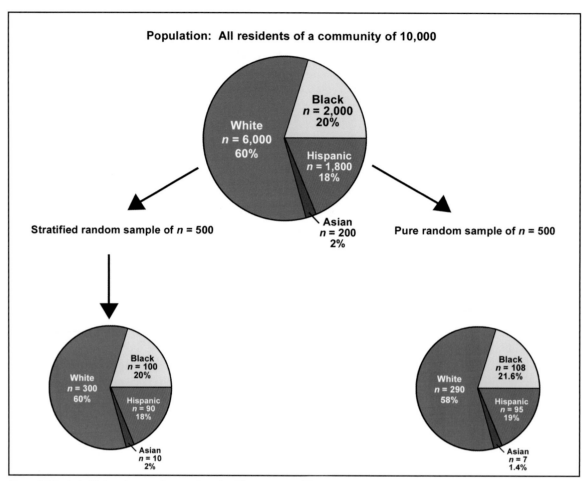

Figure 3.6.4 – *A stratified random sample guarantees that different groups will be represented in the correct proportions. With pure random samples, the sample proportions will vary somewhat from the true population proportions. In this example, Whites and Asians were slightly undersampled, while Blacks and Hispanics were slightly oversampled.*

ing that, there is a brief discussion of how to choose randomly among a set of elements.

Stratified random sampling. An approach used by most public opinion polls is to select respondents randomly, but with a constraint—namely, that the proportions of different types of respondents must fit the proportions of the population. Thus, if African-Americans make up 12% of the national population, they should make up 12% of the sample, and so on for other groups. The variables (ethnicity, in this example) that define the strata should be ones that are likely to affect the outcome of the survey, and you then randomly select persons within a stratum. The strata to choose will depend on the type of population and the type of survey. For example, national opinion polls at election time often stratify on sex, race, religion, party preference, age, and region of the country, since each of these is known to be related to voting patterns in national elections. For other populations and other issues, very different strata might be chosen. For a stratified random sample of students at your college or university, for example, you might stratify on year in school and major. The main thing to remember is that a stratified random sample will result in certain variables (the strata) being guaranteed to be represented in the sample in the same proportions as in the population (see Figure 3.6.4).

Clustering represents another modification of simple random sampling. Suppose that you wanted to collect a state-wide sample of high-school students. Getting a list of all high-school students in the state and then randomly selecting from that list would be an arduous task, to say the least. A way to reduce the problem to manageable size would be to first take a random sample of high schools, and then get a random sample of students within each school. The randomly chosen schools from which the randomly chosen samples came are thus the "clusters" for our sample.

Clustering also offers a solution to a problem encountered in telephone surveys. If you randomly sample from the listing of numbers in the telephone book you will be missing some of the 10-25% of households that have unlisted numbers. Randomly generated telephone numbers are a way around this, but at any time a large proportion of the possible numbers within a given prefix are not in use, resulting in a great deal of wasted time. A way to avoid this is to call a single number within each cluster of 100 numbers (such as 424-6300 to 424-6399). If it is not a number in use, then eliminate that cluster (e.g., 6300-6399) from further calling, since most of the rest of those numbers also will be unused. If the number is in use, then interview that person and keep calling numbers in that cluster until some pre-set number is reached (say 5 responses), then begin looking for another cluster. This is likely to reduce the number of calls to non-working numbers to only 50% or so (high, but not as high as 80%!), and it will include a random sample of unlisted numbers.

Other techniques. Other techniques of sampling are available, and books on survey research will detail them. One we will note briefly here is to combine stratification with clustering. In the example above of selecting a sample of high-school students by first selecting a sample of high schools, you might want to also impose stratification, selecting rural, small town, and big city high schools in proper proportion to the

population, and then randomly selecting your clusters of high schools from within each stratum. You might also then stratify within each selected cluster (school), so that males and females, and different classes, are represented in the correct proportions. You would then randomly sample individuals within each stratum (sex, class).

How _not_ to sample. A word of caution is needed about one method _not_ to use in selecting a sample. You have doubtless seen "reader's polls" conducted by popular magazines, television shows, and newspaper columnists, who ask their readers to call a "900" number or to fill out a card and send it in. The results are then tabulated and presented as meaningful information about the general population. _Do not be fooled._ At the absolute best, these samples are representative only of the readers of that magazine or column. They usually are not even that good, however, since the sample was _self-selected_: Only people who really wanted to do so responded. If the survey concerns anything at all controversial (say, opinions on abortion or gay marriage), the sample is probably only representative of people who read that magazine _and_ who have a strong opinion on the issue. People who do not have a firm opinion, and people who do not have an extreme opinion, are far less likely to respond to such a poll. That bias can make it appear that people are terribly polarized about an issue, when, in fact, most people hold views somewhere in the middle. The result is that such "unscientific" polls are uninterpretable. (Of course, self-selection may operate in a random sample, since not everyone will be willing to complete the survey. But unless respondents with one particular view are far more likely than others to refuse to complete a survey, there should be little systematic bias, and people with extreme views will almost certainly not predominate.) Note, no matter how strong or large the self-selected group's opinion is (e.g., of ten thousand surveyed, 90% agree), it _cannot_ be assumed to provide a useful estimate of a larger unselected population.

Sample Size

How large does a sample need to be? The easy answer is "As large as possible." But please keep in mind that **the size of a sample can never be large enough if the sample is not representative.** The selection of the sample size is rather complex—and beyond the scope of this workbook (see the references—especially Fink, 2002, or other books on survey methodology). The general approach, however, involves the notion of a *confidence interval*, which you may have encountered in a statistics course. You probably have heard the results of opinion polls on the news, reporting the percentage of people who favor or oppose some view or candidate. That discussion usually contains a statement something like "This poll has a *margin of error* of plus or minus three percentage points." The margin of error (MoE) is the same as the 95% confidence interval. A 95% confidence interval of MoE of 3% means that if 45% of the respondents in the *sample* favored candidate X, we can be 95% certain that the true percentage in the *population* was between 42% and 48% (45% plus or minus 3%). (That is, we can assume that if we repeated the poll 100 times, the sample proportion favoring candidate X would be between 42 and 48% in 95 or more of those 100 samples.) The general approach to determining sample size is to turn that on its head. Instead of asking what the confidence interval is, given your sample size, you can choose how accurate you want the sample to be (within 3%, 1%, 10%, or whatever) and then find the sample size that will yield that level of accuracy when estimating a population proportion from a sample proportion.

You should keep in mind that you do not need as large a sample if you are not interested in comparing sub-groups of the sample. For example, if you want to compare the proportions of males and females favoring a candidate or holding a given view, then a larger sample size will be needed than if you are interested only in determining what proportion of the general population holds that view. For national polls before a presidential election, the margin of error for a sample of 1500

likely voters is usually about 3%. But if the same poll is used to predict the results in a single state (where the sample size is much less), the MoE may be much larger, rendering the poll useless for state-by-state predictions.

An issue related to sample size is *response rate*. What proportion of the persons asked actually complete the survey? In national telephone surveys the response rate is usually less than 60% (Krosnick, 1999). There has been a long-standing assumption that surveys with low response rates are not representative, though recent research has questioned this assumption. Krosnick (1999) reviews the issue.

Sampling from Your School or Community

Students at your school and citizens of your community make good populations from which to sample for a class project. Several considerations in such sampling are given below.

Sampling randomly. Selection of a random sample from your school can be done fairly easily, since most schools publish a campus directory. (A few students may have asked to be omitted from that directory, but they should be few enough to cause no problems.) One scheme would be to randomly select a page number (using a table of random numbers or computer-generated random numbers), then randomly select an entry on that page. Simply continue this until you have enough names on your list, then contact each of those persons and ask them to complete the survey (by phone, by mail, or in face-to-face interviews).

A random sample of either people or households in your community may be a bit more difficult. If you plan to do a mail survey, check to see whether a city directory is published that would list all addresses. For a telephone survey, you could use the local telephone directory, the city directory, or random numbers added to the three-digit prefixes used locally. (See the discussion above concerning telephone survey sampling.)

Stratification. If you use a stratified random sample, the choice of the strata will depend in part on the nature of the survey. Some general considerations for sampling from students at your school might include the following. Stratify on sex of the respondent, matching your sample to the proportions of males and females at your school. Stratify on whether a person is a member of a fraternity or sorority, with independents and "greeks" represented in your sample in the same proportions as in the population of all students. Stratify on class standing (freshman, sophomore, etc.), again matching your sample to the proportions in the population (usually more freshmen than seniors, if some people drop out). You might also choose to stratify on the basis of college (Liberal Arts, Engineering, Business, etc.) or major—or both. The registrar at your school can provide you with a breakdown of how many students are in each college or major.

If your population of interest is the community, you will face somewhat different problems. Stratification by sex is relatively easy. You certainly want to avoid having your sample be unrepresentative in regard to "socio-economic status," but this is difficult to determine without extensive questioning that many respondents will find invasive. A good strategy to adopt would be to stratify on location within the community. If you use a map, you can keep track of the locations of the households surveyed, and you can then be sure that all sections of the community are represented. This should lead to reasonably good representation of wealth, ethnicity, and other factors.

The Surveys

Two surveys are included in the accompanying software. They are discussed briefly here. Your instructor has the full data for both surveys. In both cases, we have simplified the data to some degree.

Both of the surveys are available for you to complete in the PsychMate student software. Please note, however, that your data are NOT logged and will not be available for analysis. Because the research methods course sometimes has fairly small enrollments, even the limited demographic data collected could serve to identify individual students. Given the nature of the surveys, that is not acceptable.

One survey, "What is Sex?", which used college students as subjects, concerns their perceptions of what kinds of behaviors constitute "having sex" (Forbes, Adams-Curtis, Jobe, Quisenberry, & White, 2004). One point of this survey is that simply asking people if they have had sex may give misleading information, since the specific behaviors that are viewed as "having sex" differ from person to person. A physician asking a young patient about his or her sexual history may be making erroneous assumptions about what the replies mean!

The other survey, "Tattoos and Piercings," concerns the incidence of body piercing and tattooing among college students (Forbes, 2001). Tattooing and body piercing (other than ear-lobes) have traditionally been regarded as seriously deviant behavior by many people. Over the last decade or so, however, that has changed a lot. This survey asked students about their own tattoos and piercings, the reasons for getting them, perceptions of pierced/tattooed people, and reasons for NOT having piercings or tattoos.

NOTE: There are no "Questions" for this chapter.

References

Babbie, E. (2004). *The practice of social research* (10ᵗʰ ed.). Belmont, CA: Wadsworth Thomson Learning.

Bradburn, N., & Sudman, S. (1989). *Polls and surveys: Understanding what they tell us.* San Francisco, CA: Jossey-Bass.

Fink, A. (2002). *The survey kit* (2ⁿᵈ ed.). Thousand Oaks, CA: SAGE.

Forbes, G. (2001) College students with tattoos and piercings: motives, family experiences, personality factors, and perception by others. *Psychological Reports, 89*, 774-786.

Forbes, G., Adams-Curtis, L. E., Jobe, R. L., Quisenberry, A., & White, K. (2004). *Perceptions of behaviors as sexual, indicators of virginity, and indicators of having "had sex": Effects of participant gender and sexual history, actor gender, erotophobia, and sexism.* Manuscript submitted for publication.

Gallup, G. (1978). *The Gallup poll: Public opinion, 1972-1977.* Wilmington, DE: Scholarly Resources.

Gallup, G. (1979 to present). *The Gallup poll.* Wilmington, DE: Scholarly Resources. (Annual volumes.)

Kalton, G. (1983). *Introduction to survey sampling* (Sage University Paper series on Quantitative Applications in the Social Sciences, Number 07-035). Beverly Hills, CA: Sage Publications.

Kiernan, V. (January 19, 1999). Journal editor loses his job over a paper on how students define "having sex." *Chronicle of Higher Education, 45*, A20.

Krosnick, J. A. (1999). Survey research. *Annual Review of Psychology, 50*, 537-567.

Sanders, S. A., & Reinisch, J. M. (1999). Would you say you "had sex" if ...? *JAMA, 281*, 275-277.

Smith, T. W. (1999). The JAMA controversy and the meaning of sex. *Public Opinion Quarterly, 63*, 385-400.

Sudman, S., & Bradburn, N. (1982). *Asking questions: A practical guide to questionnaire design.* San Francisco, CA: Jossey-Bass.

HUMAN
FACTORS

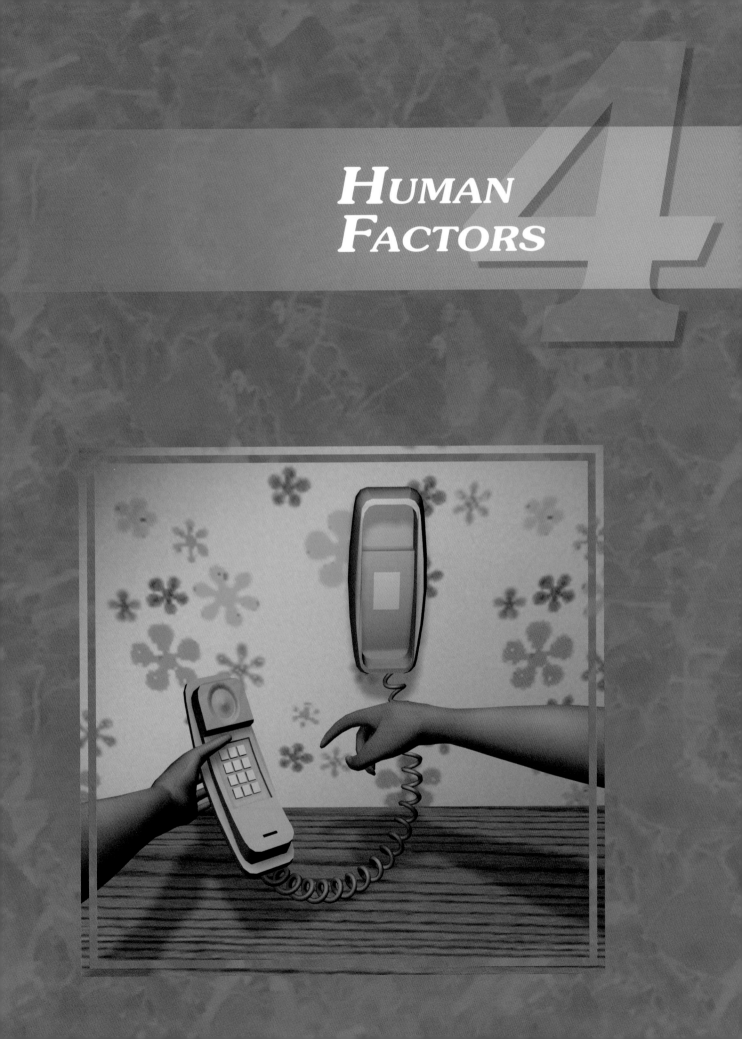

HUMAN FACTORS

4

4.1 *Human Factors in Telephone Systems*

Introduction

Human factors (or *ergonomics*) is the application of our knowledge of human abilities (e.g., memory, motor skills, attention, and so on) to the design of machines and tools for human use. Consideration of the experimental psychology of human behavior can aid in the design of many types of equipment—nuclear power plant control rooms, aircraft instrumentation, computer workstations and software, and even such everyday things as our office telephone systems.

Human factors developed as a discipline during World War II. Aircraft manufacturers found that doing research on how to arrange knobs and dials in cockpits could greatly reduce both accidents and training time. Since the 1970's, human-factors specialists have studied human-computer interaction to address such questions as which layout is best for computer keyboards and which types of "menus" work best for users of computer programs. (You will doubtless have encountered examples of both good and bad design of computer programs.)

Consider the last time you had trouble operating some machine, such as a complex copying machine. What should the manufacturer have considered about human factors in good design? The memory, learning, and problem-solving abilities of humans certainly should be considered in relation to how the machine works and what humans must do to operate it. But the world is full of machines and other things that are difficult to learn and hard to operate. Sometimes that may be inevitable, but, in too many instances, it is due to a lack of consideration of human factors.

Human factors, then, is the use of information about human abilities in the design of systems for human use. The exercise that follows illustrates the employment of human factors in system design.

While PsychMate currently has only a single experiment directly testing human-factors applications, many of the experiments in the sections on Perception and Cognition serve as part of the knowledge base for human factors. Basic studies of attention, memory, problem-solving, signal detection, and many other areas have contributed to the development of human factors.

4.1 Human Factors in Telephone Systems

Abstract

Human Factors is the application of our knowledge of human abilities (e.g., memory, motor skills, attention) to the design of machines and tools for human use. Consideration of the experimental psychology of human behavior can aid in the design of many types of equipment, including nuclear power plant control rooms, aircraft instrumentation, computer workstations and software, and even such everyday things as office telephone systems. In the experiment accompanying this chapter, two different office telephone systems are simulated, and the ease and accuracy of use of each system is measured. The first system is designed to parallel the System 85™ developed by AT&T® which is currently in use in many businesses and universities. The second is a system developed by undergraduate psychology students at the University of Pittsburgh, applying experimental knowledge of mnemonics to the problems of transferring calls, setting up conference calls, and the like. In addition to demonstrating the need for human factors consideration in design, the experiment illustrates the use of questionnaire data from a survey of subjects' impressions of the systems.

Designing better human-machine interfaces is an important application of psychology. Whenever a new machine is built for humans to use (e.g., telephones, photocopiers, video-tape recorders, computer word-processors, pilot cockpits, nuclear power plants, space stations), it is critical that humans learn to operate that machine quickly and reliably. *Human Factors* is the study and application of psychological research to processes that involve humans working with man-made systems (in Europe, the preferred term is *ergonomics*). It's likely that you have learned to use many machines, and you probably have seen examples of both good and bad human factors designs. For example, the standard touch-tone buttons of a telephone are easy to read and are spaced so that there are few times when you press the wrong key due to

movement errors. In addition, when each key is pressed, you get good auditory feedback (i.e., a unique tone) as well as tactile feedback (i.e., you feel pressure when you start to push a button and a clear stopping point when the key is at the end of its travel). The experiment accompanying this chapter examines human factors applications to the design of such a system; it was based on extensive previous research on keyboard configurations and ease and accuracy of entering telephone numbers.

Many systems are designed with little regard to human factors considerations. This occurs as a result of a lack of expertise, as well as a lack of time and care. Many nuclear power plant control rooms illustrate poor human factors design. They were often designed with hundreds of neatly arranged knobs with small labels (see Figure 1). This was done because control rooms designed this way looked neater and were slightly cheaper to build. The problem is that, in a stressful situation, an operator might turn the wrong knob and cause a serious accident (see McCormick, 1976). In some power plants, operators have tried to overcome this poor design by placing unique stimuli next to critical knobs to reduce the chance of such errors. While this might help make the controls easier to discriminate—and thus reduce error—it should be clear that the best solution would be to design the system properly from the outset. In contrast, knobs in a cockpit have different shapes and colors which provide discriminating and redundant cues (e.g., label, location, shape, and color) so that critical functions (e.g., lowering landing gear, turning off engines) are less likely to be triggered by mistake.

Consider the last time you had trouble operating some type of machine, such as a complex photocopier. What should the manufacturer have considered about human factors in good design? The memory, learning, and problem-solving abilities of humans certainly should be considered in relation to how the machine works and what humans must do to operate it.

In the exercise accompanying this chapter, you will evaluate two alternative methods of designing a phone system to enable a person to execute special functions (e.g., to send and transfer calls and to arrange conference calls). The first system is designed to parallel the System 85 developed by AT&T which is currently in use in many businesses and universities. The second system, which was designed by undergraduate psychology students, incorporates mnemonic memory techniques to simplify learning. We will refer to the two conditions as the *digit condition* and the *mnemonic condi-*

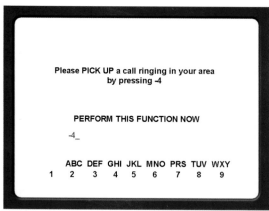

Figure 4.1.1 – *Example trial in the Human Factors in Telephone Systems experiment*

tion. In the digit condition, each function is specified by a single digit. For example, to pick up a call ringing in the area, you would type "-4". In the mnemonic condition, each function is designated by a letter code that provides a mnemonic aid or memory cue for that function. For example, to pick up a call ringing in the area, you would press "=P" (as in *P*ick-up).

The learning literature suggests that mnemonics can aid learning; hence, the mnemonic condition should be better. With a mnemonic approach, you try to give the learner a simple rule to use as a cue to retrieve the desired information. In the telephone scenario, you want to associate the proper key presses with the actions the subject thinks about when doing the experiment. An easy rule would be to press the first letter of the word describing the function. The letters could be printed on the telephone push-buttons. All you would have to learn is the proper names for the functions. (The major functions are *H*old, *T*ransfer, *F*orward, *P*ick-up, and *C*onference call.) To execute a function, you would press a special function key (e.g., the "*" on a touch-tone phone), followed by the corresponding letter key (e.g., for *H*old, you would press "*H").

If you were gambling the fortunes of a billion-dollar company on marketing a new phone system for business, would you: (a) use the digit condition, (b) use the mnemonic condition, or (c) run a ten-hour experiment to find out which is better?

Methodological Considerations

In this experiment, subjects operate two different simulated telephone systems and must learn five different functions for each in turn, including call forwarding, adding a person to a conference call, transferring a call, placing a caller on hold, and picking up a call ringing in the area. One system is based on the AT&T System 85, with minor changes to adapt it to the use of a computer keyboard rather than a touch-tone phone. The other was developed by students in an undergraduate laboratory course in research methods and was based on well-known mnemonic principles.

In the experiment, we will use the top row of numbers and the "-" and "=" keys as an alternative to the number keypad. The "-" and "=" keys represent special keys such as the "*" and "#" keys on a telephone keypad, and the top row of number keys on the keyboard are used for telephone number digits. Since telephones come with the numbers already printed on them, it is important that a comparable memory aid be provided; thus, the response key options are displayed at the bottom of the experiment screen as shown in Figure 4.1.1. This experiment does not use the numeric keypad on the right-hand side of the keyboard since it is arranged in a different order from a telephone keypad and the keys do not have alphabetic letter groups printed on them.

· · · · · · · · · · · · · · · · · · · ·
Expected Running Time = 25 minutes
· · · · · · · · · · · · · · · · · · · ·

Questions

1. What are the independent and dependent variables in this experiment? What are some important controls? Describe the counterbalancing used in this experiment.

2. What are the results? Is one system faster and/or more accurate than the other? Do subjects show a clear preference for one system over the other? If so, is that congruent with their performance?

3. What is it about mnemonics that makes it easier to learn systems that use them? What characterizes a good mnemonic?

4. Describe a system that you have had trouble learning to use and design a brief study to explore alternative designs for such a system.

5. *External validity* refers to whether experimental results can be generalized to the "real world." Certain aspects of the experiment you have completed are rather artificial. Consider problems of external validity relating to the choice of subjects, type of instruction, amount of training, and the absence of requiring subjects to talk to someone on the phone while making the responses.

Extension Experiments

1. Compare the effects of job aids (such as reference cards) on learning the digit system. What would be the benefits of pictorial, verbal, and combined reference cards?

2. How would you test reading and proofreading efficiency for text presented on a computer screen versus printed on paper (see Gould, 1968)?

3. Microwave ovens can be programmed either by entering the time directly (e.g., push 3-2-1 for 3:21) or by pressing the units (e.g., press minutes three times, tens of seconds twice, and seconds once). Which is better? Which would be better for the blind (assuming tones are sounded whenever a button is pressed)?

Advanced Questions

1. How might having job aids available (such as cards listing the special functions) affect performance?

2. How much money might the better system save a large university relative to the poorer system? Assume (a) that the university has 2,000 employees who regularly use the phone system 250 days per year and (b) that an employee would use an average of 5 special functions (as illustrated in this experiment) per day. Also assume that every failed phone action (e.g., failed transfer of a call) costs the university $1.00. Make a projection based on the relative differences in accuracy at the end of training in your lab's data. How much would be saved by using the better system?

3. Reanalyze the data, including the order of learning the two systems as a second independent variable. Do the data suggest an asymmetry of transfer? If so, what implications does this have for the validity of this experiment?

4. Discuss the advantages and disadvantages of the experimental approach to human factors design.

5. Real-world tasks often take weeks to learn. How does this complicate the interpretation of research results?

References

Card, S. K., Moran, T. P., & Newell, A. (Eds.). (1983). *The psychology of human-computer interaction*. Hillsdale, NJ: Erlbaum.

Deininger, R. L. (1960). Human factors studies of the design and use of push-button telephone keysets. *Bell System Technical Journal, 39,* 995-1012.

Gould, J. (1968). Visual factors in the design of computer-controlled CRT displays. *Human Factors, 10,* 359-376.

McCormick, E. J. (1976). *Human factors in engineering and design*. New York: McGraw-Hill.

REACTION TIME

REACTION TIME

5

5.1 Reaction Time Procedures

Introduction

Almost since the beginning of a scientific psychology, reaction time (RT)—the time required to respond to a stimulus—has been of importance in psychological research. That importance has only increased with time, and RT is now the principal dependent variable in a large number of areas of psychology.

This section of PsychMate contains two experiments within a single chapter. We review a number of issues concerning conducting experiments that involve recording RT. Aside from the independent variables that an experiment deliberately manipulates, a variety of factors can affect RT, and this chapter examines many of those confounds and how they are controlled. Any student planning to do RT research should read this chapter carefully.

One of the two experiments accompanying this chapter focuses on the effect on RT of changing the number of stimuli or responses. The other focuses on the effect on RT of changing the probability of a stimulus.

5.1 Reaction Time Procedures

Abstract

Reaction time (RT) is the time from when a stimulus appears until a subject responds to it. RT has become a widely-used dependent variable for research on cognition, perception, and other aspects of psychology. In the exercise accompanying this chapter, the basics of RT research are outlined, including blocking versus randomization, within- versus between-subject designs, number of choices, the probability of a stimulus, and the location of the stimulus. Two experiments illustrate various aspects of RT research.

*R*eaction time (RT) is a standard measure in cognitive and perceptual psychology. This is reflected in the fact that many of the exercises in PsychMate™ use RT as a dependent variable (DV). The concern for many of these exercises is how various independent variables (IVs) affect RT—that is, how RT is changed when we deliberately manipulate the stimuli in some way. But RT is also affected by many variables in which we are not directly interested. *Confounds* are those things (other than the independent variables deliberately being manipulated) that might affect the dependent variable in an experiment and, therefore, must be controlled in some way so that they do not influence the outcome.

The exercise accompanying this chapter is designed to acquaint you with some of the many variables affecting RT. Additionally, the exercise will be concerned with the stability of RT across trials, the issue of how many trials should be averaged in order to determine the "true" RT for a given condition of an experiment, and a number of other issues in RT research. The two experiments included in the exercise are designed to illustrate the operation of several controls.

Following a definition of RT, we present a discussion of the events that occur in a typical RT experiment. Next, we discuss a number of factors that can affect RT and which must be considered in designing experiments employing RT as a dependent variable.

RT Defined

For most research in psychology, RT is defined as *the time from the onset of a stimulus to the time the subject responds.* For the purposes of these exercises, this is the time from stimulus onset until a key is pressed indicating a response. It is important for comparing the results of different experiments to realize that RT as defined above may vary with the type of response required. For example, imagine the following simple experiment. The subjects are to indicate which of two letters was seen on the computer screen.

The independent variable is clarity: the stimulus was either clearly seen or masked by visual "noise" cluttering the screen. Obviously, subjects would be faster at recognizing a clear letter than a masked one.

But suppose further that we did two versions of this experiment, differing only in how the subjects respond to indicate which letter was seen. In one version, they must press the '1' and '2' keys on the computer keyboard to indicate which letter appeared. In the other version, they must press a lever to the left or right to indicate which target letter they saw. Overall RT might well be longer in the case of the lever-press, because the mechanical resistance is higher, or because the distance to be moved is farther, or because different muscles are employed in the two types of responses. In this case, we would have to be very cautious about comparing the results of the two experiments. Differences in the RTs obtained might be due solely to mechanical factors, and thus might not reflect any differences of interest. For this reason, we must be careful in comparing the outcomes of experiments using different responses. Whether a subject used a relatively fast key-press or a relatively slow lever-press will affect *overall* RT, but, in either case, the response to the masked letter would be slower than the response to the unmasked letter. In comparing experiments, therefore, the crucial issue is whether the same *pattern* of RTs is seen, rather than whether overall RT differed.

While we have defined RT as the time from stimulus onset to a response, RT is sometimes defined in other ways. In much research in kinesiology, for example, RT is defined in relation to the onset of a muscle potential (as measured by an electromyographic signal), while the time from the first electrical activity in the muscle to when the response movement itself is completed is called Motor Time. *Because RT is sometimes defined differently, and because it can depend on the nature of the response apparatus, it is important in RT research that the definition of RT and the nature of the response be made explicit and also that it be reported in the Methods section of the research report.*

RT is also sometimes classified as *simple RT* or *choice RT*. In simple RT, a subject makes one response to a single stimulus. This requires only a judgment about the presence of a stimulus; it does not involve a decision about the nature of the stimulus. When more than one type of stimulus can occur, and the subject must indicate the stimulus type by his or her choice of responses, we are studying *choice RT*. In this exercise, and throughout the PsychMate experiments, "RT" means *choice RT* unless noted otherwise.

RT Experiments— General Considerations

In developing the general considerations for RT research, we examine issues concerning the events that take place on each *trial*, how *blocks* of trials may differ, and, finally, how these combine to form the *experiment* as a whole.

What Happens on Each Trial?

Typically, RT experiments consist of one or more series (blocks) of trials. While the specific stimulus may vary from trial to trial, certain aspects of the experiment are usually the same on each trial. There is often a *fixation* mark of some kind, to let the subject know where he or she should be looking when the trial starts. *Initiation* of a trial may be under the subject's control, allowing the subject to begin a trial whenever he or she is ready. Alternatively, initiation of a trial may be automatic, controlled by the experimenter or computer. In this case, a *warning* signal is typically given to allow the subject to get ready for the trial. (Sometimes the appearance of the fixation mark acts as the warning. Sometimes a tone or other signal is used.) After a trial is initiated (either by the subject or automatically), there is usually a brief delay before the stimulus appears. This delay is called the *foreperiod* and it may vary from trial to trial or it may be fixed (unvarying). (The foreperiod is usually fixed for choice RT tasks. For simple RT, the duration of the foreperiod varies randomly so that the subject cannot "react" by anticipating the appearance of the stimulus based on timing.)

At the end of the foreperiod the stimulus is presented. Sometimes there is only a single event making up the overall stimulus. In others, there may be a series of stimuli on the screen. (When these stimuli are intended to affect the processing of the later stimulus, they are referred to as *primes* or *priming stimuli*.) In either event, timing of the reaction begins when the *imperative stimulus* (i.e., the one requiring a response) is displayed. The imperative stimulus refers to the element in the display that deter-

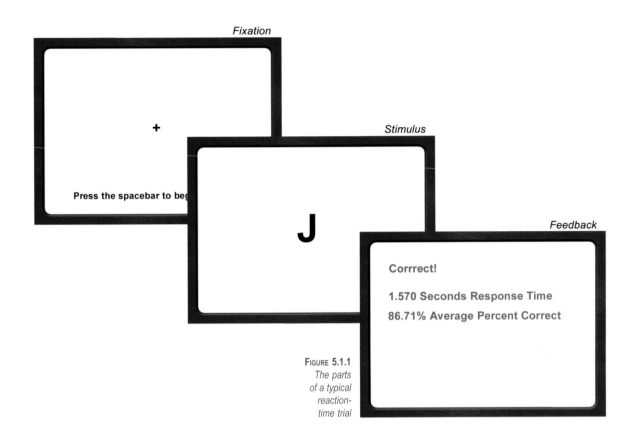

Fixation

+

Press the spacebar to beg

Stimulus

J

Feedback

Corrrect!

1.570 Seconds Response Time

86.71% Average Percent Correct

FIGURE **5.1.1**
*The parts
of a typical
reaction-
time trial*

mines the appropriate reaction (e.g., which key to press). The *stimulus duration* (i.e., how long it remains in view) will be controlled largely by the nature of the stimulus display. For example, if eye movements during the stimulus presentation could affect the experiment, a very brief (say, 100 ms) presentation is often used, since it takes some time after the stimulus appears for an eye movement to begin. If the stimulus duration is so short that the subject gets only a glance at the stimulus, the display is described as a *data-limited* display.

Another issue for defining a trial is that of how long to give the subject to respond. In most of the experiments in PsychMate, you must respond with a key-press within some limited time. The determination of this time limit for a given experiment depends on the range of RTs expected—the time limit must be set so as to encompass any legitimate trials. If the task is an

easy one, with RT on most trials being less than 500 ms, the time allowed for a response may be relatively brief—2 seconds or so. If no response occurs in that time period, the trial is counted as an omission. Many more difficult tasks, however, have typical RTs of 1-2 seconds. In this case, the time allowed for a response should be increased accordingly.

Feedback

Typically, feedback about accuracy and/or RT is given following a response. Feedback about accuracy is usually provided, informing subjects whether they were right or wrong in their choice of a response. It should be noted, though, that subjects are generally aware of having made an incorrect response. Accuracy feedback emphasizes the importance of responding correctly. Because the usual RT instructions emphasize speed of reactions, RT feedback is important since it lets subjects monitor their own performance.

Other Terminology

The *inter-trial interval* (ITI) is the time from the end of one trial to the beginning of the next. If the subjects control initiation of the next trial, they also control the ITI. When it is important to control ITI, trial initiation must be controlled by the computer or experimenter.

As noted above, in some experiments, there may be more than just a single stimulus. For example, if subjects must judge whether two letters they see are the same or different, they might see one letter and then see the second some short time later. The delay before the second stimulus is the *inter-stimulus interval* (ISI). The ISI is the time from the onset of the first stimulus to the onset of the imperative stimulus. Another term for this is *stimulus onset asynchrony*, or SOA.

What Happens in a Block of Trials?

Usually, the entire series of trials making up an experiment is divided into *blocks* of trials. This division may simply reflect time-constraints. In a long experiment, we want to be sure that subjects take occasional pauses, so we may break the entire series into shorter blocks, with rest pauses between them. More importantly, the division of the experiment into blocks may be an integral part of the experiment itself. The remainder of this section treats that situation.

Blocked Versus Random Presentation

Suppose there are two or more different types of trials being presented in an experiment (comprising two or more levels of each independent variable). A question to consider is whether these different types of trials should be presented together in each block with the two types alternating in *random* order, or whether the series of trials should be *blocked*, with all trials of one type presented, followed by all trials of the other type.

Consider two experiments in which subjects must respond by pressing the correct key to indicate either (a) which of four letters is present (four-

choice RT) or (b) which of only 2 letters is present (two-choice RT). The two experiments differ only in whether the two types of trials (two- and four-choice) occur *randomly* (within a single block) or whether they are *blocked*, with all of the two-choice trials occurring together, and all of the four-choice trials occurring together.

The probable outcome of such an experiment is graphed in Figure 5.1.2. Note that both experiments show that four-choice RT is longer than two-choice RT, which is just as expected. But the difference between two- and four-choice RT is considerably larger for blocked presentation than for random presentation. That is, *the results of the experiment depend (in part) on the choice of blocked versus random presentation of the stimulus types.* Why should this be so? In this experiment, random presentation leads the subjects to sometimes ignore whether the trial is two- or four-choice. In other words, the subjects seeing the stimuli in random order may treat many of the two-choice trials as if they were four-choice. That raises the mean RT for two-choice responses, while having no effect on four-choice responses.

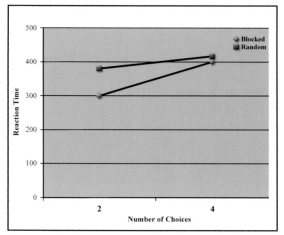

FIGURE 5.1.2 – *Typical outcome of an experiment comparing two- and four-choice RT*

In general, then, the choice of random or blocked presentation must depend on whether subjects given random ordering of trials will adopt different strategies from those given blocked order. In the case of the experiment above, subjects in the random-order experiment adopt the strategy of ignoring whether there were two choices or four and treating many two-choice trials as if they were four-choice trials. Thus, the blocked version gives us the better estimate of the actual time required for two or four choices.

When blocked presentation is used, the issue of *counterbalancing* of treatment orders is raised. In the blocked version of the two- versus four-choice experiment (two levels of one independent variable), half of the subjects would do the two-choice trials first, while half would do the four-choice trials first. This counterbalancing is designed to remove (or at least minimize) any effects of carry-over from one block of trials to the next.

Stimulus-Response Mapping

Certain variables are almost always controlled by counterbalancing. One such variable is the mapping of stimuli to responses. In some experiments, this can be absolutely crucial. In the exercise on "Perceptual Matching," for example, subjects must indicate (a) that two stimuli are the same by pressing one key or (b) that they are different by pressing another. Since one aspect of that experiment is to compare "same" and "different" responses, it is important to counterbalance the mapping of the response keys to same and different stimuli. Otherwise, we might find a difference between "same" and "different" responses and conclude that the differences in the stimuli caused the differences in RT, when it was really due only to a lack of proper counterbalancing. (Conversely, a failure to counterbalance might lead to a finding of no difference, when there really was one.)

What Happens within the Whole Experiment?

An experiment is composed of one or more blocks of trials. If the experiment is particularly long, it may be broken down into *sessions* of one or more blocks each. In that case, counterbalancing of blocks across sessions also may be required. An experiment most often begins with

instructions about the nature of the experiment and some *practice* trials. When the experiment is concluded, some form of *debriefing* is often used to show the subject the purpose of the experiment and to permit questions about it. Instructions, practice, and debriefing are considered separately below.

Instructions

The purpose of the instructions in any experiment is to let the subject know what will be happening and what the correct responses are. In RT research, instructions also should emphasize that subjects are to respond as quickly as possible while still remaining accurate. "Accurate" is typically considered 10% or fewer errors, though this would also depend on the specific experiment.

In long experiments, it is also advisable to instruct subjects that they should take occasional breaks to rest their eyes. If trials are initiated by the subjects, these breaks are under the subjects' control. Otherwise, it is a good idea to "build in" breaks by having blocks of trials that are fairly short (e.g., 5-10 minutes). Occasional breaks help to prevent subjects from just staring at the screen and pressing keys like zombies. This means that subjects will be not only less error-prone, but also that RT will be less subject to added variability due to eye strain, mental fatigue, and the like.

Practice

Most experiments ask people to do unfamiliar tasks and require them to indicate their responses by pressing keys that have no previous association with the stimuli. For example, When asked to press the "1" key if an "H" appears and the "2" key if an "S" appears, subjects must first learn to associate "1" with "H" and "2" with "S." At first, subjects will be very slow and error-prone in their responses, simply because they have to think carefully about which key to press after they identify the target letter. After a while, subjects no longer have to think about which key to press, and their responses become faster and more accurate (see the experiment on Automaticity). For this reason, we usually give considerable practice on the task before actually beginning to collect data. For the exercises in PsychMate, we typically give only about 10 practice trials, due to time limitations. Note, however, that most research gives far more practice. The effect of this practice is to reduce the variability of RT during the experiment itself.

In a short experiment, completed in a single session, one block of practice trials is usually all that is needed. If the experiment extends over several sessions, a brief block of practice trials is usually given at the beginning of each session, and the first session is often treated as a practice. If the type of stimulus display or responses change from block to block, it might also be necessary to have practice before each block of trials.

Debriefing

When an experiment is over, the subject is usually *debriefed*. The debriefing typically is a simple matter of telling the subject what pattern of RTs you expect to find and why. That is, the debriefing is used to explain to the subject what the experiment was about. In addition, subjects may be shown their individual results. A second reason for a debriefing is to get comments from the subjects about their own experience. While such comments may not be part of the data proper, they can sometimes reveal the use of strategies that the experimenter had not considered, or may even point up flaws in the design. Remember that subjects have spent some of their time during the experiment trying to figure out "what is going on." In doing so, they may notice things about the experiment that the experimenter never noticed—including problems.

How Many Trials?

Why not just have the subject respond once to each type of display, and take that single RT as the "score" for that condition? This certainly would be faster, since few trials would be needed. The problem with using this procedure, however, is that it ignores the large variability in

RT that is due to factors other than the independent variables. RT varies from trial to trial, *even if the stimulus does not.* That variability comes from momentary changes in attention, among other things. Note that we cannot pay attention evenly and uniformly for any length of time. Even when you are listening to a fascinating lecture, you will find your attention wandering from time to time. The same thing happens in RT experiments, when the subject sits doing trial after trial. Occasionally, subjects will start a trial when their attention is not focused on the task. When this happens, a very long RT usually results. Long RTs due to inattentiveness would be expected to occur about equally often for all stimulus types, so averaging a few such trials with many others creates no problem.

Another way to look at the problem of number of trials per condition is to realize that the RT on each trial provides an estimate of a subject's "true" RT for that condition. Each individual estimate is not very reliable, for the reasons given above. We therefore combine (average) a number of estimates (RTs on many trials) to provide a better (i.e., more reliable) estimate of "true" RT. If you have had a statistics course, you will have been introduced to the notion of a *confidence interval*. Recall that the confidence interval estimate of the population mean becomes more and more precise as the sample size increases. Similarly, our estimate of true RT becomes more accurate as the number of trials increases. By employing the formula for the confidence interval, you could determine the number of trials needed to have a certain level of accuracy. For most purposes, however, such precision is unnecessary. In practice, 15-30 trials per condition per subject seem to provide a satisfactory result. This is a sufficient number of trials such that a few aberrant trials will have little effect on the mean RT for that condition. In the exercises in PsychMate, there are sometimes fewer trials than this because some limitations were required to complete the exercise in part of a single class period. In actual research, on the other hand, time limitations are less of a problem, and far greater power is obtained when each subject's RT for each condition is based on a larger number of trials.

Between- Versus Within-Subjects Designs

Another issue of importance to RT experiments is that of whether the independent variables should be manipulated between subjects or within subjects. *Between-subjects* variables are ones where different subjects are tested at each level of the variable. For our example of two- versus four-choice RT, that would mean that subjects do *either* the two-choice version *or* the four-choice version, but not both. *Within-subjects* variables are those where each subject is tested at each level of the variable. For our example, this would mean that each subject does *both* two- *and* four-choice trials (either in random or blocked order).

Which method is preferred? Suppose we wanted to determine the effect of alcohol on RTs to a simple stimulus, and we have 20 subjects available. We could randomly assign 10 subjects to perform the task while under the influence of alcohol and 10 to perform it sober, then com- pare those mean RTs. This would be a between- subjects design. But why not test each subject both sober and drunk? That way we would have 20 subjects in each condition. This would be a within-subjects design. (Of course, we would want to counterbalance the order, and test some subjects sober and then drunk, and others drunk and then sober.) It should be clear that an analysis based on 20 subjects per group is more powerful than one based on only 10 subjects per group. (Note that the type of statistical analysis would change slightly, since a within-subjects design violates the assumption of independent samples. In this case, comparing two means, we would use the *t*-test for independent samples with the between-subject design, and the *t*-test for dependent ("correlated", "matched-pairs") samples with the within-subject design.)

The main thing to note about the example above is that a within-subjects design is clearly better. But there are severe limitations to its use as well. A within-subjects design works fine in this

example because if we tested subjects who were inebriated, then tested them sober a few days later, we could be fairly sure that the only systematic difference in them is in whether or not they were sober. Similarly, when comparing RT to two versus four stimuli, we can be fairly sure that making a choice between two stimuli does not have a later effect on making a choice among four stimuli (or vice-versa)—at least if we have blocked the trials. But, in many situations, we cannot make the assumption that there is no carry-over from one condition to another. For example, if we wanted to compare RT for naming meaningless shapes following two different types of training, we would have to use a between-subjects design, because if we have a subject learn something by one method, we cannot then "erase" that learning. If they performed faster following the second round of learning, is it because that method of learning is better? Or is the difference simply due to the *added* learning? Another situation in which we are forced to employ a between-subjects design is when the variable is "attached" to the person and cannot be manipulated experimentally. Variables of this kind include sex, race or ethnic background, and religion.

In general, then, within-subjects designs are to be preferred *if* we can reasonably assume that there are no carry-over effects of one level of an independent variable on performance at other levels of that independent variable. If we cannot make that assumption, we must employ a between-subjects design.

There are also some experiments that employ *both* within- and between-subjects independent variables. These are usually referred to as *mixed* designs. For example, suppose in the two- versus four-choice RT experiment that we wanted to compare the patterns of RTs for males and females. Our two independent variables would be number of choices and sex. Number of choices (two vs. four) would be a within-subjects variable, for the reasons outlined above. But sex (male vs. female) would be a between-subjects variable, since no subject could be in both groups.

Other Considerations in RT Research

A number of other factors that must be considered in designing research that employs RT as a dependent variable are discussed below. Wickens (1992, Chapter 9) provides a more detailed account of most of these same issues.

Speed-Accuracy Tradeoff

In research employing RT as the dependent variable, we usually are interested in showing that RT *differs* for different levels of the IV(s). A serious problem can arise, however, if the conditions associated with faster RT also have higher error rates. Such a condition is called a *speed-accuracy tradeoff*, because the subjects may be trading accuracy for speed. That is, they may be faster on those trials because they are pushing themselves for speed, but ignoring the higher error rate that often goes with that effort. Consider the comparison of RTs for subjects when tested drunk and when tested sober. Suppose the mean RT was 450 ms, whether the subjects were sober or drunk. Could we conclude that alcohol had no effect on RT? If the error rate was the same for both conditions, we could. But suppose further that an examination of error rates found only 5% errors when subjects were sober, but 30% errors when they were drunk. In this case, it looks as if the difference in RT is uninterpretable since subjects were responding too quickly (and hence inaccurately) when they were drunk. (The analysis developed in the chapter on Signal Detection is relevant here.)

Fortunately, in most RT research we do *not* encounter speed-accuracy trade-offs. In fact, most of the time, the fastest conditions will have the *lowest* error rates, while the longest RTs will come in conditions with the highest error rates. In this case, difficult stimuli lead to both slow and sloppy responding. In any case, it is a wise practice to examine error rates for evidence of speed-accuracy trade-offs. To avoid this problem, instructions to the subjects usually stress that they must be as fast as they can in each condition, *but without sacrificing accuracy.* That is, the error rates should be uniformly low for all conditions.

Stimulus-Response Compatibility

In most RT research, the connection between the stimulus and the response is arbitrary. We can have the subject press "<" for an "S" and ">" for an "H" or ">" for an "S" and "<"for an "H"—the mapping of stimulus to response is arbitrary. But occasionally the mapping is not arbitrary. Consider the same experiment, but using "L" and "R" as stimuli, instead of "S" and "H." If you had to press "<" for an "R" and ">" for an "L," for example, you might be both slower and more error-prone than otherwise, because of the association of "L" with "left" and "R" with "right." Making a "left" response to an "R" might well produce some response competition, resulting in a slowing of RT. Basically, any time a stimulus implies a certain direction of response (such as "L" and "R" implying "left" and "right" responses), there are potential problems of stimulus-response compatibility.

Probability of a Stimulus

In most of the experiments in PsychMate, and indeed in much research with RT as a dependent variable, we present each type of stimulus equally often. In this way, we eliminate guessing by the subject, since each stimulus is equally likely on each trial. Sometimes, however, we may present one stimulus more often than another, and this can have major effects on RT (and error rate). In general, the more frequently occurring stimulus is responded to more quickly and more accurately. Why is this so? Suppose that in the experiment on recognizing "S" and "H" we presented an "H" 80% of the time and an "S" just 20% of the time. Subjects would realize this quickly and would thus *expect* an "H" most of the time. On any trial, if the target *is* an "H," there is likely to be a fast response. But if the target is an "S," the subjects must overcome their expectancy—and their preparedness—for

"H." The result is a slow response and a high probability of error.

Because of these considerations, it is best to have the different trial types be equally likely whenever randomization is used. Unequal stimulus probabilities are best avoided unless they form part of the research itself. The effects of unequal stimulus probabilities are illustrated in the experiment *Reaction Time Procedures: Stimulus Probabilities*. In that experiment, you will complete three blocks of trials. In one, the "S" and "H" occur equally often. In another, the "S" occurs 80% of the time, while in another the "H" occurs 80% of the time.

Number of Different Responses

As illustrated in the experiment *Reaction Time Procedures: Number of Choices*, RT increases as the number of possible responses increases. This relationship has been long known. It was quantified in the early 1950's, when Hick (1952) and Hyman (1953), working independently, each noted that RT increases linearly with the logarithm (base 2) of the number of alternatives (see Schmidt, 1982 for a good discussion). What this means, in effect, is that additional alternatives will increase RT, but the effect of that increase will be smaller as the number of responses becomes larger. While this effect is not usually of much concern, it must be kept in mind when comparing the results of several experiments—if they used different numbers of response alternatives, the RTs cannot be compared directly.

Intensity and Contrast

At least for low levels of illumination, the more intense the stimulus, the faster the RT. Once the stimulus reaches an intensity where it is clearly visible, however, further increases will have little effect. Similarly, increasing contrast (the difference in intensity between the stimulus and the background) will decrease RT, up to a point where the stimulus is clearly visible. Either low intensity or low contrast would produce a data-limited display.

One common problem in controlling intensity and contrast is *ambient light* (the light present in the room). A display that may seem very weak under ordinary room lighting may seem quite bright when room lights are off and windows are covered. Because the conditions under which you conduct the exercises in PsychMate are likely to be less than ideal, we have tried to avoid experiments that would be greatly affected by ambient light. In experiments employing brief, data-limited stimulus displays, it is important that ambient light be carefully controlled.

In addition to lowering apparent intensity and contrast, ambient light may result in glare or reflections on the display screen of the computer. In this case, lights must be shielded or the computer moved to prevent such interference.

Location of the Stimulus

The location of the stimulus can have a powerful effect on both RT and error rates. *Retinal locus* (i.e., the location on the retina where the image of the stimulus falls) must be controlled by randomization or counterbalancing if the stimuli are not all presented in the same location. If one type of stimulus is presented in the fovea (i.e., the central part of vision) and another in the periphery, differences in RT might occur (or fail to occur), but they could be due to differences in the *location* of the stimuli, rather than differences in the stimuli themselves.

The Distance to the Screen

Note that as you move nearer to a display screen, the size of the image of the stimulus will increase. If the size of the image is important, the location of the subject's head relative to the screen must be controlled. This is often done by use of a chin rest or viewing hood to keep the subject's head relatively stable. See Footnote 2 in Chapter 1.1, *The Filling-In of Blind Spots: Induced Scotomas*, for a discussion of measuring image size as degrees of visual angle.

Methodological Considerations

This entire chapter is concerned with methodological considerations in RT research. It consists of two experiments: Number of Choices and Stimulus Probabilities.

● ●
Expected Running Time *(for each experiment)* **= 18 minutes**
● ●

Questions

1. What are the independent and dependent variables for the experiments you performed for this exercise? What are some important controls?

2. Examine the error rates for the different conditions of one of the experiments. Is there any indication of a speed-accuracy trade-off? What indicates that such a trade-off did (or did not) occur?

3. (For Number of Choices) What is the effect of having to choose from among four choices instead of just two? If there is an effect, why might it occur?

4. (For Stimulus Probabilities) What is the effect of changing the probabilities of the stimuli? Does RT change? Do error rates change? When one target appears only 20% of the time, do you have more errors?

References

Hick, W. E. (1952). On the rate of gain of information. *Quarterly Journal of Experimental Psychology, 4*, 11-26.

Hyman, R. (1953). Stimulus information as a determinant of reaction time. *Journal of Experimental Psychology, 45*, 188-196.

Schmidt, R. A. (1982). *Motor control and learning: A behavioral emphasis.* Champaign, IL: Human Kinetics.

Wickens, C. D. (1992). *Engineering psychology and human performance.* Columbus, OH: Charles E. Merrill.

COGNITIVE
NEUROSCIENCE

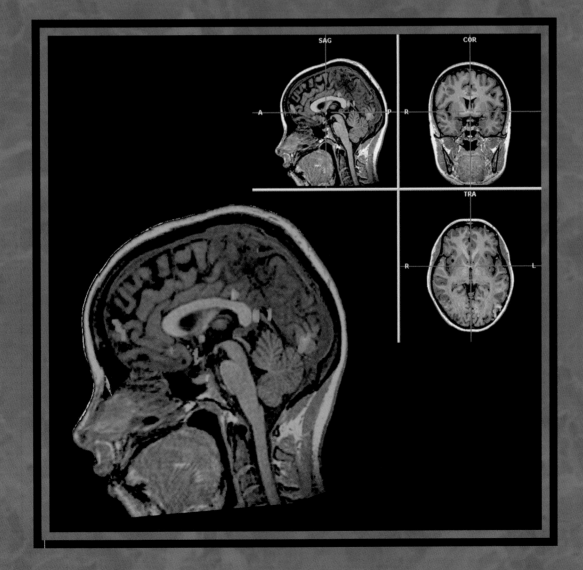

6

COGNITIVE NEUROSCIENCE

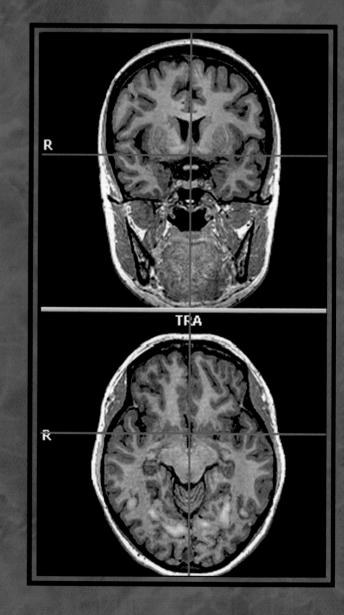

Introduction

*N*euroscience is the umbrella term adopted several decades ago to refer to the parts of biology that are directly concerned with the nervous system. It includes studies at all levels of the nervous system—from the biochemistry of neurotransmitters to the physiology of cell membranes. It also includes the study of the brain as it directly affects, and is affected by, cognition, including perception, memory, attention, and other cognitive processes. These are the concern of *Cognitive Neuroscience*.

Cognitive neuroscience shares with much of cognitive psychology the assumption that, in order to understand a cognitive process, we need to specify the series of mental operations that make up the process. Cognitive neuroscience builds on this assumption by also searching for correlations between brain events and cognitive events. Such correlations were a part of neuroscience for a century before it came to be called neuroscience. Paul Broca, in 1861, demonstrated the importance of what is now called Broca's area for speech production by showing that damage to a specific area of the brain in the left hemisphere produced a characteristic inability to speak normally, despite otherwise normal language.

Historically, the study of brain states in relation to cognitive states was largely dependent upon accidents and injuries; the study of brain activity during normal waking consciousness is a recent development. Beginning in the 1960's, the development of the electroencephalogram (EEG) made it possible to track changes in the electrical activity of the brain across time as subjects performed various cognitive tasks. Though useful, the EEG is limited in its ability to determine the location of brain activity. Since the 1980's, new techniques for forming images of the interior of the body have revolutionized medicine. Chiefly, positron emission tomography (PET) and magnetic resonance imaging (MRI) provide images of the body, and both permit the examination of changes in brain activity during cognitive tasks.

6.1 Introduction to Brain Imaging and Brain Tutor

Abstract

Brain imaging permits researchers to look inside someone's brain to try to understand cognitive processing. This chapter describes how to identify cortical brain areas and interpret the specialization of each area. We will review the major brain imaging methods of Magnetic Resonance Imaging (MRI), Functional Magnetic Resonance Imaging (fMRI), Diffusion Tensor Imaging (DTI), Positron Emission Tomography (PET), and Event-Related Potential (ERP). We will examine fMRI methods in detail to provide a basis for designing and analyzing fMRI experiments related to the experiments in which you will participate.

Overview of Brain Imaging

Brain imaging provides non-invasive methods to look inside someone's head and observe internal brain processes. The ability to track stages of processing in the brain provides a powerful tool for understanding the underlying mechanisms. Most of the experiments in Psych-Mate and most of psychology use behavioral data to understand processing capabilities. These methods are the major basis for understanding human behavior. Behavioral studies basically look at input/output relationships (e.g., visual stimuli inputs and motor response outputs). However, there is a multitude of possible mechanisms that might produce the same behavioral results, and these provide a lively basis for argument among psychologists.

The brain is a computational device with hundreds of specialized areas. Brain imaging allows researchers to look inside the brain and find what processes occur in specific areas of brain tissue. In the brain, function is often localizable (e.g., vision at the back of the brain, motor processes at the top, and language production on the left). The goal of many neuroimaging investigations is to identify where particular psychological functions are localized in the brain. There are multiple areas devoted to a given function. For example, in vision there are over 34 areas that do visual processing (Felleman & Van Essen, 1991), with specialization ranging from detection of lines, to image movement, to face recognition. Tissue in locations just millimeters apart perform identifiably different processing. Given this

Abbreviation	Technique Name	Principle Use	Spatial Resolution	Temporal Resolution
MRI	Structural Magnetic Resonance Imaging	Identify structural features of the brain	<1 mm	Not Relevant
fMRI	Functional Magnetic Resonance Imaging	Localize energy use (BOLD signal)	1–4 mm	0.1–4 s
DTI	Diffusion Tensor Imaging	Connection tracing	<1 mm	Not Relevant
PET	Positron Emission Tomography	Measure chemical density or activity	5 mm	50–300 s
ERP	Event-Related Potential	Measure electrical activity of brain	10–50 mm	0.001 s

FIGURE 6.1.1 – *Primary brain imaging techniques used in studying the human brain*

localization, we have a means to connect a function to a point in the brain. We can then see what other functions occur at that point, what other points connect into that point, and to where that point connects. This can provide a detailed map of brain function and connectivity.

Brain imaging allows the identification of function by tracking spatial activity of internal components of the brain. To use an analogy, think of the problem of someone using satellite observations to try to understand "automobile function." Automobiles move, they rest, they accept and discharge people, they go to places to receive energy (gas stations), sometimes they connect to each other (as in getting a jump-start),

and sometimes they crash, die, and are buried (in junk yards). You could set up behavioral experiments, such as seeing how automobiles function when gas is scarce or how they flow when a road is impeded. However, understanding of how automobiles operate would be greatly facilitated if you could open up the hood and track the sound, heat, vibrations, fluids, and electrical activity within the automobile in order to relate it to the behavior (e.g., speed). With such measurement tools one could understand subsystems (e.g., engine, transmission, steering, cooling system, fuel system, climate control) and the interconnections between the parts. One could determine whether the theories about "automobile behavior" are consistent with the mechanisms of automobiles.

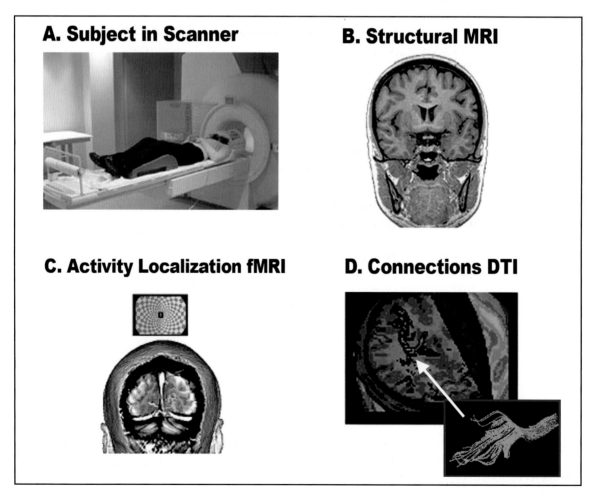

FIGURE 6.1.2 – MRI-based brain imaging methods: (A) MRI scanner and placement of subject prior to entry into the scanner; (B) Structural image showing brain tissue; (C) Functional activation image with the visual stimulus as subject is examining flashing checkerboard (grey indicates structure; color indicates functional activation); (D) Connection tracing using Diffusion Tensor Imaging of neural pathways.

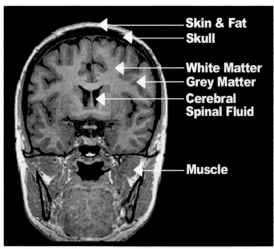

FIGURE 6.1.3 – *Structural MRI of the human head—note that different tissue types show up in different shades of gray and texture.*

Major advances in brain imaging in the last two decades have made it possible to "open up" the human brain and measure brain activity to allow interpretation of dynamic brain function. There are multiple techniques which provide different types of data. These techniques can be used individually and in combination to understand brain function. There is a growing list of brain imaging techniques. We will discuss the five major techniques used on humans (see Figure 6.1.1).

Structural Magnetic Resonance Imaging (MRI) provides measurement of physical brain structure showing cortical lobes, subcortical structures, and tissue differences such as grey matter (where the neuron cell bodies are) and white matter (where neurons output their axon fiber bundles) with sub-millimeter accuracy (see Figures 6.1.2 and 6.1.3). It involves putting a person in an MRI machine, which is basically putting the person's head in a large magnet and measuring the density of hydrogen atoms in the head. The concentration of hydrogen atoms varies with the type of tissue (e.g., the bodies of neurons have a modest concentration of hydrogen atoms and thus appear grey, while the axons of neurons have high concentrations of hydrogen atoms and thus appear white). In our automobile example, this would be analogous to taking X-ray pictures of the engine, with the density of metal showing dark areas (the engine block) and light areas (the windshield fluid holder).

Functional Magnetic Resonance Imaging (fMRI) measures the amount of energy used by neurons in the brain. Areas of the brain that have higher energy use are shown as brighter. This is measured by tracking changes in the MRI image that result from increased neuron firing, producing greater blood flow. Figure 6.1.4 shows the changes that occur in fMRI. The stimulus is presented, which increases neuron firing about 0.1 seconds later in the brain. The neuron firing stimulates the vascular system to open up to provide more oxygenated blood (known as the *hemodynamic response*), peaking about 4 seconds post stimulus. The MRI machine records the activity with a typical delay of 2 seconds to process the data. The graph shows the typical timecourse of activation. In our automobile example, this would be like taking an infrared (heat or night vision) picture of an engine and seeing where heat is generated (pistons) and where it is removed (radiator).

Diffusion Tensor Imaging (DTI) provides a method to measure fiber tracks from one brain region to the next (see Figure 6.1.2[D]). It can track neuron axon bundles that are about 1 millimeter thick. This would be similar to tracing all the wires in the car and seeing how the battery is connected to the ignition switch, starter motor, and spark plugs.

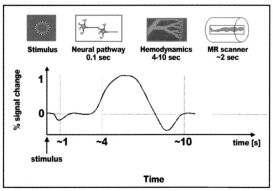

FIGURE 6.1.4 – *The top diagrams illustrate the stages of fMRI data collection. The neural response occurs at about 0.1 seconds post-stimulus, and the Hemodynamic response at about 4-10 seconds. The MR scanner reports the data typically 2 seconds after it is collected. The graph shows the activation time course.*

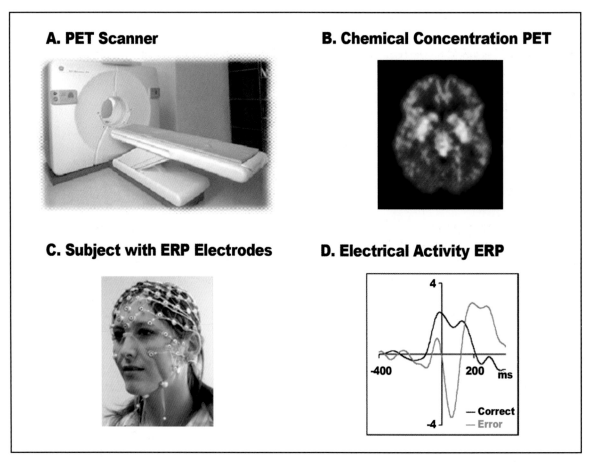

FIGURE 6.1.5 – (A) PET Scanner; (B) PET image showing concentration of serotonin receptors (Carolyn Cidis Meltzer, by permission); (C) Subject wearing ERP electrode cap (Electrical Geodesics, Inc., by permission); (D) ERP recording showing activity changes during subject response (correct versus error trials).

Positron Emission Tomography (PET) allows the tracking of specific chemicals in the brain such as oxygen or specific neural transmitters such as acetylcholine (see Figure 6.1.5[A,B]). PET involves injecting or inhaling a radioactive isotope which circulates in the blood stream. As the isotope decays, it emits high gamma rays that can be detected from a ring of radiation detectors. By counting the number and timing of the detected gamma rays, the number of radioactive molecules at a given location can be calculated. Thus you can determine how much of a chemical is at a given location. Figure 6.1.5[B] is a PET image of a low dose radioactive isotope injected into the bloodstream that indicates the concentration of 5HT (5-hydroxytryptamine) receptor sites for neurotransmission. This enables mapping the density of serotonin (5HT) receptors in the brain.

Autoradiography—tracking of concentrations of receptors—is being used to interpret disease processes such as depression. The recording period depends on the radioactive isotope involved (e.g., 90 seconds for an isotope of oxygen). Spatial resolution is typically about 8 mm. In our automobile analogy, this would be like tracking the movement of the gasoline, transmission fluid, water, and gasses.

Event-Related Potential (ERP) techniques provide millisecond measurement of electrical activity with modest spatial resolution—typically at the centimeter scale. This typically involves putting an array of tens to hundreds of electrical measurement devices (electrodes) on the scalp to measure the electrical activity at each point (see Figure 6.1.5[C, D]). Unfortunately, these measurements are quite distant from the source and the signals are miniscule, necessitating averaging over many stimulus presentations. This would be like using an electrical meter to measure electrical potentials on an automobile engine while keeping the meter at the level of the hood and never touching any lower point. You could tell with great temporal precision when an electrical signal occurred, but with only general information about the location.

All of these measurements have complementary strengths and weaknesses. They can be combined to get a clearer picture of function. For example, fMRI can show where activity is with millimeter precision for a response lasting one second, whereas ERP can tell when the activity occurs with millisecond precision, but has only centimeter spatial resolution. By combining both techniques, we can have millimeter spatial resolution with millisecond temporal resolution.

How fMRI Works to Map Brain Activity

Functional MRI (fMRI) makes it possible to form maps of cortical activity at fairly high spatial resolutions (~1-4 mm). It can track brain activity in small areas about the size of a pencil point (millimeter resolution). fMRI is just over a decade old and is becoming the most popular of the brain imaging techniques used in cognitive neuroscience. To measure activity from outside the head requires specialized equipment and use of physics and biochemistry. Functional MRI uses an MRI machine to make 3D pictures of the brain. Individual slices (an individual image is referred to as a "slice") can be taken in a tenth of a second. A full brain volume (e.g., 30 slices) can take typically from 1 to 4 seconds depending on the equipment.

Most fMRI experiments measure neural activity indirectly by measuring a property of blood flow related to cellular respiration (i.e., oxygenation). This is referred to as measuring the *BOLD* (Blood Oxygenation Level Dependent contrast) effect. The intensity of the BOLD response is influenced by the amount and type of blood in any location of the brain. Blood that is low on oxygen (deoxygenated) is paramagnetic, meaning that in a magnetic

field it becomes magnetic (like paper clips brought in contact with a magnet). This deoxygenated blood disturbs the magnetic field in the MRI machine, thereby reducing the MRI signal (and hence dimming the picture at that location). In contrast, blood that is high in oxygen (oxygenated) is non-magnetic and does not disturb the field, therefore producing a brighter image at that location (see Figure 6.1.4 for MRI signal and Figure 6.1.8 for example of an fMRI image).

The mechanism of BOLD is: 1) neurons receive synaptic input, using energy; 2) neurons send signals to the vascular system to provide more oxygenated blood; 3) more blood is provided, increasing the oxygenation level of the blood; 4) the blood becomes less magnetic; 5) the local MRI signal increases. This process takes about 4 seconds, so the signal is delayed and summed over several seconds. This occurs at the micro-vascular spatial scale, providing the potential for sub-millimeter resolution of activity.

The BOLD effect is typically reported in percent change (see Figure 6.1.4). That is, you take the recorded signal at any point, divide it by the mean and multiply by 100. Typically, the BOLD effect is small—less than one percent. Measuring the BOLD response is purely a *differencing technique*. That is, we cannot tell how active a site is, but only if it is less or more active than it was at a different time.

There is a close relationship between neural response and the BOLD signal. In animal studies, researchers have related the firing rate of neurons to the observed BOLD response. That is, a neural firing closely follows the BOLD response (see Figure 6.1.6). The figure shows data from primate studies which compared the percent BOLD response to the change in neuron firing as a function of stimulus contrast. As the contrast changed from very low contrast (5%) to high contrast (70%), the cell firing increased from 0.2 to 0.9 spikes per neuron (shown as the dots). The recorded fMRI response increased from 0.4% to 2.4%. This shows a tight coupling between neuron activity and the fMRI response.

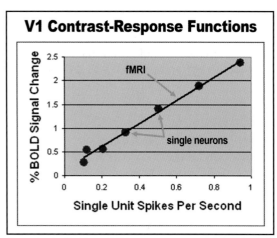

FIGURE 6.1.6 – *Relation of BOLD response to neuron firing in primary visual area (V1) neurons (adapted from Boynton, personal communications).*

The actual size of the BOLD response varies with the type of MRI magnet and scanning procedure used. The BOLD response can be considered as a measure of the underlying neural activity. Note that neural activity can both increase and decrease, so you can have both positive and negative percent change. Most observed regions show positive responses. Negative responses, when they occur, typically are suggestive of an inhibition of the area, reducing the normal firing of neurons.

How an MRI Experiment is Different from a Behavioral Experiment

Each brain imaging method typically involves specialized equipment, experimental designs, and analysis methods, and each is limited by various artifacts of physics and technology.

Equipment. MRI imaging requires an MRI machine. These machines are hospital imaging machines housed in special buildings with a typical setup costing two to four million dollars. An MRI experiment requires that the subject be placed on his or her back and moved into a long, confining tube with tightly packed pillows to minimize head movements. In addition, the subject's head is stabilized with pads in the head coil to minimize movement (see Figure 6.1.2[A]). The subject views a computer image on a projection screen within the tube and makes responses with a specialized response device so the subject

can push the keys without needing to see his or her hand. When the magnet is collecting images, it makes a very loud (110 decibels) sputtering noise similar to that of a machine gun at close range (visit ***www.psychmate.com/resources*** to hear the noise). Subjects must be screened for claustrophobia, any metal or electronics in the body (e.g., pacemakers), and the ability to lie very still.

There is no direct eye contact between the experimenter and the subject. The duration of a typical session is between 1-2 hours, during which the person is not to move. The typical session includes 10 minutes of setup, 10 minutes of structural imaging, and 30-90 minutes of functional scanning. These restrictions do require some special experimental procedures such as having the patient go to the bathroom before starting, wearing special non-magnetic clothing (e.g., hospital gowns), and training the subject sufficiently before entering the magnet. The typical data collection session currently costs about $500/hour.

Designs. Since MRI tracks signals that are slow, taking several seconds to develop, it is often best to do things for an extended period of time to get a clear image. This is analogous to taking a picture with a slow camera (e.g., 10 seconds). Think how you might use such a camera to take pictures of two friends. If they both walked in front of the camera switching places every 5 seconds you would have a blurred image with few recognizable features. However, if you had one friend stand still for 10 seconds, then they changed places in the next 10 seconds, then the second friend stood still for 10 seconds, you would have two clear images of each person for the first and last picture and a blurred picture in between. In fMRI experiments, we similarly might have the person get into one mental state, hold that state while we take an image, then change to a second mental state, and take the second image.

There are three basic fMRI experiment design types (see Figure 6.1.7). First is the *block design* in which researchers ask people to perform a given task for a period of time repetitively and

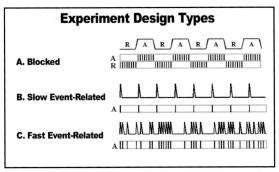

Experiment Design Types

FIGURE 6.1.7 – *Common stimulus event presentation sequences for fMRI experiments. "A" refers to active periods of stimulus presentation. "R" refers to rest periods.*

then switch—e.g., touching the fingers of the left hand for 30 seconds, then touching the fingers of the right hand for 30 seconds. This provides a clear picture of the somatosensory representation of the fingers in the brain.

A second type of design is called a *slow event related design*, which involves doing something once and then resting during the imaging period. In Chapter 6.2, *Working Memory and the fMRI*, you will be analyzing brain imaging data collected from an experiment using a slow event related design (Chein & Fiez, 2000).[22] In the original Chein and Fiez study, a trial was 52 seconds in duration. Subjects performed word encoding for 8 seconds to allow a clear image, even though most subjects could encode 5 words in 2 seconds. Note that slow event related designs can be used to assess rapidly occurring events as long as there are no intervening events (see Figure 6.1.7[B]). In our camera analogy, this would be like opening up the camera for a single event, then putting something over the lens to stop any additional events from changing the image. The image would be "dimmer" than in the block design (which allowed more light to come in to expose the film).

A third design is the *fast event related* design. In this case, researchers take lots of pictures with different combinations of events and use mathematical techniques to separate the blurred images. This typically requires many more trials to get an interpretable image. However, it is the only way to look at fast events when material is not repeated (e.g., looking at the brain after errors versus correct responses).

Block designs show stronger activation than event designs when the amount of scanning time is the same. Figure 6.1.8 shows activation from a block design (top) and a fast event design (bottom). Event designs are better for rapidly changing or unpredictable events (e.g., trials on which errors occur). However, they typically require a substantially larger amount of imaging data to get a clear image relative to block designs.

The ability to control the subject's mental state generally determines the type of design that is effective for a particular experiment (see Figure 6.1.7). If the event can be repeated, block designs are preferred. If not, slow event related designs work if the subject can slow down the processing without engaging in interfering processing. If not, it is best to do the events many times in a fast event related design and use mathematical methods to separate the event types. Note that given the high costs of scanning, researchers try to use the most efficient design possible.

Analysis. Brain imaging analysis requires the processing of large quantities of data and performing enormous numbers of statistical tests. The data from a typical session is about a gigabyte (1,000,000,000 characters) per subject collected in an hour. Analysis requires special

---

[22] This chapter provides an overview of methods and tools used in brain imaging. Chapter 6.2 introduces the PsychMate Working Memory experiment and the BrainExaminer image analysis tool. These elements demonstrate the behavioral and final analysis aspects of an fMRI experiment without requiring actual use of a scanner or extended data processing.

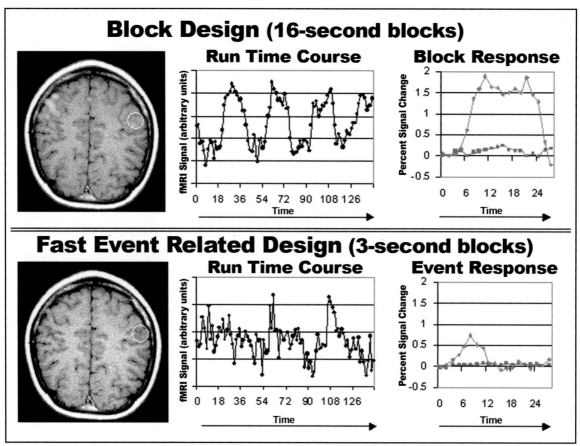

FIGURE **6.1.8** – *Blocked vs. fast event design*

programs for image reconstruction, movement correction, spatial normalization, spatial filtering, statistical analysis, and data visualization.[23]

Statistical programs are variants of the standard statistics used for behavioral data (e.g., ANOVA). The experimenter contrasts the magnitude of the BOLD response at different conditions for every location in the brain. Each location of the brain is called a *voxel* (short for **vol**ume **pixel,** which is the smallest distinguishable box-shaped part of a three-dimensional image). There is a large number of statistics performed. For example, in the Working Memory experiment there are about

10,000 voxels (each of which is about a 4x4x4 mm cube) in the image. For each location typically there are multiple statistical tests to determine if activity in that location changed across conditions. Analysis of a typical brain imaging experiment requires running tens of thousands of statistical tests (e.g., 5 tests on each of hundreds of thousands of voxels). There are computer programs that do this automatically in less than a minute.

Humans cannot look at ten thousand numbers and interpret all of the numbers. However, humans have great perceptual skills and can look

---

[23] *Image reconstruction* takes data recorded from the MRI machine antenna and produces images (as in Figure 6.1.2[B]). *Movement correction* programs take each volume of the head and move and rotate the images to align them so the intensity of each point can be compared over time. *Spatial normalization* programs take brain volumes and warp (shrink or expand) the brains so each head has the same center and the same size. *Spatial filtering* involves defocusing the activation images or applying what is called a Gaussian smoothing. This means spreading the activation of one point over a dimensional normal sphere (e.g., take each point and add half of the intensity of that point to all of its neighbors). This compensates for local anatomical variability between subjects and enables the averaging of data across subjects whose brains are not perfectly matched.

at images, rapidly identifying bright spots. *Data visualization programs* display the numbers in graphic form, similar to what you would see if you could cut into the brain and see what was inside. Typically, researchers display structural features in black and white and activation as color overlays. The typical rule is to color only those areas that are significantly more active (e.g., that would occur less than 1% of the time by chance). For example, any positive activity would be red, and, as it gets more positive, it would shift to yellow. Negative activity might be blue shifting to green. One could easily see the center of yellow with a red surround and perceive where the area of large activity is.

Artifacts. All imaging methods have artifacts. Artifacts are problems that can cause faulty results (e.g., small movements of the head). One needs to carefully review the data to identify artifacts. Possible artifacts must be corrected or, if they cannot be corrected, the subject's data must be excluded from the statistical analyses.

The brain imaging data provided for use with Chapter 6.2 is at the last step of processing—the data visualization step. The data you will be looking at will have already gone through all of the early analysis stages. You will be using the PsychMate BrainExaminer data visualization tool to interpret the results.

Interpreting Brain Imaging Results

Interpreting brain imaging data is far more than looking at pretty pictures. It requires careful consideration of the control conditions and the contrasts. For example, let's assume you do an experiment comparing people viewing pictures of faces versus pictures of houses and you find an area in the brain that shows more activity when viewing faces. Is it appropriate to conclude that this is the "face area" in the brain? Well, not until you do many comparison experiments. Faces differ from houses in many ways, and it is critical to show that it is the nature of the *face* that causes the differences in fMRI, rather than some other aspect of the stimuli.

Imaging results become stronger with carefully *planned contrasts* of related interpretations. Remember, brain imaging is a differencing technique—not showing what is happening at a location, but what is happening differently between two conditions at a location. If you see a difference between viewing faces and houses in a part of the brain, it could be due to the faces having high positive activation and houses having none, or it could be due to faces having no activation and houses having negative activation (inhibition). Both give you a positive difference. This is one of the reasons people often use a *resting control*— recording activity when presumably no task is being performed. If you compare faces to looking at a blank screen, you can tell if activity increases.

To provide evidence for a specific function for a part of the brain, you need to eliminate other interpretations. In our face example, in presenting faces, you will not know if activity is due to the stimuli being faces, as opposed to another visual pattern. There are many possibilities, such as texture, emotional expression of the face, amount of attention to the face, or eye movements when looking at the face. Eliminating these and many other interpretations requires careful, planned contrasts of faces with other types of material. The work of Kanwisher (Kanwisher, Stanley, & Harris, 1999) on the face area illustrates such careful use of contrasts. She determined that the face area (in the brain) responds preferentially when viewing faces relative to blank screens, houses, textures, other body parts, images with many grey scales, eyes, cartoon faces, and furniture. In fact, the only stimuli other than faces that the face area responded to were pet faces (cats and dogs). This suggests that this area of the brain (in the occipital lobe) is active for face processing. But this does not mean it is a face area only. The area does respond to a wide range of learned visual objects (e.g., birds in expert bird watchers).

Note, we do not know if this specialization is genetic, a function of experience, or a combination of the two. Also, even though the "face area" may be maximally activated by faces, it is also activated by other stimuli such as houses. So it is not uniquely a face area. While faces may have greater activity in this region than houses, when compared to a resting baseline, both faces and houses are significantly active. Interpretation is highly subject to the use of various controls.

Planned contrasts. Analysis of brain imaging typically involves a combination of *temporal contrasts* and *condition contrasts.* Temporal contrasts involve looking at contrasts across time periods. In the Chein and Fiez memory experiment, subjects encoded words for 8 seconds, rehearsed words for 20 seconds, recalled words for 4 seconds, and then rested, keeping their eyes on the fixation cross for 12 seconds. For analysis, 0% activation was treated as the average signal from an area during the end of the rest period. A typical temporal contrast would contrast the activation during the rehearsal period to the rest period. A condition contrast involves comparing different conditions, typically over a specified temporal period. For example, Chein and Fiez contrasted activation when rehearsing non-words versus when rehearsing short words.

Region of Interest (ROI). Most imaging experiments identify regions of interest (ROIs). An ROI is a specified part of the cortex representing a 3D space in which voxels are changing. In general, ROIs are either structurally defined or statistically defined. *Structurally defined ROIs* typically involve someone tracing the area of a structure, such as the hippocampus, on each subject's brain. This is a time-consuming process and requires expertise in brain anatomy. A much more common technique is the use of *statistically defined ROIs.* These involve defining a region based on a statistical test (e.g., ANOVA) relative to a control condition. Then, all of the

voxels that touch each other and that are above some statistical threshold of activation (e.g., have a probability less than 0.001 and with at least five voxels in a cluster), define the ROI. This ROI can be examined across time and conditions to see if there are changes in activity.

It can be problematic defining an ROI due to selection bias problems. In the Working Memory experiment, one could define an ROI based on a contrast of encoding versus control, maintenance versus control, or encoding versus maintenance. Each of these contrasts will define different areas that may or may not overlap. If you want to test an area to see if it is more active in rehearsal than encoding, what contrast is appropriate? If you use the encoding contrast ROI, you have selected voxels that show more activity in encoding and hence you do not know if the difference is due to selection bias or a true contrast. Typically, ROIs are based on representative conditions. For example, ROIs are defined based on being active in either the rehearsal or encoding condition relative to the control. In a typical experiment, there is a modest number of important ROIs, typically less than 25. It is much easier and interpretable to look at activity from a small number of ROIs rather than from the hundreds of thousands of voxels in a typical image.

Talairach Coordinates. In order to communicate results, it is critical to have a common reference coordinate system (e.g., similar to describing your location on the planet in degrees longitude and latitude). Researchers want to see if the area activated in one experiment is the same area activated in different experiments. However, the subjects in different experiments have different brain sizes. To provide commonality of reference, researchers have developed the Talairach[24] coordinate system (see Figure 6.1.9).

---

[24] Defining the Talairach (pronounced TAL-uh-RAK) coordinate system involves finding a common center point (a neuron fiber track called the anterior comissure), and then finding the boundaries of a cube containing the furthest forward, backward, top, bottom, left, and right of the cortex. Then each subject's brain images are warped (expanded and contracted) such that they have the same extent as the standardized brain. Typically, each subject's data is warped to a target brain, and all of the activation data is resampled to the target brain's size to allow between-subject averaging (i.e., averaging across subjects).

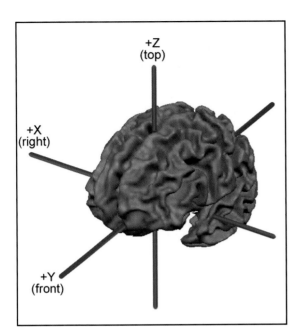

FIGURE **6.1.9** – *Planes used in the Talairach Coordinate system. The X coordinate increases from left to right, the Y coordinate increases from back to front, and the Z coordinate increases from bottom to top (figure adapted from Talairach Daemon, University of Texas Health Science Center at San Antonio Research Imaging Center).*

The coordinates are in millimeters, with X being right to left, Y front to back, and Z top to bottom. When researchers report where they found an area of activation, they typically report the location in Talairach coordinates. You will be working with the Brain Tutor visualization program that will report the locations to you.

Activity Plot. For a given ROI, one can examine the activity at that location over time.

Plots typically show the BOLD response over time across conditions. The plot represents the mean change in the MRI signal for all the voxels in a given ROI (see Figure 6.1.10). The lines represent differences across conditions. It is important to realize that there is a *hemodynamic delay* in the plotted data. That is, when a stimulus is presented, the maximal activity occurs four seconds after the stimulus occurred. This is due to the slow response of the vascular system responding to the increased neuron firing. Hence, if two events occurred at 0 and 10 seconds, you would expect to see the peak of the first stimulus at 4 seconds and the second stimulus at 14 seconds.

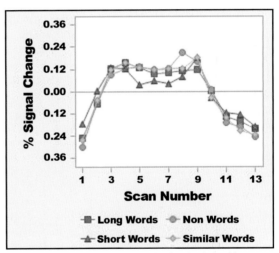

FIGURE **6.1.10** – *Working Memory activity plot showing activity across conditions during the rehearsal phase of the experiment.*

Questions

1. Describe how the major human brain imaging methods of MRI, fMRI, DTI, ERP, and PET work and what type of information is derived from each. What is the major strength of each method? How might they be combined to better understand brain function?

2. Define each of these terms: BOLD, design types (block, slow event, fast event), spatial normalization, spatial filtering, voxel, planned contrasts, temporal contrasts, condition contrasts, ROI, Talairach Coordinates, activity plot, and hemodynamic delay.

3. For each of the design types discussed (i.e., block, slow event related, fast event related), describe an experiment that would run optimally in this design. What do you need to consider when choosing a design?

4. In recent experiments on dyslexia (reading disorder), studies have found that poor readers have less activation than normal readers. What would be a series of tests that could be done to determine whether an area relates to reading, and whether the difference seen is based on factors of learning, attention, or genetics? Discuss what it means to show that normal readers have more activation than poor readers. Consider whether you think this would be a difference in brains or a difference in training and experience. What experiments might you perform to contrast those?

Brain Tutor

Abstract

Brain Tutor is an interactive application used for teaching about the structure and function of the human brain. Brain Tutor (an option on the menu for the Cognitive Neuroscience category within the PsychMate Student application) is a program developed by Brain Innovation[25] as a tutorial guide for looking at the brain in a variety of views. You can explore brain anatomy and learn to identify different structures such as lobes and gyri/sulci. You can also learn how to identify locations in the brain in the standardized coordinate system (Talairach coordinates). Learning these structures will aid you in interpreting brain activation. This section of the text is best read with the Brain Tutor program running so that you can try each of the functions described to see how they work.

FIGURE **6.1.11** – *Accessing Brain Tutor from PsychMate*

---

[25] Brain Innovation provides a variety of brain analysis tools for professional brain imaging work. See ***www.brainvoyager.com*** for details. The Brain Tutor is based on technology developed for BrainVoyager,™ a leading program for analysis of brain imaging data.

Using Brain Tutor

After launching Brain Tutor (see Figure 6.1.11), use the buttons at the base of the application (see Figure 6.1.12) to select the display mode, slicing mode, or hemispheres to display. The windows on the right side of the application provide information, tips, and instructions relevant to the display mode or area selected. The specific function of each button is described below.

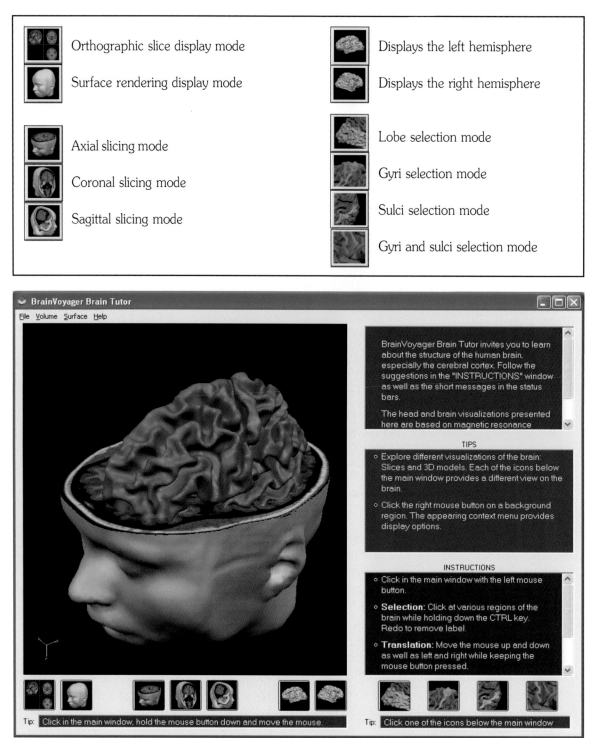

Orthographic slice display mode

Surface rendering display mode

Axial slicing mode

Coronal slicing mode

Sagittal slicing mode

Displays the left hemisphere

Displays the right hemisphere

Lobe selection mode

Gyri selection mode

Sulci selection mode

Gyri and sulci selection mode

FIGURE 6.1.12 – Information, tips, and instructions relevant to the display mode or area selected are displayed in the panels on the right.

Orthographic Slice Display Mode

The **Orthographic Slice Display Mode**, or Volume Viewer, provides three views, oriented from the side, front, and top of the head (see Figure 6.1.13). These views are named the Sagittal, Coronal, and Axial (also called Transverse) plane views, and indicate three different orientations of a particular coordinate in the brain. All of the views reflect a single coordinate position, indicated by the intersection of the blue lines. The views differ in whether the slice was taken horizontally or vertically, and whether direction of the slice occurred from the top, front, or side of the brain.

data across individuals and to compare areas of activation across studies.

Clicking the left mouse button in any one of the views relocates the cursor to a new coordinate position, and updates the other two views to reflect the same coordinate location from a different orientation. Clicking and dragging the mouse in one view will result in continuous updates in the other two views. Click in the center of the axial view, then click and drag to the lower left, and you will see the upper two images changing as you sweep through the brain image.

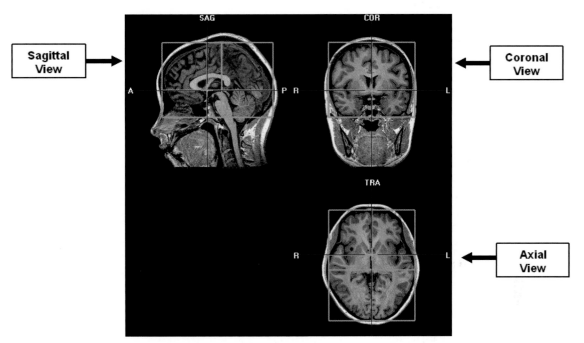

FIGURE **6.1.13** – *Orthographic slice display mode*

The boundaries of the green box in Figure 6.1.13 indicate the *Talairach coordinates*, which define a standardized coordinate space. Talairach and Torneaux (1988) created a standard, 3D spatial coordinate system based on a single human brain, defining a kind of brain atlas. Using the Talaraich system, brain images are mathematically stretched, squeezed, and warped so that they map onto a normalized space in order to account for differences in brain size and orientation. Normalization of image data allows researchers to combine functional

Surface Rendering Display Mode

In **Surface Rendering Display Mode**, three views are available, allowing the user to slice the brain along different planes (see Figure 6.1.14). The Axial (or Transverse) slicing mode cuts the brain horizontally from top to bottom. In medical terms, the top is referred to as "superior" and the bottom is referred to as "inferior." The Coronal slicing mode cuts the brain vertically from front (anterior) to back (posterior). The Sagittal slicing mode cuts the brain vertically from one side of the brain to the other.

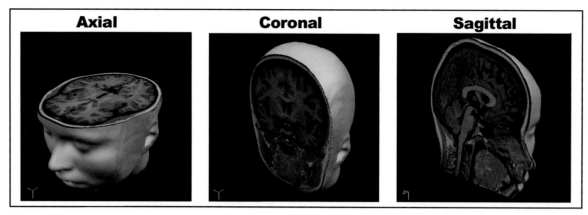

FIGURE 6.1.14 – In surface rendering display mode, slicing occurs along the three planes: axial, coronal, and sagittal.

In medical terms, there are different conventions for directions (see Figure 6.1.15). For example, front is referred to as anterior or rostral (meaning "beak"), and back is referred to as posterior or caudal (meaning "tail"). The outside is referred to as "lateral," while the inside is referred to as "medial." For example, the nose is considered medial to the eyes, and both the eyes and the nose are medial to

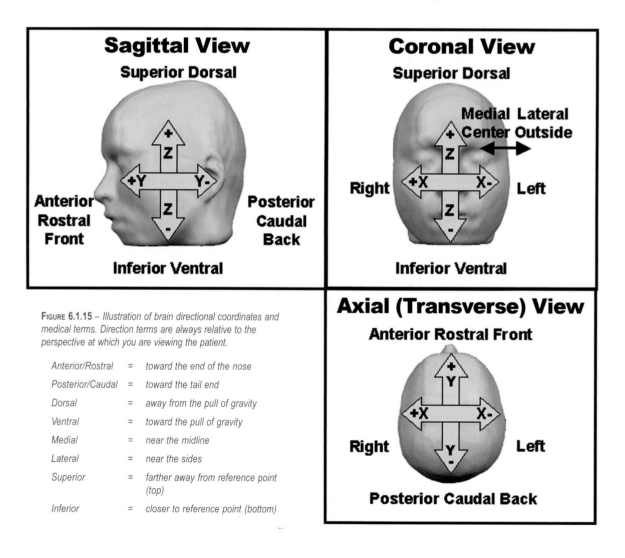

FIGURE 6.1.15 – Illustration of brain directional coordinates and medical terms. Direction terms are always relative to the perspective at which you are viewing the patient.

Anterior/Rostral	=	toward the end of the nose
Posterior/Caudal	=	toward the tail end
Dorsal	=	away from the pull of gravity
Ventral	=	toward the pull of gravity
Medial	=	near the midline
Lateral	=	near the sides
Superior	=	farther away from reference point (top)
Inferior	=	closer to reference point (bottom)

the ears. Coordinates are based on the perspective of looking at the patient in what is called the radiological convention. The right side of the patient is shown on the left side of the display, as if you were looking at the patient in an operating room, positioned at the waist, looking at the head.

Modifying the Display

While in surface rendering display mode (see Figure 6.1.14), the following commands are available:

Translation (changing position in the window) — click and hold down the left mouse button, then move the mouse to reposition the image.

Rotation (change head to different orientation) — click and drag the left mouse button while simultaneously pressing the Shift key.

Zoom in or out (increase or decrease the size of the head) — click and drag the left mouse button while simultaneously pressing both the Shift and Ctrl keys. To cut to a specific location in the brain, click and drag the mouse while pressing the right mouse button.

Use the **hemisphere buttons** to turn the display of the left or right hemispheres on or off. The hemispheres may be displayed with or without the slicing mode view by selecting Surface Rendering Mode, setting the hemisphere(s) to display, and clicking the slicing mode view button to turn it off.

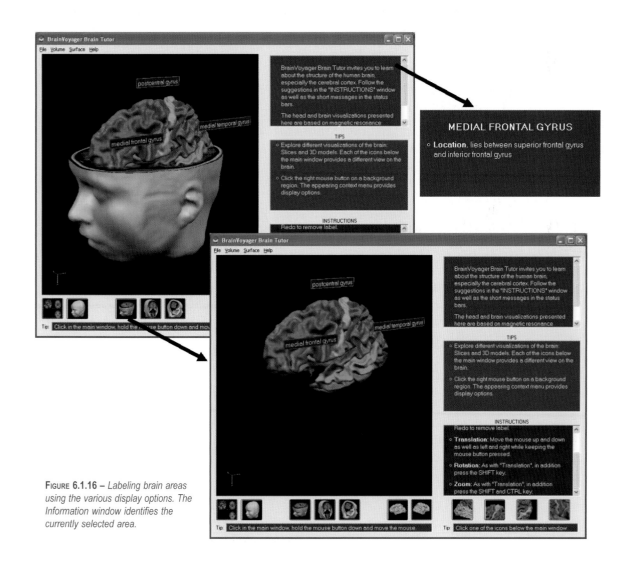

FIGURE 6.1.16 – Labeling brain areas using the various display options. The Information window identifies the currently selected area.

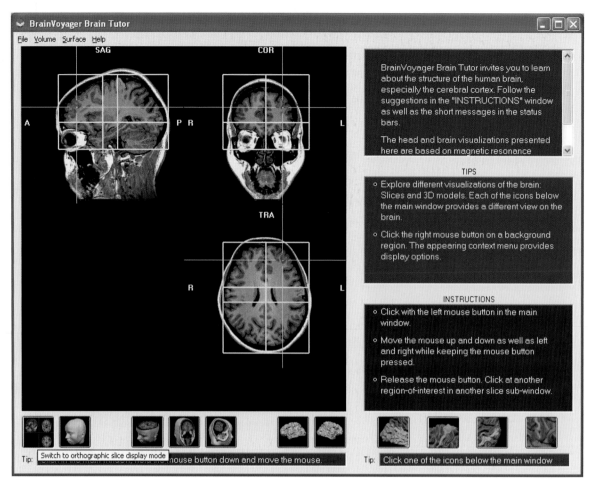

FIGURE 6.1.17 – Orthographic slide display mode identifying the location of a selected area in the planar views.

Labeling Brain Areas

Brain areas can be labeled while displaying one or both of the hemispheres (see Figure 6.1.16). Specific locations in the brain may be selected for identification by holding the Ctrl key and clicking the area with the left mouse button. Use the buttons below the Instructions window to set the selection mode for Lobes, Gyri, Sulci, or Gyri and Sulci. When a particular area has been selected, the Information window updates to display information relevant to the selected area.

Additionally, the display may be customized to turn off or display labels and other features by right-clicking one of the selection mode buttons in the lower right. After identification of specific areas of the brain, switch to the Orthographic

display mode to view the locations of the selected areas according to each of the three planar views (see Figure 6.1.17).

Reading Talairach Coordinates

In the Orthographic views, you can click on a point and read the Talairach X, Y, and Z coordinates of that point. Click "Volume" from the menu at the

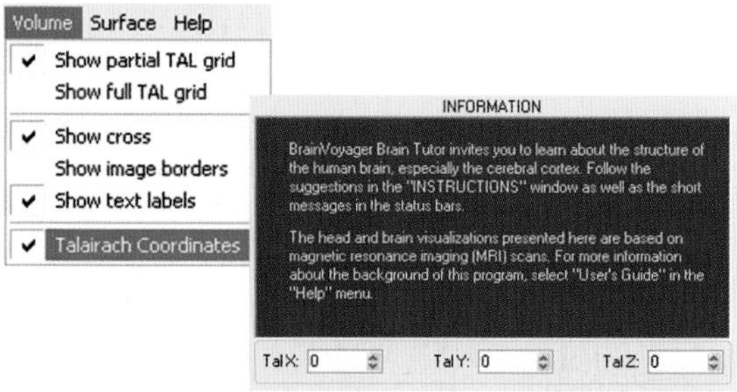

FIGURE 6.1.18 – Turning on the display of the Talairach coordinates.

top of the application, and select the "Talairach coordinates" option. A small window showing the Talairach coordinates will be displayed under the Information Window (see Figure 6.1.18).

Identifying Cortical Areas from the Talairach Position

When researchers communicate about cortical areas, they use both the Talaraich coordinate names and the names of folds of the brain. The brain is a folded structure. The *gyri* (*gyrus* is the singular form) are the outward folds (hills) of the brain (see colored areas in Figure 6.1.19), and the *sulci* (*sulcus* is the singular form) are the inward folds (valleys) of the brain. Figure 6.1.19 shows the precentral gyrus in pink, the postcentral gyrus in orange, and the central sulcus in white as the valley between the two regions.

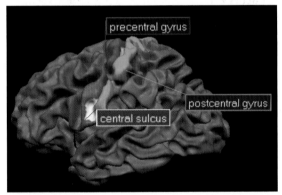

FIGURE 6.1.19 – *Gyri and Sulci (hills and valleys) in the brain.*

To go from a Talairach coordinate to the gyrus and sulcus requires several steps and often some judgment calls. Remember that the Brain Tutor is mapping the location to the folding of the generic brain, rather than to the brain on which your data were collected. So the location you get from mapping any coordinate is an approximation.[26] When mapping an individual brain to a reference brain, one expects about a centimeter variation.

To localize an ROI requires several steps (see Figure 6.1.20):

1) Turn on the Talairach fields in the Volume menu (if you have not already done so).

2) Click the gyri/sulci button on the lower right (to turn on gyri/sulci selection).

3) Click the orthographic view button in the lower left of the application window.

4) Enter the Talairach coordinates for the ROI.

5) Identify the location of the ROI by viewing the intersection of the lines in the Orthographic View.

6) Ctrl-click (left mouse button) to color/identify the gyri and sulci near the target location.

7) Make a judgment call of the nearest gyrus/sulcus to the given point (the Talairach coordinates of the ROI).

8) Ctrl-click on the closest gyrus/sulcus.

9) The name and information pertaining to the gyrus/sulcus will be displayed in the Information window.

NOTE: In the following exercises, you will be asked to provide the names of gyri and sulci given the Talairach coordinates. Text from the Information window may be copied to the clipboard by selecting the text and right-clicking to display a context menu, or simply by pressing Ctrl+C. This information may then be pasted into another application (e.g., Word) for use in preparing reports and presentations. Use the "Save display window" command in the File menu to save a picture of the current contents of the display view, or use "Save snapshot" to save a picture of the entire application window.

---

[26] Note that, for an accurate map, some researchers will identify the location on each individual rendered brain to determine the gyri and sulci on that specific subject and then report the data (e.g., a paper might report that the ROI was localized in eight subjects as being the precentral gyrus and in two subjects, the precentral sulcus).

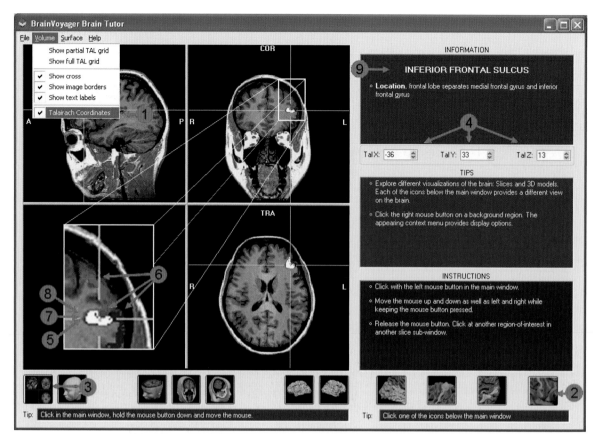

FIGURE **6.1.20** – *Steps in the localization of a region of interest.*

Exercises

1) Identify Lobes:

    a) Select Surface Rendering Display Mode.

    b) Select Axial Slicing Mode.

    c) Display the left hemisphere.

    d) Click the Lobe Selection Mode button.

    e) While pressing the Shift key, click and drag the mouse to position the head such that the display looks like the image in Figure 6.1.21.

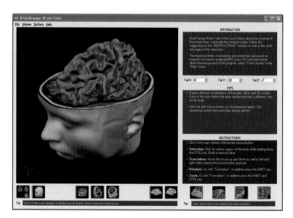

FIGURE **6.1.21** – *Appropriate display for Exercise 1 following steps a through e.*

Exercises (continued)

f) Locate each of the lobes (click with the left button while pressing the Ctrl key).

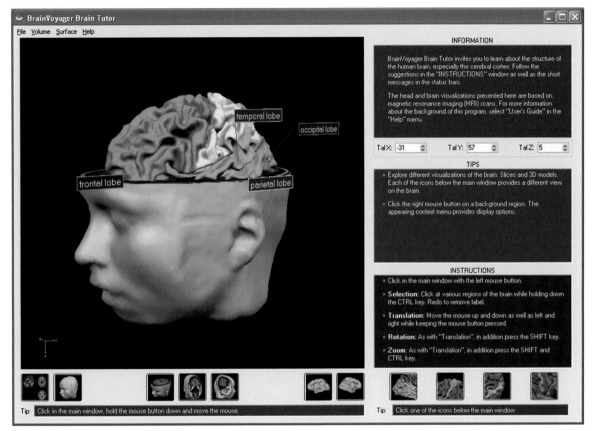

FIGURE 6.1.22 – Brain Tutor display with lobe selection.

g) Shift from the rendered view to the Orthographic view (see Figure 6.1.23). Click in different locations within each lobe and note the change in Talairach coordinates. Identify each of the lobes listed in the table following Figure 6.1.23, and enter the Talairach coordinates for that lobe. The coordinates for lobes will vary greatly because of the large volume of these areas. For the exercises (i.e., entering Talairach coordinates in the tables), select a location in the center of each lobe as an approximate location.

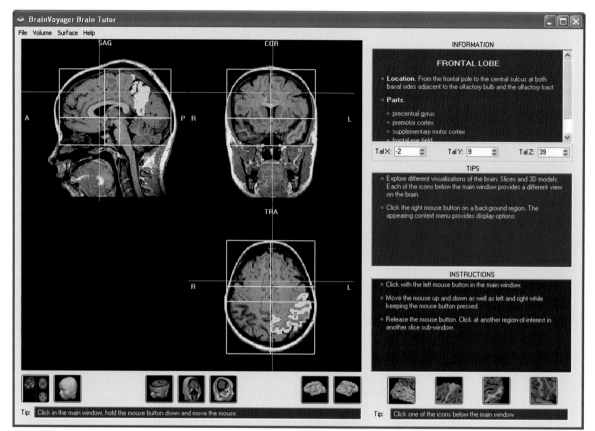

FIGURE **6.1.23** – *Selection and approximate Talairach coordinates for the Frontal Lobe.*

Lobe	X	Y	Z
Frontal Lobe	−2	9	39
Parietal Lobe			
Temporal Lobe			
Occipital Lobe			

Exercises *(continued)*

2) Identify gyri and give the Talairach coordinates of the center of the features of the left hemisphere.

    a) Select Surface Rendering Display Mode.

    b) Select Axial Slicing Mode.

    c) Display the left hemisphere.

    d) Click the Gyri Selection Mode button.

    e) Simultaneously click and drag the left mouse button while pressing the Shift key to rotate the head display as needed to locate the following Gyri. (**Note**: To locate some of the features, the head display may need to be rotated fully. Remember to use Ctrl+click-left-mouse-button to select and label features.)

Gyrus	X	Y	Z
Superior Frontal Gyrus	−11	44	34
Medial Frontal Gyrus			
Inferior Frontal Gyrus			
Cingulate Gyrus			
Precentral Gyrus			
Postcentral Gyrus			
Supramarginal Gyrus			
Superior Temporal Gyrus			
Medial Temporal Gyrus			
Inferior Occipital Gyrus			
Medial Occipital Gyrus			
Superior Occipital Gyrus			
Cuneus			
Precuneus			

3) Repeat the steps in Exercise 2 to identify sulci and give the Talairach coordinates of the center of the features of the left hemisphere. Be sure to select Sulci Selection Mode in Step *d* in order to locate sulci.

Sulcus	X	Y	Z
Superior Frontal Sulcus	–19	23	37
Inferior Frontal Sulcus			
Precentral Sulcus			
Central Sulcus			
Postcentral Sulcus			
Lateral Sulcus			
Superior Temporal Sulcus			
Inferior Temporal Sulcus			
Parietooccipital Sulcus			
Intraparietal Sulcus			
Transverse Occipital Sulcus			
Calcarine Sulcus			
Cingulate Sulcus			
Orbital Sulcus			
Occipitotemporal Sulcus			
Collateral Sulcus			

References

Felleman, D. J., & Van Essen, D. C. (1991). Distributed hierarchical processing in the primate cerebral cortex. *Cerebral Cortex, 1(1)*, 1-47.

Gazzaniga, M. S., Ivry, R. B., & Mangun, G. R. (2002). *Cognitive neuroscience: The biology of the mind* (2nd ed.). New York: W. W. Norton & Company.

Huettel, S. A., Song, A. W., & McCarthy, G. (2004). *Functional magnetic resonance imaging.* Sunderland, MA: Sinauer Associates, Inc.

Kanwisher, N., Stanley, D., & Harris, A. (1999). The fusiform face area is selective for faces not animals. *Neuroreport 10(1)*, 183-187.

Kolb, B., & Whishaw, I. Q. (2003). *Fundamentals of human neuropsychology* (5th ed.). New York: Worth Publishers.

Posner, M. I., & Raichle, M. E. (1994). *Images of mind.* Washington, DC: Scientific American Library.

Sejnowski, T. J., & Churchland, P. S. (1989). Brain and cognition. In M. Posner (Ed.), *Foundations of cognitive science* (pp. 301-356). Cambridge, MA: MIT Press.

Talairach, J., & Tournoux, P. (1988). *Co-planar stereotaxic atlas of the human brain.* New York: Times Medical Publishing.

Additional Information

For more information regarding brain imaging, a listing of links to useful websites is available at the PsychMate website (**www.psychmate.com/resources**).

Credits

Special thanks to the following institutions and individuals for contributions and/or illustrations:

Geoffrey Boynton, University of California, Santa Barbara

Brain Imaging Research Center, a joint venture between Carnegie Mellon and the University of Pittsburgh

Electrical Geodesics, Inc.

Rainer Goebel, Brain Innovation B.V.

Carolyn Cidis Meltzer, University of Pittsburgh

6.2 Working Memory and the fMRI

by Jason M. Chein, James St. James, & Walter Schneider

Abstract

Baddeley's *working memory* model of the brief persistence of the immediate past has been the subject of many behavioral experiments. The *phonological loop* used to maintain verbal information has been most thoroughly investigated. Chein and Fiez (2001) used functional magnetic resonance imaging (fMRI) to attempt to localize the brain regions that constitute this working memory subsystem. The experiment accompanying this chapter is a replication of the behavioral part of the experiment conducted by Chein and Fiez. Their fMRI brain imaging data are included so that students can explore the associated brain activation data to examine the relationships between behavior and the specialized functions in different cortical regions.

The present experiment has two purposes: (1) promoting an understanding of working memory and (2) illustrating a current cognitive neuroscience method for assessing brain function. First, we will consider a very basic phenomenon of human cognition—working memory. Working memory is the brain's system in which memories for the very recent past can be stored and manipulated in the service of ongoing cognition. In your working memory, at this very moment, you are storing the contents of this sentence and processing them into a meaningful whole. Working memory also maintains the goals of your mental activities, like your intent to perform the task of reading this chapter.

As a second goal of this chapter, we will illustrate how brain imaging allows researchers to look inside peoples' heads to examine the different functions performed by various parts of the brain. Major advances in brain imaging in the last decade have made it possible to measure human brain activity and to track the location and timecourse of the brain's activity changes. As you are reading this text, there are about a dozen brain areas engaged, performing various reading-related processes such as shape detection, the mapping of shapes to words and of words to their phonological (sound-based) and semantic

(meaning-based) representations, storing the representations, and connecting them to previously processed content. To understand brain processing, it is useful to consider how it changes along with different stages of a task. Knowing the timing of activity changes in the brain helps us to constrain the theoretical models trying to account for both the behavioral and brain-related findings.

This chapter will allow you to conduct a behavioral replication of a working memory experiment and then analyze the data collected from a related functional imaging experiment. For more details on brain imaging methods, see the enclosed summary of fMRI methods and the recommended reading in the bibliography in Chapter 6.1, *Introduction to Brain Imaging and Brain Tutor*.

In the development of a brain imaging experiment, it is the psychologist's job to be able to alter brain processing systematically, so that we can interpret the changes in activity that occur. When subjects are asked to perform a task that engages a specific cognitive mechanism, we expect the brain imaging data to show increased activity in the areas that support the engaged mechanism. The development of a behavioral paradigm that exercises different brain subsystems at different times, and which produces interpretable behavioral outcomes, is a critical step in achieving a successful brain imaging experiment.

Working Memory Behavioral Experiment

A perennial puzzle for psychology has been how to characterize the fleeting memories we have for the immediate past. William James (1890), whose *Principles of Psychology* did much to define the field, said that *primary memory*, as distinct from "memory proper, or secondary memory as it might be styled, is the knowledge of a former state of mind after it has already once dropped from consciousness" (p. 648).

> *"...What [primary] memory makes us aware of is the just past. The objects we feel in this directly intuited past differ from properly recollected objects. An object which is recollected, in the proper sense of that term, is one which has been absent from consciousness altogether, and now revives anew. It is brought back, recalled, fished up, so to speak, from a reservoir in which, with countless other objects, it lay buried and lost from view. But an object of primary memory is not thus brought back; it never was lost; its date was never cut off in consciousness from that of the immediately present moment." (pp. 646-647).*

Peterson and Peterson (1959), along with Brown (1958), revitalized the study of this type of memory with their famous experiment on the forgetting of single three-consonant trigrams (e.g., "QLD") over periods of 3-18 seconds when rehearsal was prevented by having the subjects count backwards by threes from a three-digit number. They called this phenomenon *immediate* memory—a term that nicely captures the fact that this memory is right there, and not mediated by an act of recall—not "fished up." Over the decade of the 1960's, an enormous amount of research was done on this type of memory, most often called *short-term memory*. James's secondary memory came to be called *long-term memory* (LTM). Perhaps the zenith of that approach was reached with the publication of Atkinson and Shiffrin's (1968) model of memory. However, their conceptualization quickly came under challenge on a number of fronts (Crowder, 1982).

Baddeley and Hitch (1974, and see Baddeley, 1995) proposed a different conceptualization of this brief memory, which they termed *working memory*. The basic working memory model is shown in Figure 6.2.1. Baddeley's model has a *central executive* that controls two "slave" systems for rehearsal. One of those is the *visuo-spatial sketchpad*. To illustrate the visuo-spatial sketchpad, close your eyes and visualize the rooms in your house and count the number of windows in the house. Visualize the kitchen and opening the windows individually. How did you do that? Most likely, you pictured the problem and moved your

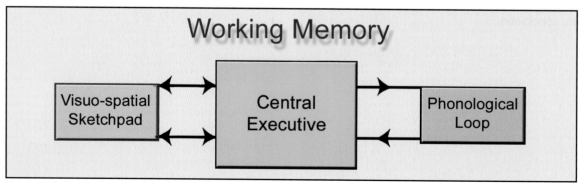

FIGURE **6.2.1** – *In this model of working memory proposed by Baddeley and Hitch (1974), a central executive controls two slave systems.*

point of attention within the visualized images. That is the visuo-spatial sketchpad.

Baddeley's other slave system is thought to support verbal maintenance and is called the *phonological loop*, or sometimes the *articulatory loop*. Baddeley (1995) suggests that this has two components. One is a brief (1-2 second) memory store of phonological information. Phonology refers to speech sounds and stresses the idea that this rehearsal loop involves internal representation of the speech sounds. The other component is an articulatory control process. Articulation refers to the act of speaking. You are familiar with this phonological loop from everyday tasks, such as looking up a telephone number and then repeating it to yourself as you make the call. Note that even a brief interruption of your rehearsal of the number will force you to look it up again. This example captures the phonological loop nicely—the memory store holds the sounds for only a second or two, and they are lost if they are not constantly refreshed by rehearsal of the sounds—either by inner (*subvocal*) speech or by rehearsing them overtly (out loud).

Basically, information in the phonological loop is assumed to decay rapidly. If nothing happens, it will decay in a few seconds. Articulation refreshes the items, preventing decay. Thus, the amount of information held in the phonological loop depends upon a balance between decay and refreshing through rehearsal. The phonological loop is the part of working memory with which this chapter and its accompanying experiment are concerned.

Evidence for the nature of this phonological loop comes from a number of sources. Conrad (1964) examined errors of misremembering that occur when subjects were shown lists of letters and asked to recall them. Errors in recall were almost always based on sound—*B* was more likely to be misremembered as *V*, which sounds like it, than by *R*, which looks like it. This makes good sense if subjects are rehearsing by articulation. In an

experiment very much like the one accompanying this chapter, Baddeley (1966) asked subjects to immediately recall lists of five words. The result is clear enough that you can probably repeat it right now. Read each of these three lists out loud (one at a time) and then immediately close your eyes and repeat it. Is one harder than the others?

List 1: PIT, DAY, COW, PEN, RIG

List 2: MAN, MAT, CAP, MAP, CAN

List 3: HUGE, BIG, LARGE, GREAT, TALL

This is called the *serial recall task* (see Figure 6.2.2); it has formed the basis for many studies of the phonological loop. Baddeley found that immediate recall was much worse for List 2, in which the words were phonologically similar—i.e., they sound alike—compared to List 1. Recall for List 3, in which the words are alike in meaning, but not sound, was as good as for List 1. (The lists are from Baddeley, 1995). Confusions in memory based on speech sounds are sometimes called the *phonological similarity effect*.

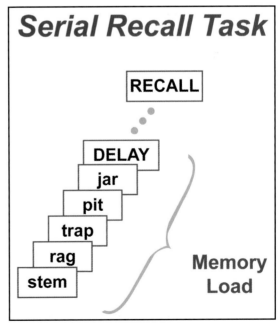

FIGURE 6.2.2 – *Illustrates the serial recall task.*

The serial recall task has been found to be more difficult (i.e., results in higher error rates) with words that take longer to articulate (e.g., SKELETON, COMPUTER, TELESCOPE) than with words that take less time to articulate (e.g., RAG, STEM, PIT). This is called the *word length effect* (Baddeley, Thompson, and Buchanan, 1975).

The serial recall task has also been used to compare recall rates of words and pseudowords. The latter are usually pronounceable, phonologically normal nonwords. An example would be CHAPE. Although definitely not a word, it *could* be—it is pronounceable and plausible (phonologically normal) as a word. (See the Methodological Considerations for more on pseudowords.) Words are recalled better than pseudowords (Hulme, Maugham, & Brown, 1991; Multhaup, Balota, & Cowan, 1996)— this is called a *lexicality effect*.

These effects are well-established, and each is thought to increase error by different mechanisms. Phonological similarity leads to increased confusion of the to-be-remembered lists, because the phonological loop is acoustically based (Baddeley, 1995). Increases in word length are thought to require a longer period for rehearsal, making it less likely that the words can be rehearsed quickly enough to prevent decay in the phonological loop (Anderson, 2000; Hulme, Surprenant, Bireta, Stuart, & Neath, 2004). Finally, the role of lexicality is assumed to reveal that there is an interaction between working memory and long-term memory. Recall of words in working memory benefits from the fact that they are already represented in long-term memory. That is, there is a semantic representation in the lexicon for a real word. Pseudowords are not represented in long-term memory (i.e., there is no entry in the lexicon for them), and thus they do not benefit from this advantage, producing the lexicality effect—see Hulme, Maughan, & Brown, 1991; Nairne, 2002.

Chein and Fiez (2001) took advantage of the relatively well-known nature of these effects to explore the brain systems responsible for different working-memory operations, as well as to examine the specific roles of these systems in encoding, maintenance, and retrieval from working memory. They divided each trial into four time periods. *Encoding* refers to the time during presentation of the list, when the subject is presumably trying to copy the items into the phonological loop. *Maintenance* is the time during which the subject is articulating the items over and over to keep the words refreshed in the phonological loop. *Recall* is the point at which subjects are asked to retrieve the items from their temporary store. Finally, a period of time after subjects finished each trial—the intertrial interval—was also recorded to provide a *baseline* brain activity for comparison.

Figure 6.2.3 shows the behavioral data from the Chein and Fiez study. Note the clear-cut effects. Relative to the one-syllable, distinct words, all others were harder to remember. You will be able to compare your class data with these data to determine whether the basic behavioral effects were replicated.

The principal fMRI findings of Chein and Fiez (2001) are shown in Figure 6.2.4, which is adapted from their Figure 4. Each plot within Figure 6.2.4 illustrates activation within a specific area of the brain. The horizontal axis shows scan number or acquisition number (each scan was four seconds in duration), while the vertical axis shows percent change. Acquisitions 2 and 3 are

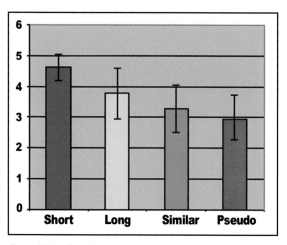

FIGURE **6.2.3** – *The effect of word type on memory retrieval based on the behavioral data from Chein and Fiez (2001). This shows mean recall and standard error as a function of stimulus type.*

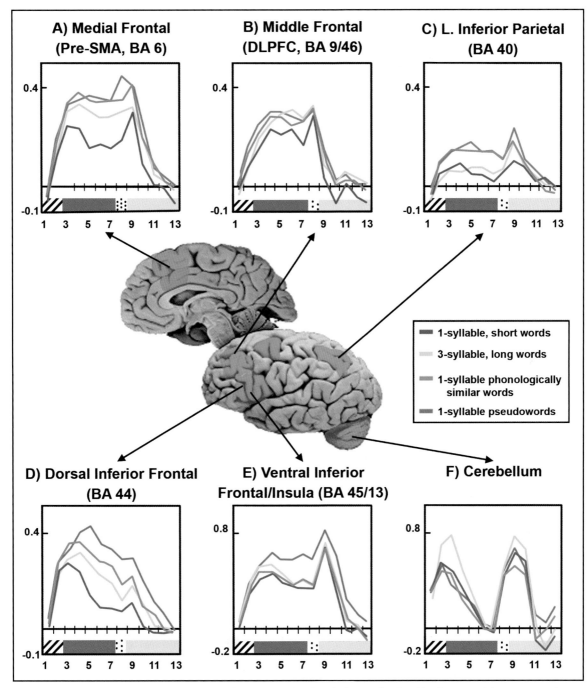

FIGURE 6.2.4 – *Brain activation in working memory task. The shaded blocks along the bottom of each activity plot represent the events occurring within a trial (refer to Figure 6.2.5 for a breakdown of trial events). Tick marks show the relative timing of scans 1-13, with each scan lasting 4 seconds in duration. For analysis: scans 2-3 = encoding; scans 6-7 = maintenance; scans 9-10 = recall; and scans 12-13 = baseline.*

A) *Medial frontal area shows an effect of difficulty (short<long=similar=pseudoword).*

B) *Middle frontal region shows a weak difficulty effect, with little differentiation across item types.*

C) *Left inferior parietal cortex shows weak effects of similarity and lexicality (short=long < similar=pseudoword).*

D) *A dorsal inferior frontal region exhibits attenuating activation across the maintenance period and a tight correspondence to performance (short<long<similar<pseudo).*

E) *A ventral inferior frontal region shows a lexicality effect (all words < pseudowords).*

F) *The cerebellum shows temporally specific activation during encoding and recall, but not maintenance.*

taken as a measure of activity during encoding. Acquisitions 6 and 7 mostly reflect maintenance of the rehearsed items. Acquisitions 9 and 10 occur at the time of retrieval or recall, and acquisitions 12 and 13 take place between trials. These final acquisitions provide the baseline (0 point) to which other acquisitions are compared in order to compute the percentage of signal change reported on the vertical (y) axis. The percent change can, therefore, be either positive (showing increased activation) or negative (showing decreased activation).

Broca's area, the supplementary motor area (SMA), and the cerebellum are all involved in the control of movement. While subvocal rehearsal does not involve overt movement, it involves many of the same processes leading up to movement. Note that Broca's area shows a peak during recall, reflecting the actual vocalization involved in saying the items out loud. The greater difficulty of articulating pseudowords can also be noted in Broca's area (see Figure 6.2.4, Graph D, "BA 44").

The SMA, which has been shown to be involved in repetitive motor sequences, shows a different pattern, with a high level of activation throughout encoding, rehearsal, and recall, but with higher levels of activation for the more difficult tasks (see Figure 6.2.4 [A]). The ease of encoding, rehearsal, and recall of the short, distinct, words seems to be reflected in the lower activation of SMA for those lists. Cerebellar activation (see Figure 6.2.4 [F]) is clearly highest during the encoding and recall phases of the task, with particularly high levels of activation for long words.

Methodological Considerations

Issues that arise in regard to the fMRI portion of the accompanying experiment are addressed in Chapter 6.1, *Introduction to Brain Imaging and Brain Tutor*. Issues regarding the behavioral portion of that experiment are addressed here.

Experiments using lists of words always have methodological considerations concerning the types of words used. In studies of the phonological similarity effect, the word length effect, and the lexicality effect, care must be taken to be sure that the only difference between the lists is in those properties— similarity, length, or lexicality. A confound that must always be addressed is that of word frequency. It will come as no surprise to you that common words are remembered better than words we seldom encounter, even when they are all unquestionably actual words (Hall, 1954), though the effect is relatively small and may reflect the level of association of the words rather than frequency, per se (Kling, J. W. & Riggs, L. A., 1971). As in the Chein and Fiez (2001) experiment replicated here, the common approach to controlling this possible confound is to use only words of relatively high frequency. All of the words used by Chein and Fiez had frequencies of above 30 per million words in written English, based on the most commonly used source for word frequency counts in English (Francis and Kučera, 1982).

The Chein and Fiez (2001) experiment also uses pseudowords, as described above. These were constructed by taking short, phonologically distinct words and swapping the initial consonant or consonant cluster (PIT and STEM become STIT and PEM). This preserves word length and letter frequency—at least across lists of words.

The version of the Chein and Fiez experiment used in PsychMate differs slightly from the original study in that it uses lists of six words, rather than the five words per list in the original. In the fMRI study, the level of distraction was high, due to the strangeness of the MRI scanner itself, the high level of noise from the magnet, the need to hold the head extremely still, and other factors. Performance on most behavioral tasks is poorer in the MRI than in standard testing. So, for the behavioral study you will perform, the list length was increased slightly to make the task harder and avoid a possible *ceiling effect*, which occurs when the task is so easy that subjects are at close to 100% recall for all lists.

Each word list is presented three times, but the analysis is based on only the last two presentations. Interference effects tend to increase with repeated presentation, so an analysis based on only the last two presentations usually shows larger differences. This *proactive interference* has itself been the subject of considerable research (Wickens, 1970).

Questions

1. What are the dependent and independent variables in this experiment? What are some important controls?

2. Consider the data in Figure 6.2.3 which shows the behavioral data from Chein and Fiez (2001). How do the differences indicate a similarity effect? A word-length effect? A lexicality effect? Do you also find these effects in your class data?

3. Explain what else might produce the similarity effect, the word-length effect, and the lexicality effect.

Analysis of the Working Memory Experiment Using BrainExaminer

Abstract

In this section, we provide the brain imaging data from the Chein and Fiez (2001) working memory experiment, enabling analysis of brain imaging data from a complete fMRI experiment. Both anatomical data and the activation data are provided. Analysis will involve the usage of tools to slice and examine brain images to relate them to a standardized brain atlas. The data include different contrasts based on different parts of the brain or Regions of Interest (ROIs). These will be analyzed at different times, examining the Encoding, Maintenance, and Recall portions of the experiment. Both the images and the activation time courses of the ROIs are available. The student's task is to explore the internal brain activity of subjects who performed the working memory task on which the PsychMate Working Memory experiment is based. The goals of this task include identifying the location of each ROI in the brain, characterizing the activation response of each region, and linking the patterns of activation with the psychological constructs of *encoding, maintenance,* and *retrieval.* The activation data differentiate according to behavioral manipulations in the experimental task, revealing the underlying properties of these regions. The data provide evidence of how information is represented, stored, and manipulated in different parts of the brain.

The Chein & Fiez (2001) study used a short term memory task in which subjects encoded five words over 8 seconds, had to remember the words for a maintenance period of 20 seconds, then were asked to verbally recall the words for 4 seconds, followed by a rest period of 12 seconds. Figure 6.2.5 shows the timecourse of the experiment.

Chein and Fiez presented four types of word lists (see Figure 6.2.6 for examples): short words, long words, similar words, and pseudowords (nonwords that sound like normal words). These were designed to test models of verbal rehearsal. For example, according to the Baddeley (1995) model of working memory, there is a rehearsal

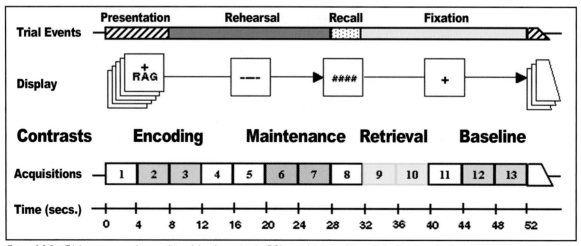

FIGURE 6.2.5 – *Trial sequence and scans determining the contrasts. ROIs are determined by statistically comparing the activity during the Encoding, Maintenance, or Retrieval period to the Baseline.*

Stimulus Word Types	
Short	cow | lot | disk | bun | rag
Long	musician | carnival | bulletin | suggestion | election
Similar	date | fate | hate | mate | rate
Pseudo-word	fow | stot | bisk | dag | vun

FIGURE **6.2.6** – *Examples of word lists used in the experiment*

buffer that cycles the phonemes of the words (e.g., in LOT, the combined sound of the /L/, /O/, and /T/ — lŏt'). Words with more phonemes (three syllable words) are predicted to have substantially more activation than short words (one syllable). Also, it would be expected that encoding and repeating words that have similar phonemes (e.g., date, fate) would produce more interference and activity than words that sound distinctly different. Finally, pseudowords do not have a lexical (word) representation. Therefore, it would be expected that pseudowords do not activate lexical or semantic representations, and would activate only the phonemic representation.

Chein and Fiez (2001) state that their goals were to use a:

> ...delayed serial recall task, together with stimulus manipulations of phonological similarity, articulatory length, and lexicality, with the following broad goals in mind: (1) to identify the neural substrates of verbal maintenance and to determine if they are selectively engaged in maintenance-based processing; (2) to further characterize the particular functions served by brain regions engaged in specific rehearsal and storage processes through an investigation of stimulus-specific and temporal effects; and (3) to

examine the response of central executive regions to changes in task difficulty stemming from the operation of the verbal maintenance subsystem. (p.1004)

The brain imaging data accompanying this chapter have been preprocessed to the stage at which activity of different brain regions can be examined, either by looking at the mean activity (activity averaged across subjects) or the activity of individual subjects. Each individual subject's brain data was passed through various preprocessing stages (see Chein & Fiez, 2001, p. 1005). These stages included:

a) movement correction to align all of the images in a run;

b) brain normalization, warping each brain into Talairach space so all of the brains are expanded or contracted to fit the standard brain;

c) spatial filtering (this defocuses the brain activation image) to account for local anatomical variability between subjects; and

d) statistical analysis to identify ROIs that were significant ($p < .0001$) and which had at least five contiguous voxels (each voxel or volume element was 3.75 x 3.75 x 3.8 mm in size).[27] (For a description of voxels, refer to the section titled "How an MRI Experiment is Different from a Behavioral Experiment" in Chapter 6.1, *Introduction to Brain Imaging and Brain Tutor.*)

The data available to you show the results from two contrasts (Encoding and Maintenance). Figure 6.2.5 shows the design illustrating three temporal contrasts, but the data was collapsed to show just the Encoding and Maintenance contrasts. (The Encoding and Recall contrasts

---

[27] The value of p indicates the probability of getting activation this strong just due to sampling or measurement error if there is really nothing going on. If it is low enough (typically, less than one chance in 10,000), then it is assumed that the activation is real and not just a statistical fluke.

FIGURE 6.2.7 – *Launching BrainExaminer from the PsychMate experiment launcher.*

showed no significant difference.) Every 4 seconds a complete image of the brain (36 slices) was acquired. The goal of this laboratory exercise is to explore the brain activity, determine which regions show specific activity, and determine how those activity patterns allow us to test models of working memory.

It takes substantial effort to characterize brain activity. Brain imaging pictures by themselves say little. As an analogy, consider examining a picture of a cutaway view of the human body. By itself, it communicates little. However, identifying the specific organs and the activity that goes on in each (e.g., lungs stream air, heart pumps blood, stomach processes food) provides a basis for understanding function. This is also true for the brain.

For the exercises in this chapter, you will be using the *BrainExaminer* data visualization and examination tool. Figure 6.2.7 shows how to launch the BrainExaminer application from the Cognitive Neuroscience category in the PsychMate experiment launcher. A Getting

Started Guide for using BrainExaminer is available at the PsychMate website (**www.psychmate.com/resources**).

As Figure 6.2.8 shows, BrainExaminer lets you look at sliced views of the brain to localize ROIs, from which you can get a plot of activation over time for the ROI. The spreadsheet at the bottom of the application display contains tables of the activation measurements and parameters for each ROI (Talairach coordinates, tissue volume, notes). You can edit fields in the ROI worksheet to answer questions about the activation.

The exercises involve several steps to interpret the results from the Chein & Fiez (2001) experiment, including both basic and advanced exercises. The major steps include identification and localization of the ROIs, and then characterizing the time course of the ROIs. Refer to the PsychMate website for a complete example of performing the exercises for a given ROI. After reading this text, run through the exercise for ROI #1 and be sure that you can match the results.

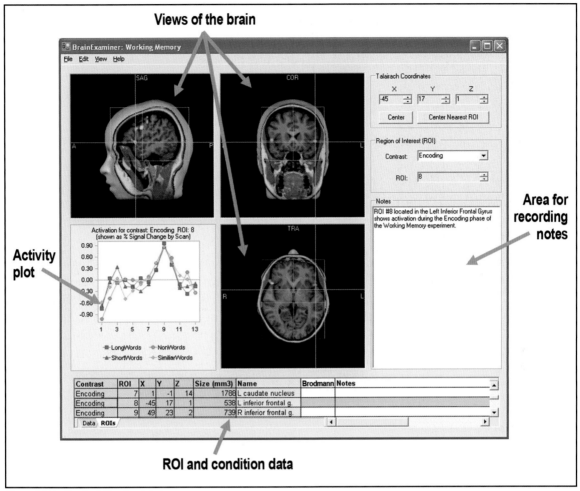

FIGURE 6.2.8 – *The BrainExaminer interface*

Brain imaging data analysis can require a substantial investment of time examining activation maps, time course graphs, and statistical results. A good place to start looking at the images is the activation data shown in each of the time period contrasts (Encoding and Maintenance).

The first stage in understanding brain imaging data is "getting your head around the data." This involves looking closely at the data and figuring out what qualitatively different patterns of activation you see in different locations. Look at the images and characterize what you see. What parts of the brain are active at different times? Which stimulus conditions show differences during the Maintenance period?

Identifying the cortical location of each Region of Interest (ROI) Using BrainExaminer and Brain Tutor

To communicate results, it is beneficial to identify the name of an ROI. As an analogy, having the longitude and latitude coordinates of a city is spatially accurate but does not communicate the description of the region as well as the city name does. For example, what could you describe about the coordinates latitude 40° 47' N and longitude 73° 58' W? In contrast, what could you describe about New York City? Similarly, brain regions are identified by names using a three-level scale similar to country, state and city. For the brain, the equivalents of these levels are hemisphere, lobe, and gyri/sulci (for cortical structures). These names are likely to be new to

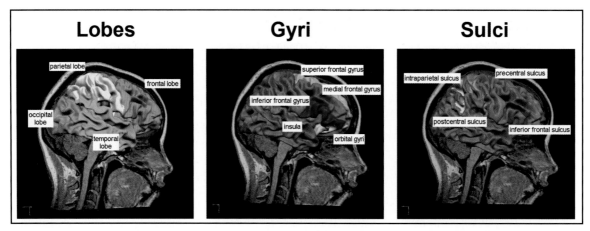

FIGURE **6.2.9** – *Lobe, Gyri, and Sulci labeling*

you so you will need a reference atlas defining them. The Brain Tutor provides such a reference atlas (see Figure 6.2.9). There is also a common naming convention called Brodmann areas, which is a numbered assignment of regions (sort of like ZIP codes for cities).

There is a special problem in brain mapping—the problem of *mapping to a common reference brain*. Each brain has some unique spatial features. First, brains are different sizes. To compensate for this, brains are spatially normalized by rescaling them into a common Talairach

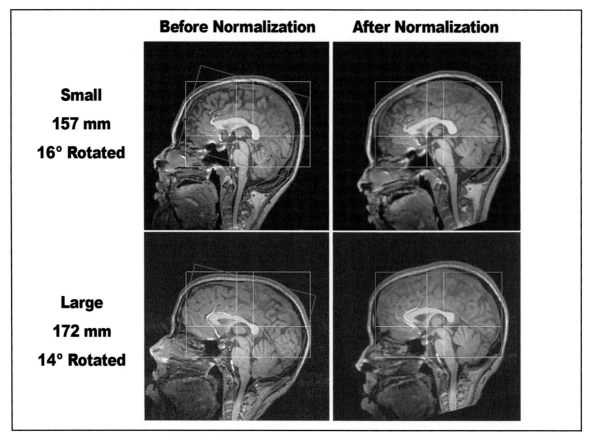

FIGURE **6.2.10** – *Sagittal view of a small brain (157 mm front to back) and a large brain (172 mm front to back). The red rectangles show the bounding box of the brain covering the front-back and top-bottom of the cortex. Notice how the red rectangle was rotated and stretched to align with the fixed normalized white box. After normalization, each brain has the same size and orientation.*

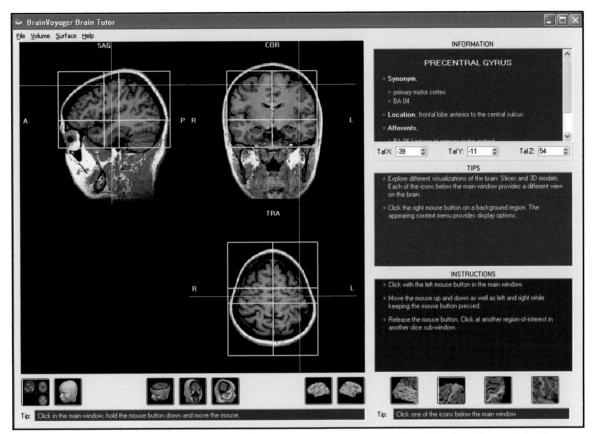

FIGURE 6.2.11 – *Mapping Talairach points to the nearest cortical structure (e.g., lobe, gyrus, sulcus). Enter Talairach coordinates obtained from BrainExaminer into Brain Tutor and Ctrl+click to select the nearest gyrus/sulcus. (Brain Tutor will adjust the Talairach coordinates to the surface of the closest structure.)*

space (e.g., each brain is expanded or shrunk such that it is the same size with a front to back size of +70 to -100 mm). Figure 6.2.10 illustrates Talairach normalization, which corrects for differences in the cortex or skull size. Correcting for brain size is valuable in that it allows us to localize brain areas across people, within a centimeter (i.e., identify the same location in different brains to within approximately one centimeter of spatial accuracy).

Talairach normalization does **not** correct for the fold patterns of the brain. The brain is a half meter square surface that has been folded and compressed to fit inside the head (think of taking a square sheet the size of your shoulders and crumpling the sheet to the size of your fist to fit it inside your skull). The problem is, each person's crumple patterns are different. When mapping

an individual brain to a reference brain, one expects about a centimeter (0.4 inch) variation.

When examining the Talairach activation mapping of brain structures (gyri/sulci), you may find the Talairach point of the activation to be in the *white matter*. In the MR images, the white matter appears light grey and makes up the interior of the cortical lobes (see Figure 6.1.3). At the surface of the cortex is the grey matter, which appears dark grey, and identifies the cell bodies. Activation occurs in the cell bodies (because they use the energy provided by the blood oxygen) and cannot occur in white matter. Hence, when you find activation in white matter, it indicates some degree of localization error (e.g., the location of the average activation is different from the standard brain, probably related to variation in folding patterns). When this occurs, the location assignment is ambiguous, and could be assigned to two areas. Some papers will describe location in terms of just the gyrus. Some will report both areas or go back to each individual brain and report how many subjects were localized in each gyrus/sulcus. Figure 6.2.11 localizes ROI #1 from the BrainExaminer Working Memory spreadsheet to the left precentral gyrus. However, moving a few millimeters in any dimension might identify the precentral sulcus or the medial frontal gyrus.

For these exercises, you will be provided the ROI-related data and the BrainExaminer and

Brain Tutor programs. To complete the exercises in this chapter, you will use the Brain Tutor and BrainExaminer applications. BrainExaminer provides three-dimensional brain imaging data for each region of interest, allowing the user to visually assess the location and integrity of the activity. Refer to the BrainExaminer Help system for information regarding the use of BrainExaminer and its capabilities. The Help system also provides detailed instructions for completing the exercises.

At the bottom of the application (see Figure 6.2.8), you will see a series of spreadsheets related to the ROIs that have been identified for

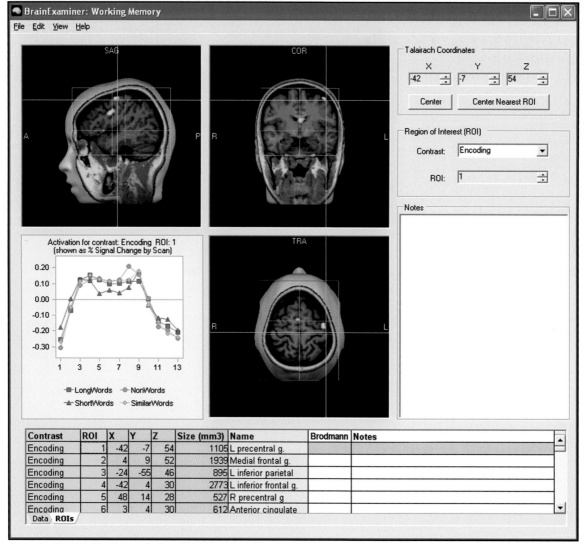

FIGURE 6.2.12 – BrainExaminer application with ROI #1 selected.

the Working Memory experiment. There will be spreadsheets corresponding to individual exercises. Completion of the exercises will involve filling in missing information in the spreadsheets, by using the BrainExaminer and Brain Tutor applications to localize and characterize the activation at each ROI.

For each ROI, you will use BrainExaminer to identify and localize the ROI, determine Talairach coordinates, and examine the activation timecourse. Use Brain Tutor to familiarize yourself with the brain regions and to identify the cortical structures associated with each ROI.

To localize an ROI requires several steps. Select the ROI tab, and then click in a row to select a specific ROI. Notice that the planar views and Talairach coordinates update to indicate the location of the center of mass of the ROI, and the timecourse activity plot updates to show the associated activity in that ROI across conditions (see Figure 6.2.12).

Once you have visualized the ROI and obtained its Talairach coordinates using BrainExaminer, you will then use Brain Tutor to cross-reference the location of the ROI with the labeled structures (lobes, gyri, sulci) in the standard brain.

Exercises

Exercises specific to the Working Memory experiment are located within the BrainExaminer Help system. To view the exercises, select the Working Memory Exercises option from the Help menu. Review the examples and instructions within the Help system to complete the exercises using BrainExaminer and Brain Tutor. The exercises will lead you through the following steps:

1. Identify the cortical location of each ROI.

2. Characterize the activation of each ROI individually.

3. Compare activity across regions and contrasts.

4. Relate the activation data to the behavioral data and models.

Advanced Exercises

In the advanced exercises included in the Help system, you will examine the timecourse variability between individual subjects and specific contrasts (Encoding and Maintenance).

References

Anderson, J. R. (2000). *Cognitive psychology and its implications* (5th ed.). New York: Worth.

Baddeley, A. D. (1966). Short-term memory for word sequences as a function of acoustic, semantic, and formal similarity. *Quarterly Journal of Experimental Psychology, 18*, 362-365.

Baddeley, A. D. (1995). Working memory. In M. S. Gazzaniga (Ed.), *The cognitive neurosciences* (pp.755-764). Cambridge, MA: MIT.

Baddeley, A. D., & Hitch, G. (1974). Working memory. In G. A. Bower (Ed.), *The psychology of learning and motivation* (Volume 8, pp. 47-89). New York: Academic Press.

Baddeley, A. D., Thomson, N., & Buchanan, M. (1975). Word length and the structure of short-term memory. *Journal of Verbal Learning and Verbal Behavior, 14*, 575-589.

Chein, J. M., & Fiez, J. A. (2001). Dissociation of verbal working memory system components using a delayed serial recall task. *Cerebral Cortex, 11*, 1003-14.

Conrad, R. (1964). Acoustic confusions in immediate memory. *British Journal of Psychology, 1964*, 75-84.

Crowder, R. G. (1982). The demise of short-term memory. *Acta Psychololgica, 50*, 291-323.

Francis, W. N., & Kučera, H. (1982). *Frequency analysis of English usage: Lexicon and grammar.* Boston, MA: Houghton, Mifflin.

Hall, J. F. (1954). Learning as a function of word frequency. *American Journal of Psychology, 67*, 138-140.

Hulme, C., Maughan, S., & Brown, G. D. (1991). Memory for familiar and unfamiliar words: Evidence for a long-term memory contribution to short-term memory span. *Journal of Memory and Language, 30*, 685-701.

Hulme, C., Surprenant, A. M., Bireta, T. J., Stuart, G., & Neath, I. (2004). Abolishing the word-length effect. *Journal of Experimental Psychology: Learning, Memory, and Cognition, 30*, 98-106.

James, W. (1890). *The principles of psychology.* New York: Henry Holt.

Kling, J. W., & Riggs, L. A. (1971). *Experimental psychology.* New York: Holt, Rinehart, and Winston.

Nairne, J. S. (2002). Remembering over the short-term: The case against the standard model. *Annual Review of Psychology, 53*, 53-81.

Wickens, D. D. (1970). Encoding categories of words: An empirical approach to meaning. *Psychological Review, 77*, 1-15.

Appendix A. PEAK (Psychology Experiment Authoring Kit)

• •

Introduction

In academic courses such as the one in which you are enrolled, students are tasked with understanding empirical methodology and the nature of scientific inquiry. However, in many lecture courses, while there is an abundance of description, there tends to be a shortage of hands-on opportunities. PsychMate offers the extremely valuable opportunity to "do" research through participation in experiments as subjects, as well as the ability to design, create, and run your own experiments, collect data, and follow the experiment through the analysis. The ability to create and implement your own experiment allows you to take intellectual ownership and thereby greatly facilitates the learning process. In addition, it allows you to learn to apply empirical methods in a wide range of inquiry (e.g., human factors, learning, social interaction) that can be applied in business, medicine, education, and social services.

• •

This appendix provides a brief overview of how the Psychology Experiment Authoring Kit (PEAK) is used to create new experiments. Complete documentation and a Getting Started Guide are available through your online PsychMate account.

FIGURE A.1 – *PEAK Splash Screen*

Within PsychMate, PEAK is a novel spreadsheet-based interface allowing students and researchers to create their own experiments, and to do so quickly and efficiently. There are many experiment editor products available for the purpose of generating novel experiments, most of which are too cryptic to be learnable within a reasonable amount of time (typically requiring more than ten hours of study to build a simple first experiment). Hence, these approaches are neither practical tools for completing a research project during a single term, nor for accomplishing the goal of effectively teaching research methods. PEAK is a new interface approach that builds knowledge of experiment creation upon the foundation of basic spreadsheet skills which most users already possess or which they can easily develop in a minimal amount of time. In empirical tests, we have found that students can learn to create experiments in about two hours of going through the introductory materials and the Getting Started Guide. The online version of these materials can be found at the PsychMate website which is accessible through your online PsychMate account.

The PEAK application provides a spreadsheet-like interface (see Figure A.2), with which most students are already familiar. PEAK provides a transparent interface in which all key variables, events, and specifications are illustrated in a well-structured, single-page, spreadsheet interface. This provides a pedagogical tool for understanding key experimental concepts, such as independent and dependent variables, counterbalancing, and precise procedural control. The system is designed to accommodate experimental paradigms covering much of the current computer-

EXPERIMENT LEVELS:

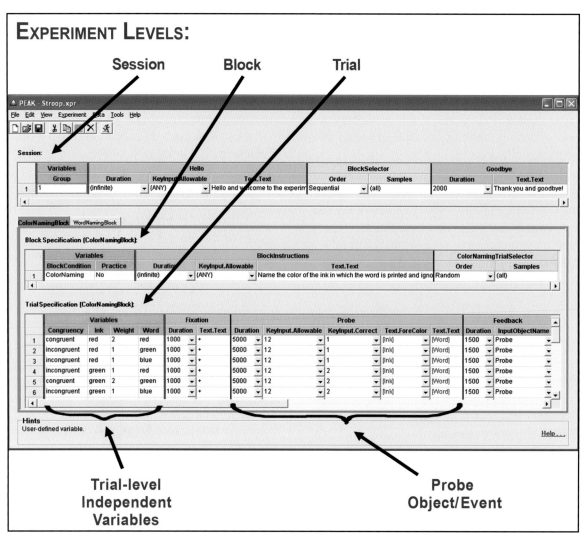

FIGURE A.2 – *PEAK interface illustrating a color Stroop task. The Probe object/event is defined as presenting a text stimulus (Text.Text) for up to 5 seconds (Duration), accepting the 1 or 2 keys for response (KeyInput.Allowable), and scoring the answer for correctness (KeyInput.Correct). The Variables column lists Congruency as a trial-level variable marking the congruency between the stimulus text and the forecolor in which it is presented (Text.Forecolor).*

ized experimental literature. After the experimental design is determined, the user implements the desired experiment by creating objects and then setting properties for those objects within the PEAK interface. Instead of detailed knowledge of computers and programming, the user is required simply to understand basic spreadsheet editing skills and, thus, can focus on implementation of the experimental design.

PEAK provides the user with the ability to define each experimental event independently. Implementing an experiment using the PEAK interface

is a matter of setting up slides to represent the events of the experiment, then setting the appropriate properties to define those events. Slides offer the ability to define events such as presenting stimuli (text, images, sound, or any combination thereof), collecting responses, scoring the responses, and providing feedback to the subject. A slide can be considered a kind of toolbox from which the user selects the appropriate tools and determines how they are used. For example, to define the presentation of a stimulus event, the user would set the text, image, and sound (or combination of these elements) to be presented as the stimulus, set the duration of the event, and define the parameters of the input to be collected (e.g., which keys are allowed, the correct answer, how long the subject has to respond).

Within the PEAK interface, columns represent the specific events and specify values of the independent variables of the experiment (e.g., instructions, fixation presentation), as well as the properties relevant to those events (e.g., text color, allowable keys, duration of display). The rows of the spreadsheet represent individual trials and levels of the independent variables.

Getting Started Using PEAK

The PEAK documentation (Figure A.3) is a series of exercises designed to introduce the PEAK interface, and also to bridge the gap between conceptualization of the experiment and its implementation using the software package. The Getting Started Guide leads the user through a series of exercises involving the creation of storyboard procedures to represent the experimental procedure. During the storyboard process, the user first conceptualizes what each level

of the experiment would look like as a sequence of events on paper and identifies the pertinent property settings for each event. The user is guided through the process of identifying how an experiment is broken down into levels (i.e., session, blocks, trials) and how the independent variables then define the values of each block or trial.

For example, in order to illustrate a color Stroop experiment, the student is given the following description of the trial procedure:

> *You will be presented with a fixation slide for 0.5 seconds, and then a probe slide composed of a picture with text superimposed. Respond by pressing the key for the picture (1-fish, 2-horse, 3-pie) while ignoring the text. The probe slide will be presented until the subject responds. Then, feedback will be displayed for up to 3 seconds concerning the accuracy and reaction time of the response.*

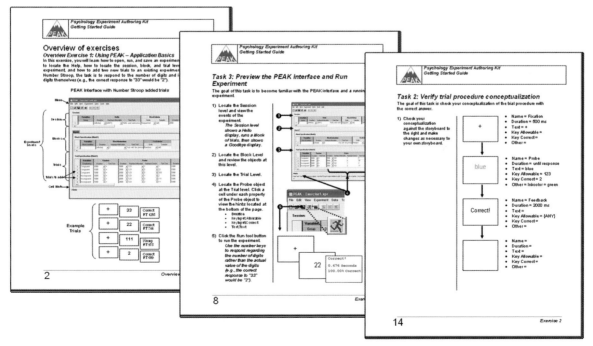

FIGURE A.3 – *Example pages from the PEAK Getting Started Guide illustrating storyboard exercises, as well as exercises focusing on the use of PEAK.*

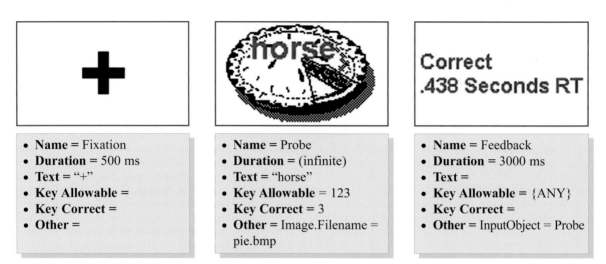

- **Name** = Fixation
- **Duration** = 500 ms
- **Text** = "+"
- **Key Allowable** =
- **Key Correct** =
- **Other** =

- **Name** = Probe
- **Duration** = (infinite)
- **Text** = "horse"
- **Key Allowable** = 123
- **Key Correct** = 3
- **Other** = Image.Filename = pie.bmp

- **Name** = Feedback
- **Duration** = 3000 ms
- **Text** =
- **Key Allowable** = {ANY}
- **Key Correct** =
- **Other** = InputObject = Probe

FIGURE A.4 – *Storyboard representation of the events of the trial procedure and property settings specific to each.*

From this description, the user is guided through the process of creating a storyboard to represent the events of the trial procedure. This involves identifying the necessary objects to represent the fixation, probe, and feedback events, as well as the relevant property settings for those objects (see Figure A.4). In the storyboard display, the rectangles indicate what the subject would see. The text below each shows the property settings that determine how the information is presented and how data is collected.

This storyboard representation of a single trial then directly translates to the PEAK interface as a single row of information (see Figure A.5). After conceptualization of the single-trial procedure, the student is able to quickly expand the experiment to run multiple trials and fill in the appropriate levels of the independent variables.

Conclusion

The innovative approach of the PEAK interface, combining skills users already possess with documentation designed to bridge the gap between experimental design and computer implementation, provides users with the tools necessary to obtain a meaningful understanding of experimental methods and to quickly and efficiently conduct their own research projects.

The PEAK Getting Started Guide, including a Quick Reference outline of steps to follow when implementing an experiment, is available at the PsychMate website (**www.psychmate.com/resources**), which is accessible through your online PsychMate account.

Fixation		Probe						Feedback	
Duration	Text.Text	Duration	Image.Filename	KeyInput.Allowable	KeyInput.Correct	Text.ForeColor	Text.Text	Duration	InputObjectName
500	+	(infinite)	pie.bmp	123	1	Blue	horse	1500	Probe

FIGURE A.5 – *Single-trial representation of the trial procedure.*